Dear Becki

As the tit[le]

Devotions for Everyday life

As you go forward in your
life, we pray that this book
helps you daily on the
many situations that come
up. Wishing you well in
whatever you do.

"You can do it"!

With love
The Lemkes

M000118842

Published by Straight Talk Books

P.O. Box 301, Milwaukee, WI 53201

800.661.3311 • timeofgrace.org

Cover image: © de santis paolo/Thinkstock

Printed in the United States of America

ISBN: 978-0-9910967-8-7

Hope

IN A MOMENT

devotions for everyday life

Dedication

It is with a grateful heart that I dedicate this book to the members of my congregation, St. Marcus Lutheran Church in Milwaukee. They have been patient and cheerful supporters of Time of Grace ever since we began in 2001. They have tolerated my frequent absences for travel and writing. I derive enormous blessings from their energy, love for each other, passion for outreach, embrace of our crazy diversity, entrepreneurial spirit, and respect for the Word. May God continue to smile on this place and keep it a place where people are connected with him and with each other in joyful love and service.

Introduction

Is your life as insane as mine? How many excuses come to mind for not doing some Bible study each day? I have plenty and I bet you do too. That's why I call these mini-devotions Grace Moments, because they take only a moment to read. Each one brings you a nugget of God's Word, a story, and an application for your faith and life.

God gave us his Word as protection for our heads, so we learn to think straight; as protection for our hearts, so that the attacks of Satan and the inevitable hardships and disasters of life won't crush us and cause us to despair; and as a headlight, so we can peer ahead into the darkness and see a path.

His Word brings the assurance of forgiveness of our many sins, a sense of being worth something to our Father in heaven, and clues toward the purpose for which he put us on this earth.

Let me encourage you to carve out a little time each day for the Word. It is my hope that these Grace Moments will help you stay connected to your Lord, to hear his powerful and gentle voice, to ponder his amazing deeds in human history, and to find your place in his agenda.

Pastor Mark Jeske

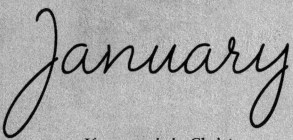

January

If anyone is in Christ,
he is a new creation;
the old has gone,
the new has come!

2 Corinthians 5:17

Making changes

There is no better time than right now to make life changes. Don't argue with me. You know that various aspects of your life still aren't under control. This is the perfect time to reflect on the past and its imperfections and look ahead to new beginnings.

It's important to remember that God accepts you unconditionally, as is. The mercy and forgiveness of Christ washes over you even though you don't deserve it. Grace is 100% God's doing. But having brought you to faith, implanting his Holy Spirit in you, and lighting your mind with the Word, God refuses to settle for your past lifestyle. What needs to change?

The new year typically is a time when we make new commitments, plan new activities like working out more, spending more time with the kids, eating healthier, and spending more time with the elderly ones in the family. All good. But let me suggest to you that the reverse can be as good or better: to make a list of things you intend to *stop doing:* **"Now you must rid yourselves of all such things as these: anger, rage, malice, slander, and filthy language from your lips. Do not lie to each other, since you have taken off your old self with its practices and have put on the new self"** (Colossians 3:8-10).

If the people around you could get you to stop doing four things, what four would they be?

_____

_____

_____

_____

Less angry, more gentle

Does an angry person live in your house? Does an angry person live in your mind?

Anger makes for interesting TV and movie plots, but it is a terrible internal acid that corrodes your soul. It won't drain itself. You must choose to let go of it. You are not a prisoner of your emotions. You belong to Christ now, and his Spirit in you is mightier than your old sinful self.

Adam and Eve's oldest son resented the second son. That resentment, unchecked, morphed into hatred, then an evil plot, and finally first degree intentional homicide. God gave him a wake-up call while there was still time: **"The LORD said to Cain, 'Why are you angry? Why is your face downcast? If you do what is right, will you not be accepted? But if you do not do what is right, sin is crouching at your door; it desires to have you, but you must master it'"** (Genesis 4:6,7). He didn't master it. It mastered him.

Take a moment right now and take inventory of your own angers. You can't wipe away your memories as though they were computer files to delete. But with God's strength you can choose to let go of your anger. You too must master it.

_____

_____

_____

_____

_____

JANUARY 3
Less bitter, more content

Do you ever catch yourself starting sentences with the phrase "Just my luck"? Do you see yourself as doomed? Are you a brooder over past failures? Do critical comments from other people linger long in your memory? Do you feel cheated in life? Are you surrounded by other people whose lives are carefree and easy?

The extract from all that stew is a bitter bile that sits in your stomach and wells up your throat. If you are looking for and expecting disappointments and brokenness and failure in your life, you will find them every time. The amount simply depends on the time you spend looking. In our broken and sinful world, there is plenty everywhere. If you approach life with that mind-set, however, you will make yourself miserable and probably others too. **"See to it that no one misses the grace of God and that no bitter root grows up to cause trouble and defile many"** (Hebrews 12:15).

If on the other hand you go about looking for gifts from God, boosts and treats and blessings, you will find them too. If you look for kind and decent people, daily guidance from the Word, and assurance of your worth and value to God, you will find that too. If you inventory your marvelous assets from heaven more than obsess over what you don't have, you will experience a contented heart.

You will also have more friends.

_____

_____

_____

_____

_____

Less critical, more encouraging

Did you have a parent who was a perfectionist? Would your spouse or kids say that you are one? Perfectionists seem to have it all together, but actually the reverse is true. They (we?) are really insecure and obsess over behaviors and dust bunnies and kitchen crumbs and gutter leaves and dandruff.

Perhaps we're so hungry for praise that we nitpick other people to make ourselves feel less bad. The irony is that being hypercritical does the opposite of what we want. It drives others away, and it leaves us just feeling emptier and even more anxious. Even when you say nothing, when you just think your critiques, you feed your own insecurity.

Here's a secret: the people you are criticizing are probably even more broken inside than you are. Here's another: people will respond much more to your words of encouragement than words of criticism. I believe that you will find that you can love people into good behavior more than you can scold them out of bad behavior. **"Do not let any unwholesome talk come out of your mouths, but only what is helpful for building others up according to their needs, that it may benefit those who listen"** (Ephesians 4:29).

If you look for things in other people to praise, you will always find them.

_____

_____

_____

_____

_____

Less selfish, more giving

I know why I'm not very interested in you or your needs—it's because my stories are so much more interesting to me, my plans are more important, and my needs are much more urgent. Hey—just lookin' out for number one (me, that is). If I don't take care of myself, who will, right?

If you hear yourself saying or thinking any of the above with me, we both need a trip to the woodshed with the apostle James: **"If you harbor bitter envy and selfish ambition in your hearts, do not boast about it or deny the truth. Such 'wisdom' does not come down from heaven but is earthly, unspiritual, of the devil. For where you have envy and selfish ambition, there you find disorder and every evil practice"** (James 3:14-16).

Lord, turn me inside out. You, my hero, came not to be served but to serve and to give your life as a ransom for many. You have redeemed me not to be a pampered starlet but a helper of others. You have gifted me and lifted me so that I may do the same for other people. Help me learn true love, to be willing to spend myself to make other people's lives better. Help me believe that I gain by giving, win by yielding, and become satisfied by serving.

Jesus, make me more like you. Please start today.

JANUARY 6
Are you all in?

Ever watch the "poker channel" on satellite TV? Perhaps you are a poker player yourself. In each game, perhaps after hours of ups and downs, a player will decide to bet everything. It's called going "all in." He pushes his whole stack of chips into the center of the table, knowing that he's either busted and out or will claim the whole pot.

The Magi who came to visit the newborn King, *their* King, were not just curious astronomers on a casual journey. They were from the Parthian (Persian) Empire, a bitter enemy of the Romans who had put King Herod on his throne and whose soldiers could be seen every day on Jerusalem's streets. For the Magi to travel hundreds of miles behind enemy lines was to risk their very lives. They were all in.

They brought gifts that showed not just casual friendship but the deepest worship, fit for a king. Their hope in the Messiah had taken them from darkness to light, from death to life. **"They saw the child with his mother Mary, and they bowed down and worshiped him. Then they opened their treasures and presented him with gifts of gold and of incense and of myrrh"** (Matthew 2:11).

Has it cost you anything, anything at all, to be a Christian? Could your gifts to your Savior be called kingly? Is your worship life an occasional and casual thing, or are you ready to go all in?

_____

_____

_____

_____

_____

He will be like Jesus

Have you ever noticed that your praying tapers off when you have a guilty conscience? Guilt makes us slink away from God's presence instead of running to meet him. That's why the gospel of Jesus' forgiveness is so thrilling to our hearts and so necessary to hear on a daily basis to sustain our faith-relationship with the Father. Through God's grace we are washed clean each day; through God's grace we find joy in our relationship with him all over again.

One of the greatest things about life in heaven someday is that we will be pure and sinless forever. Never again will we hurt or disappoint our heavenly Father. Never again will we feel shame and guilt.

The Bible says in 1 John 3:2, **"What we will be has not yet been made known. But we know that when** [Jesus] **appears, we shall be like him, for we shall see him as he is."** You know what? I can't wait to be like Jesus. I am thrilled that my physical body will be restored from all its damage and imperfections. I am even more excited that my heart and soul and mind will be as pure as Jesus' also.

In heaven I will never hurt anybody again. In heaven I will never hurt my God again.

_____

_____

_____

_____

_____

JANUARY 8
Built to work

"Kids today have a terrible work ethic." A friend of mine who is a small business owner said that as he was groaning about the terrible time he was having getting his new hires to show up on time and do a job right. What's been your experience? Was my friend right?

"My Father works, and I work," Jesus said once. Work is essential to the essence of our God. The first thing God did upon creating the first man was to put him to work. Right away on day one of the existence of the human race, Adam was commissioned to take inventory of the fauna in his new habitat and give each animal a name appropriate to its appearance and function.

We are God-designed and God-built for labor. Hard work helps us appreciate the value of money and invites God's blessings. **"Lazy hands make a man poor, but diligent hands bring wealth"** (Proverbs 10:4). **"He who works his land will have abundant food, but the one who chases fantasies will have his fill of poverty"** (Proverbs 28:19).

One of the greatest legacies parents can give to their children is to teach them how to work, defer gratification, keep their word, obey a boss, participate in a team, and finish a job.

_____

_____

_____

_____

_____

Waking up

One of the most miserable sights in America is the televised press conference called by a politician who has been caught with a prostitute, gay lover, congressional page, or intern. He or she struggles, squirms, makes excuses, evades direct questions, and looks miserable. Sometimes the politicians appear on camera standing next to ashen-faced spouses.

Think how much damage can be done to people's lives with a moment of impulsive and reckless sin. If only they had thought about that potential damage *before* they acted on their selfish impulses. If only someone had awakened them from their immoral stupor *before* they did all that harm to the people in their families.

That's the essence of learning by words instead of pain. *Now* is the time to listen to God's Word. *Now* is the time to take his words to heart. *Now* is the time to wake up and remember what's at stake. **"Blessed is the man who finds wisdom, the man who gains understanding"** (Proverbs 3:13).

What would your best friend tell you that you need to change in your life? What does God's Word tell you about where your life is at the greatest risk? How will you pray today for God's help in those changes?

_____

_____

_____

_____

_____

I love to worship you, Lord

I love being in your house, Lord. I know I can worship you anywhere, and I do. But there is nothing like being in your house with other believers. I love the choirs and instruments. I love the hymns and the prayers. I appreciate the messages that come from your Word, and I love giving gifts, acknowledging you as the ultimate Giver of all.

I love being with other people who care about you as much as I do. **"Praise the Lord. How good it is to sing praises to our God, how pleasant and fitting to praise him!"** (Psalm 147:1). I love being able to go public with my praises and let the world know I am proud to be your child. I claim you; thank you for claiming me.

Father, you are the Designer and Maker of all. Lord Jesus, you are our Redeemer, living, dying, and rising to win back your lost brothers and sisters. Holy Spirit, you are the energy source and the wisdom in my life. I acknowledge you; I appreciate you; I depend on you; I worship you; I praise you. The joy I feel in your house will sustain me until I can praise you face-to-face. I will love to worship you in heaven too.

_____

_____

_____

_____

_____

I'm exhausted

There are two kinds of tired. One kind is the way you feel after a vigorous aerobic workout or after putting in long hours at work but getting some important things done or as you look around at a really clean house. That's happy tired, glowing tired. People who are happy tired sleep well.

The other kind of tired is when you have been giving and giving without ever being acknowledged. Or when you realize that all your work will be wasted. Or when you have overcommitted, trying to do it all, and weeks of sleep deprivation take a nasty toll. Or when illness or worry has kept you from getting a decent night's sleep.

Is that you right now? If it is, you need some Sabbath rest from the Savior. He promises rest to all who are weary and burdened. What are you carrying right now that's too heavy for you? Drop it on him—he shares your life's yoke with you, you know. If you have guilt, he will forgive. If you feel weak, lean on his strength. If you feel lost, listen to his voice.

Here are words for your head as it hits the pillow: **"I will lie down and sleep in peace, for you alone, O Lord, make me dwell in safety"** (Psalm 4:8).

_____

_____

_____

_____

_____

JANUARY 12

In the eye of the beholder

One of the great improvements in city life has been the disappearance of X-rated movie houses. Those sleazy joints offered voyeuristic thrills for sad and lonely men, but were also magnets for robbery and prostitution.

Alas, their disappearance is not because of a great rise in stable and happy marriages with fulfilling sex lives. They have been replaced, and their influence greatly multiplied, by the rise of shops selling X-rated DVDs, and even more so, the rise in easy availability of online pornography. By some estimates, more than 25% of all web traffic is porn-related.

Those temptations will be with us forever—we can't control porn accessibility. What we can control is our desires and behaviors. Christian men need to stop rationalizing and making excuses. Jesus' words were never more urgently needed than right now: **"You have heard that it was said, 'Do not commit adultery.' But I tell you that anyone who looks at a woman lustfully has already committed adultery with her in his heart"** (Matthew 5:27,28). We need to put our time and energy not into adulterous virtual fantasy but into real relationships with real women, building strong marriages.

Christian women need to recognize the enormous power that comes with their sexuality. Wives do well to ponder Paul's important insight: **"The wife's body does not belong to her alone but also to her husband"** (1 Corinthians 7:4). Use that power carefully.

_____

_____

_____

_____

I'm afraid that my life is pointless

When you were a kid, did you ever build sand castles? I did, and it was fun to watch my kids build them too. They invested many hours in setting up plastic soldiers and stick artillery for their imaginary wars. But the castles and forts didn't last long. Other kids running around on the beach kicked the towers over. Waves, sun, and wind eroded them into shapeless lumps of sand.

Do you ever feel that futility with the things you have tried to build in your life? Have you experienced the bitterness of business failure? Have you tried multiple careers and never quite found the groove? Are there a lot of broken relationships in your past? Is it a struggle to find things in your life that you are proud of?

What may be missing is your reference point. When your measuring stick is yourself, your wealth, your ego, your prestige, or your comfort and pleasure, you may indeed feel as though your strength was spent in vain.

When God is at your core, when he is your central reference point, everything changes. **"Whatever was to my profit I now consider loss for the sake of Christ. What is more, I consider everything a loss compared to the surpassing greatness of knowing Christ Jesus my Lord, for whose sake I have lost all things. I consider them rubbish, that I may gain Christ and be found in him"** (Philippians 3:7-9).

_____

_____

_____

_____

The strong bear with the weak

Everybody hates bullies. I would imagine that most men have painful memories of playground humiliations by older and bigger boys. I would imagine that most women have painful memories of being made to feel homely by a clique of prettier girls.

While our memories of being bullied are strong, I doubt that we are even half aware of the pain we have inflicted on others. Our culture glorifies the strong and beautiful and has only contempt for the weak and plain.

Does it surprise you to know that Satan tempts those who have their lives together spiritually to look down on weaker believers? I have never heard anyone admit to the sin of being a Pharisee, but the spirit of those arrogant, judgmental church people will never die. I know it's in me, and it may live in you too.

Here's a better way: **"We who are strong ought to bear with the failings of the weak"** (Romans 15:1). That means in humility realizing that I'm no better than anybody else. That means I daily recognize my need for a Savior and am daily grateful to Christ. That means I can choose to be as patient with the strugglers around me as Christ has been with me. That means I can choose to extend a word of encouragement or a helping hand instead of a sneer. Who is in need of your mercy today?

_____

_____

_____

_____

_____

JANUARY 15
Courageous mothers

When the subject of adoption comes up, there is generally a good vibe when the transplanted child succeeds in the new home. We may be dimly aware of the strains and expense on the adoptive parents, and we acknowledge that the day a child finds out he or she was adopted can be traumatic. But we rarely think much about the birth mother and her grief, since we rarely know who she is.

Think about an Israelite woman named Jochebed. She and her husband, Amram, had the terrible misfortune to live as slaves in Egypt at the very time that the pharaoh had declared the death penalty on all boy babies. **"She became pregnant and gave birth to a son. When she saw that he was a fine child, she hid him for three months. But when she could hide him no longer, she got a papyrus basket for him and coated it with tar and pitch. Then she placed the child in it and put it among the reeds along the bank of the Nile"** (Exodus 2:2,3).

This woman is a hero. She sacrificed her own mother-needs and put her son Moses up for a watery adoption to give him a chance to live. She suffered the terrible loss that her dear little Moses would now call another woman "Mommy." Her plan worked, and God used this noble act to have his future leader raised and educated in the Egyptian royal court.

_____

_____

_____

_____

_____

God and my salvation

David, king of Israel, was a great military hero. He knew the hardships and thrills of military life. David was also a liar and poseur. He knew from firsthand experience how unconfessed sin builds up like a dark cloud overhead. It never goes away by itself. Time does not heal all wounds. Debts incurred do not just disappear; they linger and accrue interest.

How great the relief that pours into a sinner's heart when he trusts God enough to confess his sin, trusts his precious promises of forgiveness, and trusts that the guilt really is gone. **"I acknowledged my sin to you and did not cover up my iniquity. I said, 'I will confess my transgressions to the LORD'—and you forgave the guilt of my sin"** (Psalm 32:5).

Enjoying God's forgiveness is better than finding out that all your credit card balances have been paid. It's better than your very last mortgage payment. It's better even than finding out that your cancer is not coming back.

Being forgiven means getting your life back. Your joy back. Your optimism back. Being forgiven takes all the pressure off our lives since we don't have to try to get it all now. Being forgiven means having an eternity you can look forward to.

_____

_____

_____

_____

_____

JANUARY 17
Crabgrass

Dear Lord, I don't thank you enough for my husband. Come to think of it, I don't thank him enough either. He brings a lot of stability into my often turbulent life. I know I take him for granted. I often get upset, and then I see with such clarity all his faults, faults I just can't seem to forget. When I'm angry, all my past irritations come flooding back and just keep accumulating.

Lord, I need your forgiveness and your help. Help me let go of all my past guilt and anger. I need to listen to your description of a happy home: **"Your wife will be like a fruitful vine within your house"** (Psalm 128:3). Help my husband see me as a beautiful and fruitful vine, not constant crabgrass taking over every room of the house.

Bless my husband today. Help him find fulfillment in his work. Help him feel respected, both in his workplace and especially in our home. Help him be the spiritual leader I want to see in our family, and help me to be more patient when I don't get what I want as fast as I want. Help me to explain clearly what I need from him, and give me the grace to dial in to his needs as well.

I want to thank you today for my husband. And thank him.

_____

_____

_____

_____

_____

Aaron and his sons were priests then

The features of the Old Covenant that God designed for his minor children involved many visual dramas to help them understand crucially important spiritual truths. One was the priesthood. People are by nature sinful. They are largely ignorant of God's works and rebellious against what little they do know. Sin separates people from God. It makes us unfit for his presence during our lives and completely unfit to live in his heaven. People can't bridge that gap by themselves.

They need a priest. Until Christ came, human priests served as temporary substitutes. God told Moses, **"Have Aaron your brother brought to you from among the Israelites, along with his sons . . . so they may serve me as priests. Make sacred garments for your brother Aaron, to give him dignity and honor"** (Exodus 28:1,2). Aaron and his sons were set apart, ritually washed, dressed in specially woven priestly garments, and anointed with specially prepared oil.

They represented the people to God—praying, offering sacrifices, leading worship. They represented God to the people—announcing grace and mercy, reaffirming the covenant relationship for time and eternity.

But Aaron and his sons were sinners too, and the validity of their work depended on another greater Priest to come.

_____

_____

_____

_____

_____

Christ is our Great High Priest now

You and I are sinners with needs just as great as anybody of Old Testament times. We can't bridge the chasm between us and God any more than they could. But the need for human priests passed away with the coming of the Great High Priest, Jesus Christ. His great work on Calvary offered the One Sacrifice. No more are needed.

"Day after day every priest stands and performs his religious duties; again and again he offers the same sacrifices, which can never take away sins. But when *this* priest had offered for all time one sacrifice for sins, he sat down at the right hand of God" (Hebrews 10:11,12).

By joining together God and man in himself, Christ is still our Priest now and always. He still mediates between holy God and sinful people, providing that critically important bridge between earth and heaven. He still intercedes for us, reminding his Father that there is no more condemnation for those who believe in him. He still guarantees that all your prayers are received, heard, and answered at the very throne of God.

And get this—he invites all believers to think of themselves as his assistant priests, bringing the mercy of God to fearful and troubled people in their lives.

Only good girls are welcome

A persistent church disease is that congregations behave like country clubs instead of field hospitals. The spirit of the Pharisees has never died. Good boys, i.e., respectable achievers with money, are desired. Bad girls, not so much.

Those quiet visitors to your church, who sit in the back and try not to be noticed, are there not because they are really successful and are looking for a wider audience to appreciate their life performances. They are much more likely to be hurting and broken, looking for forgiveness and acceptance and hope. They know they need God, and they would love a loving community.

Joshua's scouts' innkeeper turned out to be a bad girl. Rahab was a prostitute, but she wanted something better for herself and her family. She figured out who the spies were and told them, **"I know that the Lord has given this land to you. . . . Give me a sure sign that you will spare the lives of my father and mother, my brothers and sisters, and all who belong to them, and that you will save us from death"** (Joshua 2:9,12,13).

That bad girl became a good girl. She ended up marrying a leader of the tribe of Judah named Salmon, which makes her King David's great-great-grandmother and an ancestor of the Savior.

Are "Rahabs" welcome at your church?

_____

_____

_____

_____

_____

Jesus is faithfulness

"Take This Job and Shove It" is an old Johnny Paycheck country music song that expresses the longings of millions of people who hate what they do and would like to quit. Every day people give up on their relationships as well, running and walking away from stress and pain. Every day people give up on their own lives and end them.

People are often weak and fickle. Jesus is not. Of all the things you worry about, you *know* that Jesus will always be there for you, always loving you, always forgiving you, always guiding and steering events in your life to shepherd you home. You *know* that he is rock-steady, willing and able to endure the worst to be able to give you the best.

His commitment to you is based not on your worthiness or performance but on a decision he made from all eternity to go after you and reconnect you with your Creator. **"Let us fix our eyes on Jesus, the author and perfecter of our faith, who for the joy set before him endured the cross, scorning its shame, and sat down at the right hand of the throne of God. Consider him who endured such opposition from sinful men, so that you will not grow weary and lose heart"** (Hebrews 12:2,3).

How are you doing right now? Don't quit! Fix your eyes on Jesus. Hang on!

_____

_____

_____

_____

_____

Audit!

Ever been through an IRS audit? Ever gone through a comprehensive job performance review? a third-party department audit? No fun. I'm told that they are miserable experiences.

Jesus told a parable about a shrewd manager who was being audited: **"There was a rich man whose manager was accused of wasting his possessions. So he called him in and asked him, 'What is this I hear about you? Give an account of your management'"** (Luke 16:1,2).

Either through mismanagement or through fraud, the rich man's business had lost serious money. The manager knew that the books would reveal his role in the losses, and his heart sank.

You may or may not like to hear this, but Jesus told this story to encourage you to see yourself as a manager, not an owner. All your stuff is really God's, and he seems to think that you are accountable to him for the way in which you accumulate it and spend it. Is he Lord of your checkbook? your portfolio? your real estate? your management philosophy? If he audited you today to analyze how you are managing his property, would you be proud or terrified? If he audited you today, would he conclude that you are proud to work for his business?

_____

_____

_____

_____

_____

Your real home is heaven

Being a cooperative citizen in America is really not such a terribly heavy burden, is it? But what if you were black or Native American and lived in the overtly racist times in our country? What if you had to live in a country today that would not allow you to live and share your faith, that seized excessive taxes, that imprisoned people without formal charges or access to attorneys? Could you still be a good citizen?

Many of the heroes of faith listed in Hebrews chapter 11 had to live lonely and isolated faith lives—think of Abraham and Sarah in Canaan, for instance, or Joseph in Egypt. But what sustained their faith and helped them get along with other people is that they were encouraged by God's wonderful Word and promises. They knew that their hardships were only temporary, and they decided to be useful to God in whatever situation they found themselves in, knowing that they had a far better life to come.

"They were longing for a better country—a heavenly one. Therefore God is not ashamed to be called their God, for he has prepared a city for them" (Hebrews 11:16).

You know, you can probably bear almost anything if you know it's temporary. Hang on! It's almost time for the grand surprise.

_____

_____

_____

_____

_____

JANUARY 24
Pure is better

The U.S. government's Food and Drug Administration is tasked with overseeing the safety of things we buy to put into our mouths. Purity is a big deal—even small amounts of certain toxins can cause illness and death.

It is a good thing that your eternal destiny isn't riding on the degree of moral purity in your heart. The disobedient spirit that lost Paradise for Adam and Eve lives on inside us. It is only through the forgiveness that Jesus bought for us on a cross that we can be considered righteous.

What, then, did Jesus mean with his sixth Beatitude? **"Blessed are the pure in heart, for they will see God"** (Matthew 5:8). King David explains in Psalm 24 that one with a pure heart is he **"who does not lift up his soul to an idol"** (verse 4). God has infinite patience with our sins against his laws, but he will not tolerate despising his gospel or inventing something else to worship. It is in the Bible alone that he reveals himself. Sinners like us have pure hearts when we listen to the God of the Bible and believe him. Through faith in the gospel, Paradise is regained and we will be able to do what now is impossible: we shall see God.

Create in me a pure heart, O God, one completely dedicated to you.

_____

_____

_____

_____

_____

We're still one body

One of our crosses to bear until Jesus returns is the fractured and fragmented nature of the outward Christian church. Though the invisible network of all true believers grows quietly through the Spirit's faithful gathering, outwardly there seems to be disunity, competition, and criticism among denominations.

Some of that is good. Public teachings that contradict the Bible should be identified so that the gospel is not diluted or poisoned. Simultaneously every denominational leader should listen humbly to the critiques that other Christians offer as a healthy corrective to smugness and groupthink.

But it is never right to imagine that your own tribe is the chosen and all others are merely false prophets. Concern for true and careful scriptural teaching must always be balanced by a kind and respectful attitude toward other Christian groups and denominations, even when there are disagreements. Especially when there are disagreements.

Jesus' disciples once were outraged that someone else was working their side of the street, was driving out demons in Jesus' name. They told him to stop **"because he was not one of** [them]. **'Do not stop him,' Jesus said. . . . 'Whoever is not against us is for us'"** (Mark 9:38-40). Can you walk that line—holding fast to the Bible's truths but also genuinely appreciating the work that other Christians are doing?

_____

_____

_____

_____

_____

Broken pots wanted

Who can stand proud, arrogant, gas-filled witnesses for Christ? I don't like listening to them and neither do you. However, I sure don't mind humility. I will pay attention when someone is willing to admit, "I've been a bozo and a fool, but God showed mercy on me. It is my pleasure to share that mercy with you."

That's why God uses broken pots like you and me. Your flaws, cracks, stains, and chips don't disqualify you. In fact, people who can testify about God's mercy shown to the unworthy sound a lot more refreshing than someone who pretends never to have sinned.

Here is the truth: **"Because of his great love for us, God, who is rich in mercy, made us alive with Christ even when we were dead in transgressions"** (Ephesians 2:4,5). It was for just such a sinner as you that Christ came, for just such a time as right now. This is the soundtrack that you can have playing in your life. You can accept and even like yourself because your worth to God isn't based on your performance.

The grace message in your ears will also help you to be less judgmental about the chips and flaws in the other "pots" in your life.

_____

_____

_____

_____

_____

Fate

Do you ever feel trapped by an evil *destiny*? Does it ever seem that your future has already been decided by unknown forces and that you are locked into bad outcomes? Do you feel *doomed* to repeat the sins of your parents and grandparents? Do you talk as though your whole life were in the grip of *fate*?

You have a lot of company. Great literature abounds in stories of people "destined" for tragedy. Oedipus' horrible future was told him far in advance. Macbeth found out from three witches that he was doomed. Romeo and Juliet were "star-crossed" lovers. Guiseppe Verdi wrote an entire opera called *The Force of Destiny.*

But that's all romantic baloney. Fate doesn't exist. The idea is based on Roman mythology—the three Fates were imaginary goddesses who determined everyone's life trajectory. Here's the real power behind your life: **"I trust in you, O Lord; I say, 'You are my God.' My times are in *your* hands"** (Psalm 31:14,15).

You are not a puppet that's operated by a divine puppeteer. You are not a marionette, dancing to strings pulled by a cruel or indifferent master. You were designed and created to be a child of the Most High, designed in God's image, designed to think and act and to love and will in perfect accord with God's holiness and purity. God is the guiding force in your life. And your choices do matter.

_____

_____

_____

_____

Jesus is gentleness

The God who rained water on Noah's world and burning sulfur on Sodom's world can indeed be stern and violent. At the same time he can be gentle as a lamb. Isaiah had prophesied that the coming Savior would have a gentle touch with broken sinners.

One such woman, caught in adultery, expected to be stoned to death. Jesus rebuked the hypocrisy of her accusers and attackers, and they slunk away. She expected at least a severe tongue-lashing from the Teacher, but instead she got a second chance and a helpful admonition: **"Jesus straightened up and asked her, 'Woman, where are they? Has no one condemned you?' 'No one, sir,' she said. 'Then neither do I condemn you,' Jesus declared. 'Go now and leave your life of sin'"** (John 8:10,11).

He himself was fully human and experienced everything we must go through—physical exhaustion, severe satanic temptation, verbal and physical abuse, and hate-filled condemnation by the very authorities who were supposed to protect him. He knows our weaknesses and does not despise us for them. Even his rebukes are meant not to beat us down but to steer us away from spiritual suicide.

His goal is not condemnation but restoration. Let his gentle voice comfort your heart. Let his gentle tone be in your voice when you speak to other sinners.

_____

_____

_____

_____

_____

JANUARY 29
I've got the winter blues

Do you know anybody who suffers from Seasonal Affective Disorder? Some people call it "winter blues"—they get irritable, moody, sleep more, eat more, and feel depressed. Psychologists have investigated the effect of diminished sunlight on people's emotional health. The farther north you live, the darker the winters get. I know some people who need light therapy to get through these months. Sunlight produces vitamin D in our skin. Snowbirds often describe the feeling of healing when they first arrive in Florida or Arizona after Christmas and feel the sun on their skin.

People need Sonlight too. When the glory of Christ does not touch our faces by coming off the pages of the Bible, when we haven't been listening to God's voice, Satan plants depression and self-hatred. Paul writes, **"You were once darkness, but now you are light in the Lord. Live as children of light (for the fruit of the light consists in goodness, righteousness and truth) and find out what pleases the Lord. . . . Wake up, O sleeper . . . and Christ will shine on you"** (Ephesians 5:8-10,14).

Here is good news that generates spiritual vitamin D (meaning Delight) in our lives: Through Christ, God thinks you are beautiful, fun to be with, and desirable to have in his everlasting family. Through Christ, your sins are forgiven, your prayers are all answered, your pains are temporary, and your joys are eternal.

_____

_____

_____

_____

Jesus is joy

In popular culture the devil's followers have all the fun and religious people are pitied as dry, sad, cheated, uptight, moralistic, crabby, judgmental, rigid hypocrites. Billy Joel sold a million records with his bouncy piano accompanying this philosophy: "I'd rather laugh with the sinners than cry with the saints; sinners are much more fun . . ."

That's just a shabby excuse to go against your conscience and be selfish. In fact, Jesus is joy, not gloom, and a relationship with him gives you a reason to hum a tune all day long. Jesus himself projected such a joyful and celebratory vibe in his public ministry that he was criticized for not being sober and grim-faced enough. **"They said to him, 'John's disciples often fast and pray, and so do the disciples of the Pharisees, but yours go on eating and drinking.' Jesus answered, 'Can you make the guests of the bridegroom fast while he is with them?'"** (Luke 5:33,34).

The gospel of our forgiveness makes us all optimists. Satan is defeated, our sins forgiven, our guilt washed away, our debts paid, our future guaranteed. The Great Power of the universe is our Friend, Healer, Counselor, and Father. Our graves will be only comfy beds where our bodies take a little nap.

Grace has triumphed over condemnation, and mercy has triumphed over judgment. Let's have some cake! And a song! Somebody tell Billy Joel how much fun we are.

_____

_____

_____

_____

You have a purpose

Why does the universe exist? Why is there soil? an atmosphere? moonlight? iron ore? saltwater? gravity? whales? corn?

The answer is *you*. God made all these things and everything else to provide a beautiful home for you and for the other six billion people. It is his heartfelt desire to have a joyful personal relationship with each one of us on earth, and his heart is restless until we all love him back.

We were made for him; that is our purpose. **"Remember these things, O Jacob, for you are my servant, O Israel. I have made you, you are my servant; O Israel, I will not forget you. I have swept away your offenses like a cloud, your sins like the morning mist. Return to me, for I have redeemed you"** (Isaiah 44:21,22).

One of the most significant parts of your mission on earth is to help God find and reclaim his lost children, people who are living their lives disconnected from him, who may spend eternity disconnected from him. When you dare to speak up to bring others back to God, you are speaking God's words. You are helping carry out God's agenda. You are helping God's kingdom come. You are doing God's work.

_____

_____

_____

_____

_____

February

Greater love has no one than this,
that he lay down his life for his friends.

John 15:13

FEBRUARY 1
Listen to your parents and friends

Everybody is capable of self-deception. There is nothing like a strong romantic attraction to slow down your brain processes. When you want a relationship really, really badly, you can become quite blind to things other people can see. You run the risk of making a lifelong commitment to someone who may later cause you immense pain.

How does your boyfriend treat his parents? Is he courteous and respectful toward you? What is her reputation when she is away from you? Does she tell the truth? Does she keep her promises? Does he build you up when he's away from you?

Although still common in places like India, arranged marriages are long out of style in America. But I'll bet Isaac was eternally glad that his father helped him find a wonderful woman like Rebekah to be his life partner. Abraham commissioned a trusted servant to find a godly woman for his son: **"I want you to swear by the LORD, the God of heaven and the God of earth, that you will not get a wife for my son from the . . . Canaanites, among whom I am living"** (Genesis 24:3).

Do you trust your parents and friends enough to ask for their advice about the people you are interested in dating? If they give it, will you listen?

_____

_____

_____

_____

_____

FEBRUARY 2
God never forgets

Quick—who won the last three Super Bowls? Unless it was your favorite team in all three, you might struggle with a ready answer. Memories blur together; only sports nerds obsess over the record books while the rest of us just plan to enjoy this year's game.

I am glad that God's memory is better than mine. He tracks the rise and fall of nations, the growth and decline of cities, the ebb and flow of population and wealth. He monitors rainfall and snowfall, remembering to keep the seasons in the rhythms he promised to Noah.

More important, he remembers every one of the promises and commitments that he has made over the centuries. Not a one will fail; not a word will fall to the ground. When the priest Zechariah's tongue was finally loosed after his enforced nine-month silence, he burst into praise to his God who had come **"to show mercy to our fathers and to remember his holy covenant, the oath he swore to our father Abraham: to rescue us from the hand of our enemies, and to enable us to serve him without fear"** (Luke 1:72-74).

God's infallible memory will ensure that he remembers to show mercy to you as well. His memories of his baptismal covenant with you are vivid, and you too can serve him without fear. He will never forget you.

_____

_____

_____

_____

_____

FEBRUARY 3
Less me, more you

Dear Lord, of all the changes I know I need to make in my life, the biggest is to have more you in my heart and less me-me-me. I'm surrounded by idols, intrigued and entranced by things to chase and have and worship. But they are trash compared to the thrill of having you.

Without your help I would become my own idol. I would seek my own pleasures, pursue my own comfort, soothe my own insecurities, and try every way I could to make myself bigger. My friend St. Paul has a better way: **"Whatever was to my profit I now consider loss for the sake of Christ. What is more, I consider everything a loss compared to the surpassing greatness of knowing Christ Jesus as my Lord, for whose sake I have lost all things. I consider them rubbish, that I may gain Christ and be found in him"** (Philippians 3:7-9).

I owe you the design and creation of my life. You gave me parents and shelter, food and friends, an education and a purpose. I live in your world, not vice versa. I owe you my lifelong thanks for the bloody rescue from Satan and hell. I have peace of mind, cleansing from sinful guilt, and the help of your Spirit who lives in me. I have been washed and fed, taught by the Word, and protected by the heavenly host. Lord, you are my all in all.

_____

_____

_____

_____

_____

FEBRUARY 4
Mother-love models grace

Most people know the experience of being chewed out by a boss or put down by fellow workers. Abuse from people around us starts early. Every schoolkid knows what it is like to be picked on; gossiped about; or mocked because of his or her clothes, shoes, grades, hair, or speech.

Where do children go when they've been made to feel worthless, stupid, and ugly? You know the answer: they go to Mom. Mothers have great restorative power in their soothing words and hugs. A child needs to know that even if the world is against me, Mom will always love me, be proud of me, and think I'm somebody.

King David, warrior and poet, compared the peace he enjoyed with his God to the utter serenity of a small child with his mother: **"But I have stilled and quieted my soul; like a weaned child with its mother, like a weaned child is my soul within me"** (Psalm 131:2).

Moms, it is you who make God believable and real to small children. It is from you that your children learn about unconditional love, daily forgiveness, and a feeling of self-worth. When they've learned it from you, they will find it believable that God could love them the same way and more.

_____

_____

_____

_____

_____

FEBRUARY 5
God sees and hears and acts

It was my privilege to teach in a high school for two years. How different the classroom looks from the front! When I was a student, slouching down low in the back seat in the corner, I thought the teacher wouldn't be able to see me dozing, doodling, or doing other homework. Ha! You can see everything from the front.

Sinful mortals sometimes assume that God must not be tracking what's happening on the surface of planet Earth. Perhaps they fear that the wicked are getting away with murder. Perhaps they fear that their own needs go unnoticed by a distant deity.

Au contraire. **"When you pray, go into your room, close the door, and pray to your Father, who is unseen. Then your Father, who sees what is done in secret, will reward you"** (Matthew 6:6). God's ability to monitor details of earthly life is staggering. The Bible says that he has counted every hair on your head and that no sparrow can fall from the sky without God being aware of it and granting permission.

Wherever you live, wherever you go, no matter the trouble, your God can see what's happening in your life. Whether you speak, sing, whisper, or think your prayers, your God can hear them all. Messages sent—messages received. Always.

_____

_____

_____

_____

_____

The American dream

Are you an American? Do you feel entitled to a full share in the American Dream? You know what I mean—a guarantee that you will be better educated than your parents, make more money than your parents, live more luxuriously than your parents. Every day in every way things are getting better and better. And of course your kids will surpass you.

Do young Brits, Nigerians, and Luxembourgers have national expectations? Where did our notion come from? An American historian in 1931 theorized that it came from the Puritan ethic of hard work and frugality and that the belief accelerated with the opening up of the endless frontier and discovery of gold. Somehow that desire has morphed into a feeling of entitlement; and like all entitlements that don't happen, it leaves people disappointed and sullen.

Be careful what you dream for. **"People who want to get rich fall into temptation and a trap and into many foolish and harmful desires that plunge men into ruin and destruction. For the love of money is a root of all kinds of evil"** (1 Timothy 6:9,10). It may please God to load up your life with assets and resources; he then will expect huge things of you.

On the other hand, it may please him to prepare you for unique service to his plans by subtracting wealth from you.

Does God hate gay people?

Perhaps you have seen pictures or video clips of the protesters. They travel all over America from their small Kansas church, and though they picket many different places and occasions, they seem to favor military funerals. Their placards shout that God hates gays.

Nobody's personal opinion on human sexuality needs to mean a hill of beans to you, including mine. But God's does. The Creator of people, of gender, and of marriage itself reserves to himself the right to define the purpose and parameters of sexuality. Romans chapter 1 (have you ever read it?) leaves no doubt about God's intent for marriage and sexuality as being limited to one man and one woman, committed to each other for a lifetime.

But it is a terrible mistake to identify one sin as somehow greater or more grievous than all the others. God condemns heterosexual sin as well. In fact, 1 Corinthians chapter 6 lists a whole range of rebellious human behavior that brings God's judgment. **"That is what some of you** *were.* **. . . . Flee from sexual immorality"** (1 Corinthians 6:11,18).

The glorious gospel reveals to us that in mercy Christ died and rose again to bring forgiveness for all sins to the world. Those who believe it, have it. They also have God's promises and God's commands and God's power to make changes in their lives.

_____

_____

_____

_____

_____

Give peace a chance

"God helps those who help themselves." That phrase has been repeated so often that many assume it comes from the Bible. It has a certain gut-level "truthy" feel to it, doesn't it? It sounds like it could be one of the Proverbs, motivating people to get off their sofas and become go-getters. God said nothing of the sort. Not that he smiles on laziness, but generally we don't need any encouragement to be self-seeking and aggressive on our own behalf.

Where we do need encouragement is in damping down our appetite for conflict, whether enjoying watching others fight or getting into it ourselves. We all know the mad fever of an adrenaline rush; we all love to be right; we all feel the need to "stand up for myself," "don't get pushed around," "teach 'em a lesson."

Here's a better way: **"Blessed are the peacemakers, for they will be called sons of God"** (Matthew 5:9). This is learned behavior—don't assume that attitude will automatically appear in your brain. You need to choose Christ's values and mission over Satan's for your personal behaviors. Any fool can egg on a fight. It takes a Christ-follower to find joy in steering people away from conflict and toward reconciliation.

It takes a Christ-follower to admit one's own faults, yield more than demand, and keep one's voice soft. Go ahead, kids—try this at home.

_____

_____

_____

_____

I'm afraid

When you wake up in the middle of the night in a cold sweat, what is your worst personal fear? Come on, admit it. Everybody has fears. When you're little, it's the monsters lurking under your bed. When you're a teen, it's being rejected and having no friends. Young mothers worry about their babies. New homeowners worry about being swamped in debt. Later your issues might be infertility, rebellious children, business failure, or an unfaithful spouse.

Whatever your fears may be, God is there for you when you need him. The Bible says, **"'Because he loves me,' says the Lord, 'I will rescue him. . . . He will call upon me, and I will answer him; I will be with him in trouble'"** (Psalm 91:14,15).

"Let go and let God" is a somewhat overworked cliché, but it's still true. Psalm 91 guarantees that the supreme power in the universe is interested in your struggles, cares about you in a personal way, and will get involved to help at just the right time. There is nowhere you can travel where his watchful eye cannot track you; there is no trouble so deep that his arms are too short to pull you out.

Gosh, I feel better already.

_____

_____

_____

_____

_____

It's great to be poor

One television series that you will never see is called *Lifestyles of the Poor and Obscure*. Millions and millions of people are trying to crawl *out* of poverty and to make something of a name for themselves. Who wants poverty?

Jesus began one of his greatest teaching discourses, the Sermon on the Mount, with a list of attention-arresting, outrageous statements to teach people how God works. These Beatitudes ("Blesseds") reveal how and where God does his gospel activity, where our true wealth lies, and where God's favor rests.

He began, **"Blessed are the poor in spirit, for theirs is the kingdom of heaven"** (Matthew 5:3). There is nothing especially desirable about economic poverty, but being poor *in spirit* means recognizing that you are born a moral beggar before God. Born sinful, flawed, broken in mental capacity and willpower, we are in desperate need of a spiritual rescue before the great judgment comes howling down on all evil.

It is only when we recognize our spiritual bankruptcy, when we realize the danger and despair of our own moral performance, when we know the taste of fear and emptiness that the message of Christ's death and resurrection becomes our dearest treasure. No one appreciates the promise of forgiveness and immortality like sinners who know they're dying.

We have a place in the kingdom of heaven!

_____

_____

_____

_____

FEBRUARY 11
Falling into Jesus' arms

*"Do not go gentle into that good night,
Old age should burn and rave at close of day;
Rage, rage against the dying of the light."*

The above lines are from Welsh poet Dylan Thomas' most famous poem. He wrote them as he watched his father, a once vigorous soldier, grow weak and frail. Thomas' words grip our hearts—we all dread dying, and we fear the dying of those we love. Thomas' own "light" was extinguished in 1953, and he probably did not go gently.

I get his point. Dying is the last human adventure on this earth. Dying exists in God's once immortal human race as a punishment for human evil and rebellion. It is not nice or natural.

But Jesus has changed everything. By taking on himself the guilt and blame and condemnation for human sin, the dying process loses its terror and fear and becomes merely the fall into Jesus' arms. Here are sweet words from a man in his 90s: **"Do not be afraid of what you are about to suffer. . . . Be faithful, even to the point of death, and I will give you the crown of life"** (Revelation 2:10). You can go gently when you know Christ is waiting for you.

_____

_____

_____

_____

_____

FEBRUARY 12
God and my plans

What do you want from life? Which of your achievements gives you the most satisfaction to remember? What do your friends and family hear you dreaming about and longing for? What do your coworkers think you want as your most important goals?

Have you always known what kind of career you wanted? Are you a late bloomer? Did you finally find yourself in grad school? Did you have to go to work right out of high school? Did any of your initiatives crash and burn? Are you in the family business? Did your family provide absolutely no help? As you look ahead in your life, what's important to you? What do you want? What are your plans?

Wherever you plan to go, whatever you want to do, make sure that God is your partner. **"Show me the way I should go, for to you I lift up my soul. Teach me to do your will, for you are my God; may your good Spirit lead me on level ground"** (Psalm 143:8,10).

For illustrations that will stick in your mind, read the book of 2 Chronicles in the Bible. When the kings abandoned the Lord, everything they tried to build fell apart. When they sought the Lord and listened to him, there were no limits to what he would do for them.

_____

_____

_____

_____

_____

Jesus is self-control

I wish I could say that I am revolted by temptation to sin. I wish I could say that I hate and fear and reject Satan's tempting voice. I wish I could say that I always see the dangers of sinful rebellion and run in the other direction. But I can't say any of those things, and I doubt if you can either.

I nurse grudges because I like the self-righteous superiority. I snap and bark irritable words, enjoying the adrenaline rush. I like lying because it is easier than admitting weakness and failure. I know hard work pays off in the long run, but laziness always pays off right now.

One of many reasons why I love and worship and need Jesus is that by living my life as a human being, he stepped in for me and showed the self-control and self-discipline I too often lack. He not only suffered for me. For over three decades in advance of Calvary he defeated the devil every day, refusing to reenact Adam and Eve's and my rebellions. **"We do not have a high priest who is unable to sympathize with our weaknesses, but we have one who has been tempted in every way, just as we are—yet was without sin"** (Hebrews 4:15).

Just say no? Impossible for me, but accomplished by Jesus. Are you as grateful as I am?

_____

_____

_____

_____

_____

Will you be mine?

"It is not good for the man to be alone," said God on the sixth day of creation. He proceeded to create a second gender, made also in his image and likeness. Eve's creation day was also her wedding day. Mindful of Satan's relentless sexual temptations, St. Paul advised that everyone should have a spouse.

In the Middle Ages, respect for the blessed virgin Mary grew to such an extent that perpetual chastity was thought to represent a higher form of existence than marriage. Cloisters and monasteries filled up with earnest men and women for whom romance and marriage were now forbidden.

But romance, love, and sexual desire were all designed by God. Within the bounds that he set up, they are beautiful and holy. King Solomon wrote a musical, the Song of Songs, about the joys and passions of romantic love. Although there was no way to preserve the musical notation, the surviving libretto in Scripture shows God's approval of and sanctification of the love between a man and woman. **"How beautiful you are, my darling! Oh, how beautiful! Your eyes are doves"** (Song of Songs 1:15).

I hope that you get at least one Valentine's Day card today. May this day remind you of romantic days in your past, and may the Lord grant you some sweet romantic days in your future.

_____

_____

_____

_____

_____

FEBRUARY 15
I keep doing the same sins

I hate having to scold my children repeatedly for the same acts of disobedience. Why do they still track mud through the house? Why do they still throw their clothes all over, "forget" to make their beds, and expect the maid to do all their dishes? I get frustrated when I have to correct them over and over and over.

And then it dawns on me, Lord, that you might be letting me experience how you feel about the way I treat you. Do I seem like a slow learner to you? stubborn? empty-headed? You have been so patient with me in the past—you keep blessing me even when I clearly don't deserve it.

I need even more patience from you than my children need of me—**"Do not withhold your mercy from me, O Lord; may your love and your truth always protect me. For troubles without number surround me; my sins have overtaken me, and I cannot see"** (Psalm 40:11,12).

Help me throw out the idols in my life, the things I love and trust and value more than you. You are my true treasure—help me see that serving and obeying you are the paths to true happiness. Lord Jesus, my Great High Priest, intercede for me every day so that grace and mercy from heaven will never cease washing through my heart and mind.

_____

_____

_____

_____

_____

FEBRUARY 16
She's a prize

Dear Lord, I don't thank you enough for my wife. Come to think of it, I don't thank her enough either. She brings many unique strengths and values into our family, things I don't or can't provide. I have learned a lot about people and relationships from her; she has made me a better man.

At the end of the book of Proverbs you describe a fictional woman and all the benefits she brings to her husband and family. Those words can help wives strive for improvement and excellence, but it is even more important that they inspire her beneficiaries (the kids and me) to appreciate her even more. **"Her children arise and call her blessed; her husband also, and he praises her"** (Proverbs 31:28). I am a poor, miserable sinner and do not deserve anything from you. I am grateful for your gift of a life partner. Help me become a better husband. Help me do what you invite and praise her more.

Bless her today, Lord. Shelter and protect her with your holy angels. Don't let her worries and fears steal her joy. Don't let her caring heart allow constant emotional storms inside her. Help her to be patient with me and to find satisfaction in all she does to build our family and home.

I want to thank you today. And thank her.

_____

_____

_____

_____

_____

An attitude of service

I had just finished praying with a seriously ill woman. I stepped out into the hospital corridor to talk with her son for a while. "John," I said, "you'll have to take care of the house while your mom is so sick. You'll have to keep it clean and make her meals."

He shook his head. "That's not my style," he said.

We all like to be waited on. We all think we deserve to be pampered. Working cheerfully for others is a foreign concept. Serving others is not our style by nature. It is learned behavior, and some, like John, apparently never learn it.

Jesus himself is our hero. He said once, **"The Son of Man did not come to *be* served, but *to* serve, and to give his life as a ransom for many"** (Matthew 20:28). If the omnipotent Lord finds fulfillment in doing things that bring benefit to other people, maybe that's a clue how I will find satisfaction in my life. Isn't that just like Jesus' way—that I will find joy in giving joy? That I will get by giving? That my needs will be met by my serving others?

Who needs you right now?

_____

_____

_____

_____

_____

Jesus is kindness

Commerce functions on some basic principles: You get what you pay for. You get paid what you earned. What goes around comes around.

It's not too hard to see how these principles dominate how we treat one another. Give people what they deserve. If they disappoint you, leave them. If they fail you, cut your losses and let them sink or swim on their own. If they hurt you, get your revenge. If they're "foreign," fear and suspect them until they prove themselves.

One gospel principle, which is a fruit of the Spirit, goes against our natural instincts but is a powerful force for building God's kingdom. It is the call to *treat people better than they deserve.* Jesus both taught that concept and lived it: **"When a Samaritan woman came to draw water, Jesus said to her, 'Will you give me a drink?' The Samaritan woman said to him, 'You are a Jew and I am a Samaritan woman. How can you ask me for a drink?' (For Jews do not associate with Samaritans)"** (John 4:7,9).

Though her ethnic group rejected most of the Bible, though her personal moral life was in severe disarray, Jesus engaged her on her terms, spoke kindly with her, and helped her find salvation that day at the well. His mission was not to criticize her but to win her heart. Mission accomplished.

_____

_____

_____

_____

_____

The power of one

In 841 B.C. the kingdom of Judah almost collapsed. With the assassination of the king, the queen mother, Athaliah, seized power and killed off every other member of the royal family, including her grandchildren. But baby Joash was spirited away by his aunt and hidden in the temple. The high priest, Jehoiada, used his authority and leadership to guarantee the toddler's safety.

After six years of Athaliah's ruinous reign, Jehoiada brought out the boy Joash and had him crowned king. **"Jehoiada then made a covenant between the Lord and the king and people that they would be the Lord's people. He also made a covenant between the king and the people. All the people of the land went to the temple of Baal and tore it down. They smashed the altars and idols to pieces"** (2 Kings 11:17,18).

Under Jehoiada's regency, Joash developed into a wonderful king. He repaired the temple, continued the spiritual reformation that Jehoiada had begun, and peace returned to Judah. But finally Jehoiada passed away at the incredible age of 130. The nation's wheels came off again—without the high priest's strong presence, Joash listened to new advisors and backslid into Baal and Asherah worship.

Jehoiada is my hero. He was just one man, but he helps me believe in the power of one.

_____

_____

_____

_____

_____

God will help

Christians who care about mission work are sad about all the people who have not yet heard about their Savior Jesus. They are even sadder about people who once believed and have now fallen away from their faith.

Are you trying to encourage someone back to the faith? You are not alone in your efforts. Remember first of all that God is loving your efforts. Winning hearts and minds and souls of people is God's number-one agenda item after all. He wants to help you. He will help you.

"Those whom I love I rebuke and discipline. So be earnest, and repent. Here I am! I stand at the door and knock. If anyone hears my voice and opens the door, I will come in and eat with him, and he with me" (Revelation 3:19,20).

It is God who creates faith in people's hearts. It is the power of God's Word that draws fallen-away sinners back home. You aren't freelancing on your own, of course. You are representing God, and your words carry God's love and sweet invitation.

God also is active, sometimes in ways we can't see, to use hardship in people's lives to tenderize their hearts. Nothing happens by accident. Everything is potentially useful for God's loving purpose.

_____

_____

_____

_____

_____

FEBRUARY 21

I wish I were rich

It is human nature to want what you don't have. The have-nots want to have. Mo' money is always mo' better. Materialism's twin sin is envy of the rich, and envy easily morphs into resentment. Have you ever noticed how soon political discourse every election season degenerates into manipulation of class resentments?

There is nothing glamorous or desirable about poverty. The Bible has great wisdom to help people endure it, but it is certainly no one's life goal. How much better is it for us simply to admire people with wealth (assuming it wasn't stolen), realizing that somebody worked hard, saved with discipline, invested wisely, and brought imagination and a value proposition to the marketplace and was rewarded.

How much better to seek your own wealth in a godly way. The Bible teaches us the dangers of materialism, but at the same time urges us to work to build our family's financial security. **"Lazy hands make a man poor, but diligent hands bring wealth"** (Proverbs 10:4). The Bible, particularly the book of Proverbs, promises that the Lord increases the assets of people who trust and believe in him.

To be sure, rich people can be oppressors of the poor, but they can just as easily be great benefactors to ministries and schools and organizations that bring social services to people in need. We need partnerships, not class envy.

_____

_____

_____

_____

_____

FEBRUARY 22
Don't go it alone

I don't have to tell you how many ways people's lives fall apart. Sometimes the devil hassles and attacks you from the outside, and sometimes you have an amazing capacity to sabotage your own life.

God knew this, and that's one of the reasons why he invented the church—so you would have a spiritual family. We are on a pilgrim journey, and being together is better than being alone. That's why the Bible tells us, **"Let us not give up meeting together, as some are in the habit of doing, but let us encourage one another—and all the more as you see the Day approaching"** (Hebrews 10:25).

You and I know people who think, "I don't need anybody. I don't need to go to church. I don't need any of this Bible stuff. I can handle my own life by myself." The bad news is that Satan knows how to go after the lone and solitary ones. Just as wolf packs prey on solitary sheep. It's when you're by yourself that you may start believing the lies he whispers that say you are no good and will never amount to much, that no one—and certainly no God—could ever love you.

That's why you need to get involved in the lives of people around you. As pilgrims we need fellow travelers so we can all keep an eye on one another. Even the Lone Ranger had Tonto.

_____

_____

_____

_____

_____

FEBRUARY 23
Love your enemies? Really?

It takes no great spiritual powers to love your spouse, your parents, your children, and your friends. Christians aren't the only ones to appreciate people who are kind to them — anybody can turn on charm when it's to his or her advantage.

It takes a Christian with Spirit-power within to love people who are not nice to you. The same Savior whose first words from the cross were "Father, forgive them" said this to his disciples on the Mount: **"You have heard that it was said, 'Love your neighbor and hate your enemy.' But I tell you: Love your enemies and pray for those who persecute you, that you may be sons of your Father in heaven"** (Matthew 5:43-45).

People who are rude to you, bad-mouth you, hurt you, even betray you are not really the enemy. They are victims of the enemy. Every person who does you some ill was designed by the Creator to be beautiful, good, and an heir of heaven. Some of them can be won back to God's ways, but that never happens by revenge, retaliation, or payback.

Here is a powerful way in which you can love Jesus back for the way in which he loved the unlovable (i.e., you): by returning evil with kindness, abuse with prayer, and hatred with love.

_____

_____

_____

_____

_____

I'm happy when I'm sad

"Thank you, sir! May I have another?" Only in the demented fraternity world of *Animal House* do people request more pain. People turn to movies, food, alcohol, and pills to *escape* and *lessen* the pain in their lives.

Perhaps, then, it comes as some surprise to hear Jesus attaching rewards to sadness. **"Blessed are those who mourn, for they will be comforted"** (Matthew 5:4). It's not that he is encouraging us to go after pain and tears and misery. Rather he is giving comfort to those who are suffering now and are fearful that the punishing has only begun. We should not view our troubles now as angry judgments from God, or signs that we aren't really saved. People whose lives right now experience bitter disappointments should not feel cheated. We will not experience heaven on earth.

Instead, we can bask in the promises Jesus makes about the future because as God he is already living there as well as now. The harder our lives are now, the more joyful they will be in heaven. The God who promises to work *all* things, even hardships, together for our good (Romans 8:28) guarantees that heaven will be worth the wait. He himself knew that his path to glory lay through Calvary's cross, and in the same way, after earth's breakdowns, collapses, and frustrations, we will enjoy an Easter rising of our own.

_____

_____

_____

_____

_____

FEBRUARY 25
Jesus is love

We have three potted hibiscus trees that spend summer in our backyard, but only two bear those big gorgeous red flowers. The third is nice and bushy, has great leaves, but doesn't feel like producing no matter what I do.

In the last paragraph of Galatians chapter 5, St. Paul lists nine "fruits of the Spirit," i.e., features and characteristics of our lives that show a living faith and the indwelling of the Spirit. These fruits are not optional; God rightly expects to see these behaviors in our lives.

Not a one of them comes naturally; they are all learned behaviors, taught by God's Word and empowered by the Spirit working through our faith. We need to choose them and choose to grow in them. Our Lord Jesus not only expects them; he enables them with Spiritual energy.

And he modeled them himself. The first fruit Paul lists is love, love that is willing to spend itself to make somebody else's life better. Let me invite you today to recommit yourself to be a joyful imitator of Jesus himself, drawing inspiration and motivation from his fruitful life on our behalf. **"My command is this: Love each other as I have loved you. Greater love has no one than this, that he lay down his life for his friends. You are my friends if you do what I command"** (John 15:12-14).

_____

_____

_____

_____

_____

Remember the Sabbath Day then

God built regular rhythms into the lives of the believers in the Old Covenant, and none were more important than the weekly *Sabbath* ("sha-BATH" in Hebrew means "rest"). The cycle was built off God's initial creation cycle, in which he called the entire universe into being from Sunday to Friday. He called the first Saturday a day of rest, during which he enjoyed his perfect creation and enjoyed his perfect relationship with the first people, Adam and Eve.

For his minor children, God instituted a weekly legal observance: **"Observe the Sabbath, because it is holy to you. Anyone who desecrates it must be put to death; whoever does any work on that day must be cut off from his people. For six days, work is to be done, but the seventh day is a Sabbath of rest"** (Exodus 31:14,15).

There are lesser reasons for this law, which is the Third Commandment: God here sanctions the concept of downtime, recharging the body. Work is good, but God doesn't expect it seven days a week. It is good also to have some family time.

The greatest reason, however, was to give emphasis to the Israelites' greatest treasure, and that was their relationship with God. The key to their Saturday Sabbaths was not in not working, but in setting aside time for worship and praise, learning from the Word, and enjoying their place in God's family and favor.

FEBRUARY 27
Remember Sabbath now

The wording of the Third Commandment has confused a
lot of Christians. God's "Big Ten" are an extremely handy
summary of his will for how he wants us to treat him (#1-3)
and one another (#4-10). Even though the wording is found
in the Old Testament (Exodus 20), they express timeless
moral truth, not just temporary ceremonial law.

Except for #3. Sabbath is timeless; the Sabbath *day* was
intended to be a temporary regulation. St. Paul helped
Christians who grew up in the Old Covenant make the
transition: **"Do not let anyone judge you . . . with regard to
a religious festival, a New Moon celebration or a Sabbath
day. These are a shadow of the things that were to come"**
(Colossians 2:16,17). You are free to worship God on any or
all days of the week. You may choose to work for a company
that wants you on the job every Saturday. You can work
around the home on Saturday without sinning.

Why? Because what matters is not really the *day* but
Sabbath, i.e., your happy relationship with God. What
matters is enjoying God's love for you and loving him back.
What matters is worship. What matters is trusting and
believing in Jesus with all your heart. Here is his Sabbath
promise to you: **"Come to me, all you who are weary and
burdened, and I will give you rest** [i.e., Sabbath]**"**
(Matthew 11:28).

Does anyone really love me?

How many movies have been made about lonely people looking for love? How many songs have been written about lonely people looking for a little affection? There is an ache inside each of us for love, in some ways a bottomless pit. We are hungry for acceptance. We are dying to be felt valuable by someone else. We all need to matter to somebody.

We need a safe place where we can lick our wounds and be liked anyway. We need a safe place where we can let our guard down and not be taken advantage of. We need to know that there is somebody who will always have our back. We need encouragement when we're down.

Has a cry like this ever arisen from your heart? **"You know how I am scorned, disgraced and shamed; all my enemies are before you. Scorn has broken my heart and has left me helpless; I looked for sympathy, but there was none, for comforters, but I found none"** (Psalm 69:19,20).

In love God allows us to be hurt like that. One of his reasons is to help us build our emotional self-confidence first on him and not on ourselves or anybody else. The first step in finding the love we crave is believing his blood-stained love letter to us.

_____

_____

_____

_____

_____

March

I tell you the truth,
whoever hears my word
and believes him who sent me
has eternal life.

John 5:24

Jesus is peace

One of the greatest works of art ever is da Vinci's *Last Supper*, a fresco painted into fresh plaster above a doorway in a Milan monastery. It depicts an evening that was one of the worst in the lives of Jesus' disciples. Jesus spent hours prepping his Twelve for coming hardships. He would be arrested, abused, and killed. They would fall into the hands of Jesus' own tormentors and suffer too. Their own faith would fail.

But all this would be happening according to the Father's plans. **"I have told you these things, so that in me you may have peace. In this world you will have trouble. But take heart! I have overcome the world"** (John 16:33). The operative words here are "in me." When you are connected in faith to Jesus Christ, you become linked to all his victories. You become a winner like him *no matter how things look at the moment.*

Jesus gives us peace. Jesus *is* peace. Even when we don't understand what's going on, he knows. Even when we feel out of control, he's in control. Even when we grieve over all our pain and troubles, he smiles and assures us that he is working all things together for our good.

His agenda is not for him to stay here forever in our broken and dying world. It is to lift us up to *his* world, his bright, alive, joyful, peaceful world. I feel good!

_____

_____

_____

_____

_____

A servant wife

Two generations ago married women were generally referred to by both their husbands' names, e.g., Mrs. John Smith. One generation ago that was passé and wives' own first names appeared—Mrs. Judy Smith. Yesterday's trend was for married women to keep their maiden names even after marriage. Today's fashion is just to live together and not bother to be married at all.

In these times, the Bible's teachings about gender roles in marriage must seem quaint and antiquated at best and slavery at worst. **"Wives, submit to your husbands as to the Lord"** (Ephesians 5:22). Wow! Seriously?

Yes. God really means it and not because the Trinity is chauvinistic. It's because he designed male and female to dance together most gracefully when a kind and gentle man leads and a loving and supportive wife chooses to let go of some of her autonomy and let him lead.

Why do this? It's not because men are smarter or more important. Wives, you aren't doing it primarily for him. You are doing it "as to the Lord." Jesus would never lie to you. Jesus would never hurt you—his ways are always good and always bring his blessings. Remember—joy is in serving, not being served.

_____

_____

_____

_____

_____

I feel so overwhelmed

Lord, help! Some days I am so overwhelmed and exhausted that I want to give up. I'd run away, but I am too tired. I can't keep up. I don't know how much longer I can keep juggling my job, marriage, children, house, bills, and all the other demands put on me.

Many days I feel like a failure in each area of my life. I can't work on improvement when every day I'm just reacting to the next crisis or problem. I don't feel proud of anything I do. I just can't get ahead. **"Save me, O God, for the waters have come up to my neck. I sink in the miry depths, where there is no foothold. I have come into the deep waters; the floods engulf me. I am worn out calling for help; my throat is parched"** (Psalm 69:1-3).

Lord, please help me! Send relief from heaven. I know you want me to be self-sufficient. I know you want me to stand on my own two feet. But my burdens are more than I think I can bear. I appeal to your love. I appeal to you as my Father. Do what all good fathers do when their children are going under; come with your greater strength and bring help. I call to you and trust in your mercy and wisdom. Please come today and help me!

_____

_____

_____

_____

_____

I'm full of doubts

What are the most serious obstacles to your faith? Materialism? Busyness? Evolutionary science? Pleasures?

How about stamina? When God makes you wait and wait and wait some more for his providence, does that grind down your confidence? Have you had some long stretches of poverty or illness or unemployment? David said, **"How long, O LORD? Will you forget me forever? How long will you hide your face from me?"** (Psalm 13:1).

As God sees it, faith is like a muscle that needs a good workout to get stronger. Yeah—no pain, no gain. What often keeps us from developing the faith stamina we need is memory loss—we forget all the times that God did answer our prayers, when God did come through for us, when he did just what he said he would.

Waiting is okay. God is always on time. David answered his own question later in the same psalm: **"I trust in your unfailing love; my heart rejoices in your salvation. I will sing to the LORD, for he has been good to me"** (Psalm 13:5,6).

_____

_____

_____

_____

_____

Your Father's compassion

You know the story of the prodigal son, right?—son asks for inheritance, son spends inheritance foolishly, son travels home looking for his father's mercy. If this were reality TV, here's how the story would continue: "But while he was still a long way off, his father's security guards spotted him and relayed the message. The father gave strict orders that his wastrel offspring was never to set foot on the family estate again, and if he tried, the dogs should be set on him."

Here's how the Bible describes the father, your Father: **"But while he was still a long way off, his father saw him and was filled with compassion for him; he ran to his son, threw his arms around him and kissed him"** (Luke 15:20).

There is hardly a more beautiful description in the entire Bible of *grace,* which is God's decision to love unlovable people because of Jesus' willing death on Calvary. Jesus wants you to know that you can always count on the Father's mercy, because it is not based on your performance.

Compassion means that the father felt his son's shame and pain. And get this: he didn't make his son crawl. The father *ran* to embrace his prodigal bonehead. Wouldn't you like to be in your heavenly Father's embrace right now?

_____

_____

_____

_____

_____

My children are my treasures

Dear Lord, thank you for my children. I know I don't thank you enough. They are miracles of your design, and they have brought incredible joy and delight into my life. How blessed I am to be their gateway into the world!

I grumble too much about the strain and cost and work involved in raising children. Lord Jesus, you sacrificed so much for me—it is a privilege to worship you by being willing to sacrifice for my children. They are worth everything I have invested in them. Forgive my irritability, self-centeredness, and blindness. Help me stay patient, sweet-tempered, and full of praise. Give me the grace to let them develop according to the way you designed them, not as props in my personal fantasies.

Your Word reminds me, **"Sons are a heritage from the Lord, children a reward from him"** (Psalm 127:3). In my better moments I do feel rewarded. They have changed me, and most of those changes are for the better. Open my heart and mind to embrace what they bring.

Lord Jesus, bless and protect them. Let all the skills and talents and aptitudes you built into them emerge. Let them be useful to you, for your agenda, for your glory. I am proud of them; I am grateful to you. My kids are my treasures.

_____

_____

_____

_____

_____

Too ashamed to pray?

When I was a kid, we always knew that when the dog slunk around the house and avoided our eyes we would soon find an "accident" in the living room. When you know that you have done wrong and offended someone, it is a powerful deterrent to wanting to have a close and intimate conversation with that person. Guilt makes you want to run away. When we are guilty of unconfessed and unforgiven sin, one of the first casualties is our desire to pray.

Here is the beauty of a relationship with our God that is based not on *our* performance and behavior but rather on *his grace,* that is, his decision to love and forgive us unconditionally. Jesus came to this earth not to pin medals on spiritual superstars but to rescue sinful and ashamed fools like you and me. He said once, **"Come to me, all you who are weary and burdened, and I will give you rest"** (Matthew 11:28).

When you are aware of your shortcomings, when your conscience makes you sick inside, when you are too ashamed to pray, that is the very best time to pray and claim the forgiveness that was bought for you for just such a time. God's mercy is bigger than your sin. He will never despise a broken and contrite heart (Psalm 51:17); in fact, his particular specialty is in healing broken hearts and providing rest for restless spirits.

_____

_____

_____

_____

_____

Leaving a legacy

Has it ever occurred to you that buying life insurance on your own life is one of the most selfless things you can do (assuming you don't cash out of the policy for your own benefit while you're still living)? All of your payments are investments in the future that will provide confidence of financial security to your heirs during your lifetime and actual financial security when you die. But *you* won't see the money—*they* will.

A distressing number of your and my neighbors and fellow church members have no financial legacy plans, no insurance beneficiaries, no will. In the case of believers, this is not only bad financial management; it is bad Christian stewardship. If you die intestate, no ministry or community charity can receive a dime from your estate. If you have no written and signed plan, a state-appointed lawyer will make the decisions.

Successful people are rarely completely self-made. Their education, value system, and financial security began decades, maybe many generations, before they were born. It is a great gift to arrange that the next generations in your family can start on a hill, not have to work their way out of a hole.

"A good man leaves an inheritance for his children's children" (Proverbs 13:22). How have you benefited from past generations? What kind of legacy will you leave?

_____

_____

_____

_____

_____

Devoted to worshiping together

One thing I love about the first wave of the early Christian church is the passion. They were so excited about their faith that they couldn't wait to go to church. Nobody needed to argue them into it. The pastor didn't have to beg or pressure them. Parents didn't have to bribe the children with promises like, "All right, if you go to church, we'll all go to McMoses afterward." Nobody had to threaten the teenagers, "You better go to church or you're not getting the horse and wagon for two weeks."

Instead, **"all the believers were together and had everything in common. Every day they continued to meet together in the temple courts"** (Acts 2:44,46).

Every day! They just did it. They loved hearing the truth, loved being with other people, loved sharing the Lord's Supper, loved sharing their faith, loved getting encouragement from others. They had everything in common. And because they couldn't wait for Sunday to roll around, they met together—every day.

This Sunday, when the snooze button on your alarm clock is calling your name, rejoice with those who say to you, **"Let us go to the house of the Lord"** (Psalm 122:1).

_____

_____

_____

_____

_____

You go first; I'll wait

"I am Oz, the great and powerful! Who are you?"

"If you please, I am Dorothy, the small and meek."

In one of many biblical themes running through that marvelous movie, the small and meek Dorothy turns out to be a witch slayer and hero.

L. Frank Baum, author of *The Wizard of Oz*, got that idea from Jesus. **"Blessed are the meek, for they will inherit the earth"** (Matthew 5:5). Jesus' mother had learned that as well—when she learned she would be the mother of the Savior of the world, she marveled at how God knocks down the lofty from their perches and in due time lifts up the lowly (like her).

Not too many people believe that today. It's a dog-eat-dog world. Our society has no admiration for the meek—they are *losers,* soon to be roadkill. Have you ever felt small and insignificant? Rejoice! God knows exactly where you are and does not think any less of you.

In fact, once when Jesus was looking around for a visual image of servant-leadership, he selected a child from the crowd and held the child up as someone for his ambitious and sometimes-arrogant disciples to emulate. He wants his people full of his Spirit, not full of themselves. Can you see how this takes all the pressure off our lives? We don't have to get it all now . . .

_____

_____

_____

_____

_____

I feel wounded

One of the benefits of being a kid in a multiple-child family is that you learn to take abuse. Not that that's good — but it is helpful. We all need to develop some coping skills for deflecting and shedding put-downs, while still preserving our self-confidence.

But sometimes nasty arrows get past our defenses. They find our weak spots, and we can't seem to pull them out. How about you? Are you bleeding right now? Has your wife crushed your feeling of manhood? Has your husband made you feel homely? Have your teenagers figured out that they are stronger than you now? Have you been dumped by the person you were hoping to marry? Have you been demoted? fired?

The Lord Jesus took his human body to heaven with him, and his human heart hurts when we hurt. **"O Lord my God, I called to you for help and you healed me"** (Psalm 30:2). He can help us remember without hating. He can help us believe in ourselves again. He can help us feel like the winners we are, even when we've been called losers.

A carpenter told me once that when wood splits along the grain, once it's been glued and clamped it will be stronger than before. Do you suppose that Jesus sometimes lets you be wounded so that his healing will leave you stronger too?

_____

_____

_____

_____

_____

Jesus is patience

No matter which human activity you pick, no two people move at the same speed in performing it. People don't run at exactly the same speed, drive, mature, or learn at the same speed. They don't progress in their faith identically either. In your life right now, you are ahead of others in your spiritual growth and maturity. How will you treat those behind you?

St. Paul tells us that one of the fruits of the Spirit is patience. Patience means that you have empathy for those who struggle at things you've mastered. Patience means that you don't despise people for being weak. Patience means that you share insights and wisdom that you have picked up so that the other person can advance.

Jesus was often disappointed by the slow progress his disciples were making, and he occasionally scolded them. But he always stayed engaged, always loved them, always stayed committed to their growth. The afternoon of his magnificent resurrection he encountered two confused and grieving disciples who didn't recognize him. **"He said to them, 'How foolish you are, and how slow of heart to believe all that the prophets have spoken! Did not the Christ *have* to suffer these things and then enter his glory?' And beginning with Moses and all the Prophets, he explained to them what was said in all the Scriptures concerning himself"** (Luke 24:25-27).

Jesus didn't give up on us. Let's not give up on those behind us.

_____

_____

_____

Smell the roses

When you're a kid, you're always waiting for something. Waiting to be old enough to try out for the team. Waiting to get your license. Waiting until the prom. Waiting to get accepted into the college you want. Waiting to have enough money to buy a car.

It's good to be focused on a goal. It's bad to be so into what you want that you no longer enjoy the place you are right now. What are you longing for right now? Is the wait driving you crazy? Does God's "slowness" make you doubt his love? his power? his wisdom?

David had to wait for seven *years* after his coronation to be fully accepted as king of Israel. During part of that time, he had to live in exile, waiting, waiting, waiting for God to do something. He learned from experience that God's ways are worth the wait. **"I am still confident of this: I will see the goodness of the LORD in the land of the living. Wait for the LORD; be strong and take heart and wait for the LORD"** (Psalm 27:13,14).

You've heard the old saying about smelling the roses? Walk a little slower. Look around a little more. Notice the people around you—some were sent directly by God. Listen first; talk later. Tip waitresses well. Take time to hug people. Let God's plans ripen, knowing that they are all good plans.

_____

_____

_____

_____

_____

Are you hungry?

"You can call me anything you want; just don't call me late for dinner," goes the old gag, probably from vaudeville days. What are you hungry for right now? Food? Attention? Amusement? Challenge? As if we didn't have enough trouble keeping our appetites in check, we face a daily barrage of advertising—print, billboards, online, radio, TV—that tries to hit an emotional trigger within us to get us to buy stuff.

Popular culture teaches us that all our appetites are normal and legitimate and get first priority. Soft drink manufacturers tell people, "Obey your thirst!" There is money to be made selling people what they want.

What do you want? What are you hungry for right now? May I invite you to ponder Jesus' words: **"Blessed are those who hunger and thirst for righteousness, for they will be filled"** (Matthew 5:6). Do you have a craving for your friends' approval? Do you have a craving for God's approval? If you don't have God's approval over your life, nothing will work right. If you have God's righteousness, bought for you with the blood of Christ and guaranteed to you through his wonderful Word, you have everything important. Everything else you really need will be provided at the right time.

You will be filled.

_____

_____

_____

_____

_____

MARCH 15
I'm angry with God

We all have bombs dropped on our lives—nasty setbacks that shake us up. Some families have had atomic bombs fall—major house fire, catastrophic illness in the breadwinner, disastrous investments, or worst of all, a child-sized casket.

Satan will always exploit openings like that: "How can you still believe that your so-called heavenly Father loves you? If he could have stopped it, why didn't he?" The psalm writer Asaph wondered uneasily, **"Has his unfailing love vanished forever? Has his promise failed for all time? Has God forgotten to be merciful?"** (Psalm 77:8,9).

God understands our anger. It is born of ignorance of the majesty of his power, the tenderness of his love, and the infinite depth of his wisdom. True enough—we may not be able to figure out exactly what he's up to at any given moment. True enough—he doesn't always explain himself in advance. But we do have his splendid track record to go on.

That's why Asaph went to the Word when he needed reassurance that God's plan would still work out: **"I will meditate on all your works and consider all your mighty deeds. With your mighty arm you redeemed your people"** (Psalm 77:12,15).

_____

_____

_____

_____

_____

Jesus is goodness

Thirty miles northeast of Mexico City lie the great pyramids of Teotihuacan. The temples at the top were sites of great religious intensity and sometimes featured human sacrifice. Victims were decapitated or had their hearts cut out to propitiate one of the eight major gods and goddesses. Favor from the gods had to be bought by human effort.

The Bible tells us that favor with God was indeed bought with blood, but it was the blood of God himself that was shed for us. The Bible also tells us that a God who would make that ultimate gift must care for us deeply and will give us the smaller things we need as well.

What do you suppose was Jesus' first miracle? Not a dramatic healing or resurrection. He rescued a bridal couple from the embarrassment of running out of wine at their reception. **"Jesus said to the servants, 'Fill the jars with water'; so they filled them to the brim. . . . 'Now draw some out and take it to the master of the banquet.' They did so, and the master of the banquet tasted the water that had been turned into wine"** (John 2:7-9).

Here you see what Jesus thinks of us. He likes us! He likes to help us in big and little ways. He exerts his omnipotence on our behalf. He is full of goodness *to us*!

_____

_____

_____

_____

_____

Stranger in a strange land

Satan never stops trying to steal our stuff. He has managed to turn Christmas into a frenzy of commercialism and Easter into nothing more than a spring festival with green plastic grass, bunnies, and chocolate eggs. And somehow he managed to take the heroic story of Patrick and turn it into an excuse to drink a lot and pretend to be Irish.

The truth is that Patrick was British. Kidnapped by Irish raiders, he was forced to work as a shepherd in Ireland. He escaped, but *chose* to return and made it his life's work to convert the wild Celts to Christianity. His story is an echo of Joseph, whose resentful brothers sold him as a slave. **"When the Midianite merchants came by, his brothers pulled Joseph up out of the cistern and sold him for twenty shekels of silver to the Ishmaelites, who took him to Egypt"** (Genesis 37:28).

Joseph suffered many indignities, the worst of which was prison for a crime he didn't commit. But he came to love his adopted country and eventually rose to become chief assistant to the pharaoh. His wise leadership averted famine in the Near East.

This St. Patrick's Day you may choose to make merry with friends, wear some green, dance to some great music, and laugh a lot. But I hope you will also take a moment to remember heroes like Joseph and Patrick who chose to love their enemies and bring them God's mercy.

_____

_____

_____

_____

A servant husband

Sometimes leadership is thought of as power to get what you want, power to control others, power to manipulate. Christ-leadership, that is, servant leadership, has as its goal making the other person's life better. In God's world, husband-leaders are in charge *first* of the well-being of their wives and children. Their position of leadership in the family is for the benefit and well-being of the family.

Here's the plan: **"Husbands, love your wives, just *as Christ loved the church"*** (Ephesians 5:25). Notice the role model for husbands. God doesn't say that husbands should love their wives as James Bond "loved" his girlfriends or as Hugh Hefner "loves" his Playmates.

Christ made our forgiveness and salvation his first priority, more important than his own comfort, preferences, and even life itself. He literally loved us to death—his death.

Husbands, God has asked your wife to let you lead. Is your leadership worthy of that sacrifice on her part? Can she see Jesus in the way you are doing it? Does she feel used and bossed around or built up and precious? Does your leadership make her feel secure, valuable, and honored?

_____

_____

_____

_____

_____

God and my fears

On every piece of money that you can lay your hands on are four powerful words.

Alas, Americans only partly believe them. Our national behavior suggests to me that our confidence is in George. Washington, that is. The only thing better than money is more money. But our currency's testimony is simple and powerful. Blessed are those who do what our money says: In God We Trust.

The giver of all life, owner of all wealth, and manager of the universe is not so very concerned with what's in your wallet. He cares more about what's in your heart. He can replace lost wealth in the snap of his divine finger. But only you can choose to trust in him. **"When I am afraid, I will trust in you. In God, whose word I praise, in God I trust; I will not be afraid. What can mortal man do to me?"** (Psalm 56:3,4).

If you need help with growing your ability to trust God for everything, don't ask a young person. He or she hasn't lived long enough to see and understand the divine patterns. Find someone with gray or white hair. They have learned how God always helps people through their hardships and in that way to overcome their fears and live confidently.

_____

_____

_____

_____

_____

Teach them God's Word and will

The mosquitoes that poke me all summer do not have to go to mosquito college to learn how to drill for red gold. That ability is simply in them from the moment they are hatched. All of the behaviors needed for a successful blood extraction operation are preinstalled in their tiny mosquito brains.

But knowledge about Jesus doesn't come to people mosquito-style. I think some parents think that the Christian faith self-implants and self-develops in their children, but when they're wild and rebellious teenagers, the parents wonder what went wrong.

Children aren't born knowing there is a God. They will soon find out how evil the world is and will discover also the presence of evil in their own minds. But they have no innate knowledge of their Savior Jesus. If he is to come and live in their little hearts, children need you to tell them. Moses instructed the believers in his day not to neglect sharing information about God's words and mighty deeds, but rather to **"teach them to your children, talking about them when you sit at home and when you walk along the road, when you lie down and when you get up"** (Deuteronomy 11:19).

When you speak God's words in your home, they are as powerful as if God himself were speaking to your children. God's words bring power to drive out Satan, create faith, and build your child's capacity to know and choose what is good and God-pleasing in life.

_____

_____

_____

_____

I'm confused

"What do I do now?" Have you ever groaned that question? What could be worse than confusion? Sometimes our choices in life all seem bad or they all seem dreadfully hard or there are so many different choices. Do you stick with a difficult boyfriend? Do you rat out a friend who is doing something illegal? Do you do an intervention in the life of a friend who is on a destructive behavioral path?

Do you help a child do math problems or make her figure them out on her own? Do you protect a coworker or tell the boss? What do you do about your daughter's problem pregnancy? How can you cope with bankruptcy?

Well, guess what? God guides your walk. He cares enough about your life to provide foundational principles to help you deal with life's toughest questions. Do you feel surrounded by darkness and unsure what to do? Let him speak to you.

The Bible says in Psalm 119:105, **"[Lord,] your word is a lamp to my feet and a light for my path."** There you will find eternal and true principles about how to think about money, love, sex, your job, your family, and yourself. God's Word evaporates confusion.

_____

_____

_____

_____

_____

Spending

Are you a skinflint or a spender? Some of you pinch your pennies hard enough to make Lincoln cry. Like Ebenezer Scrooge, you would rather shiver in a cold office than "splurge" on more coal. But others, probably many more, absolutely love spending. What is it about spending money that is so addictive?

Well, it's fun to be pampered, to spoil yourself, to indulge. Having stuff is good. Having more is better. We imagine that we will impress other people with our new clothes or toys. Jesus warned that loving spending would lead to loving money, a deadly form of idolatry. He said, **"Be on your guard against all kinds of greed; a man's life does not consist in the abundance of his possessions"** (Luke 12:15).

How can you tell if you are a problem spender? (1) Do you get into family fights over spending? (2) Do you charge more purchases than you can pay off each month? (3) Do your impulse purchases mean that you have no money left for more important things like education or your offerings to the Lord? (4) Are you under water in consumer debt?

How can you be set free from addictive spending? Make spending decisions jointly with your family—a fiscal buddy system. Pray to the Spirit to help you grow in the grace of contentment. Remember that your money really belongs to the King and that you are merely a manager in his company.

_____

_____

_____

_____

Persecution complex

Do you get a little disoriented from all of Jesus' "upside-down" statements? Are you ready for another? Here is a paradox that is hard to accept at first: **"Blessed are those who are persecuted because of righteousness, for theirs is the kingdom of heaven. Blessed are you when people insult you, persecute you and falsely say all kinds of evil against you because of me. Rejoice and be glad, because great is your reward in heaven"** (Matthew 5:10-12).

Satan hates Christ, and his followers hate Christians. Until Christ returns, spiritual warfare is our lot. But here's the great news: Satan has already been defeated, and all his assaults on the church will fail. Here's more: God works his saving agenda both through our comfort and our pain, both with our outward successes and our hardships. One African church leader recently attributed the rapid growth of his church body to the amount of suffering they had endured.

My heart goes out to Christians who suffered persecution in Roman times, dying in the Coliseum, burned at the stake, and crucified like Christ. My heart goes out to Christians today who are driven into exile, beaten, imprisoned for their faith, and killed.

Jesus himself assures us that these are not signs that we are losing. Just the reverse—we are blessed for everything we suffer for Jesus, and great is the reward waiting for us.

_____

_____

_____

_____

_____

MARCH 24
Cut 'em some slack

How I love it when people cut me some slack! When the state trooper lets me off with a warning instead of slamming me with an expensive ticket . . . when my wife overlooks my grouchy remarks . . . when my coworkers cover for me and smooth over something that was my fault. Why is it so hard for me to do that for others?

Maybe it's because I don't want to enable bad behavior in others. Maybe it's because I am so doggone insecure that I think I stand a little taller if I cut other people down to size. Maybe it's because I feel morally superior when I can catch people in their sins and gloat an internal "Aha!"

My Savior Jesus made the supreme sacrifice of bearing the wrath of God for human sin in his holy body for one purpose and one purpose only—to purchase for me the forgiveness of my sins. It is he who now commissions me to be his agent, his broker, in sharing that forgiveness with the people around me. **"Blessed are the merciful, for they will be shown mercy"** (Matthew 5:7).

Perhaps I'm afraid that if I do that I will weaken the rules. Jesus wants me to know that when I do that, I open the floodgates of *his* mercy coming down over my head. Who in your life needs your mercy today?

Their culture is disgusting

It isn't hard to criticize what you don't understand. If you don't get around much, other people's culture and behaviors can sure seem weird, if not downright disgusting. Americans traveling abroad have been known to freak out over bathroom plumbing that looks nothing like home. The thought of eating seaweed and fish eggs has made some of our fellow Yankees green.

Long-lost son Joseph, now vice-pharaoh of Egypt, explained why his father's family wouldn't have to worry about assimilation and disappearance as a nation if they all came to Egypt to live. The Israelites would keep their identity, Joseph said, because **"all shepherds are detestable to the Egyptians"** (Genesis 46:34). Kind of brings back memories of the American West, doesn't it? Cattlemen always hated the sheepmen, and the sheepmen vigorously returned that fear and contempt.

My hope for you is to be of maximum use in God's plan to draw people not like you into his kingdom. As Mark Twain said, "Travel is fatal to prejudice, bigotry, and narrow-mindedness. . . . Broad, wholesome, charitable views of men and things cannot be acquired by vegetating in one little corner of the earth all one's lifetime."

You can't share the Word effectively with people you don't love and accept.

_____

_____

_____

_____

_____

Tell the truth

"In wartime, truth is so precious that she should always be attended by a bodyguard of lies." You know who said that? I bet you think it was Hitler or Goebbels. Actually, it was Winston Churchill.

Not that human beings need much urging or rationale for lying, even from Churchill. We were all born children of Satan, and Satan's native language is lying. Jesus called him the "Father of lies, a liar from the beginning." Truth telling is learned behavior, and it's hard. From young on, children learn how easy it can be to evade responsibility, divert blame, cause trouble for others, and get things through lies.

But lying isn't just a cute and understandable strategy for problem management. Lying poisons our minds. Persistent lying hardens our consciences and leaves us so confused that we no longer can recognize the truth. **"The Lord detests lying lips, but he delights in people who are truthful"** (Proverbs 12:22).

Lord, anoint my lips today. Let me choose to speak the truth, and let me bite back a lie, even when it costs me something.

_____

_____

_____

_____

_____

Am I old and useless?

In Jaques' famous "all the world's a stage" speech from Shakespeare's *As You Like It,* he roguishly describes the stages of human life, the final phase of which sounds pretty grim: "The last scene of all, that ends this strange eventful history, is second childishness and mere oblivion, sans teeth, sans eyes, sans taste, sans everything."

Solomon presents a similarly gloomy view of what old age does to the body. He speaks in unusual metaphors for muscles, eyes, ears, and teeth: **"The sun and the light and the moon and the stars grow dark . . . when the keepers of the house tremble, and the strong men stoop, when the grinders cease because they are few, and those looking through the windows grow dim. . . . All their songs grow faint"** (Ecclesiastes 12:2-4). Lord, how will I manage when I am old? Will there still be a use for me?

Scripture tells us many stories of how useful God's seniors are. Paul was still a traveling missionary in his 60s, Abraham first left Ur for Canaan in his 70s, Daniel shivered in the lions' den in his 80s, and St. John wrote the matchless book of Revelation in his 90s. God's seniors can find serenity in knowing that in heaven their bodies will ache no more, but they should stay ready and alert in case God calls them to significant service yet on this earth.

_____

_____

_____

_____

_____

MARCH 28
Be gentle

The two greatest missionary heroes of the age of the apostles were Peter and Paul. Both had an enormous impact on the early church, gathering believers and planting congregations. They both left behind profound writings that anchor the doctrinal portion of the New Testament.

And yet both had much in their pasts to be ashamed of. Peter denied knowing or believing in Jesus on the dreadful night of Jesus' arrest and trials. For the rest of his life, the crowing of a rooster at dawn must have given him bad flashbacks. Paul spent his earliest adult years violently persecuting Christians, and the mental images of his cruelties were never far away. Only God's grace made him somebody and kept him going.

Those painful memories kept both apostles humble and kept their words soft when they sought to restore others whose lives were unraveling: **"Brothers, if someone is caught in a sin, you who are spiritual should restore him *gently*"** (Galatians 6:1).

Shaming and shunning only push people farther away from their Savior. Be kind to sinful fools. You were one once, and a time may come when you are one again.

_____

_____

_____

_____

_____

Trusting what you can't see

Zarephath is a village outside of Israel, located in what is today the coastal country of Lebanon. A widow there was God's chosen agent for the preservation of his prophet Elijah during a time of severe drought in Israel. She had lost her husband and provider, and now she and her one son were themselves near starvation.

Elijah put her and her faith to a severe test: "Feed me first," he told her. "God will provide for you." She took a deep breath and agreed. Sure enough—her flour bin and oil jar were miraculously replenished each day, and the three had enough to eat.

Sometime later her son died. In bitterness of spirit she feared that his death was a punishment for her past sins. Elijah assured her that no such punishing was going on and interceded with God to restore the boy's life.

Humbled and grateful, the widow exclaimed, **"Now I know that you are a man of God and that the word of the Lord from your mouth is the truth"** (1 Kings 17:24). I want to learn from this remarkable woman—to trust God's promises while danger still threatens and to give him the glory when he sends relief.

Are there any unthanked gifts and miracles in your life?

_____

_____

_____

_____

_____

MARCH 30
Removing the curse

In one of the local hospitals here in Milwaukee, the top floor is where fetal alcohol babies go. The problem with those babies is they inherited something that was not originally their personal choice. They inherited an alcohol dependency from their mothers who drank, and their lives will never be normal as a result.

Well, I've got news for you. You and I are "fetal sin" babies. We can whine about it, tap dance around it, make excuses for it, or think about something else as a distraction, but we cannot get rid of our congenital evil virus. We all come from the same set of first parents, who in the Garden of Eden thought that being connected to God was demeaning slavery. Now we all live under God's triple curse of pain, death, and judgment.

Astoundingly, the same God who condemned their rebellion also designed a rescue plan. The prophet Isaiah explained the great messianic plan more clearly than anyone in the Old Testament: **"He was pierced for our transgressions, he was crushed for our iniquities; the punishment that brought us peace was upon him, and by his wounds we are healed"** (Isaiah 53:5).

It is this message of love and forgiveness that a dying world needs and that your congregation can bring to your community.

_____

_____

_____

_____

_____

You make the first move

Say these words right now out loud: "It was my fault." "I'm sorry." "You were right."

That was a struggle, wasn't it? Those words come hard out of my mouth, and you probably don't say them very often yourself. We like to be right. We like the moral high ground of remembering clearly the faults of others. We excel at justifying our own words and actions and can easily find fault with the other guy.

We would rather prolong an argument than enter a discussion where we might have to admit wrong. Jesus stunned his hearers yet again when he showed them that reconciliation with a brother or sister is even more important than going to church. **"If you are offering your gift at the altar and there remember that your brother has something against you, leave your gift there in front of the altar. First go and be reconciled to your brother; then come and offer your gift"** (Matthew 5:23,24).

It does not show spiritual strength to hold out and give the other person the silent treatment. That in fact is lazy and weak. We show spiritual strength *by going first.* And don't initiate that conversation by criticizing the other person for his or her faults. Jesus' way for that conversation to begin is to admit your own mistakes and sins, listen humbly, and ask for forgiveness.

You may then be surprised, for gospel kindness melts cold hearts.

_____

_____

_____

_____

April

I am the resurrection and the life.
He who believes in me will live,
even though he dies.
And whoever lives and believes in me
will never die.
John 11:25,26

APRIL 1
Don't talk about a cross

Jesus disappointed just about everybody with whom he came into contact regarding the kind of Messiah they wanted and expected him to be. He didn't move fast enough for his mother, infuriated the religious establishment, and even scared his disciples by his death-talk. They wanted none of that: **"From that time on Jesus began to explain to his disciples that he must go to Jerusalem and suffer many things. . . . Peter took him aside and began to rebuke him. 'Never, Lord!' he said. . . . Jesus turned and said to Peter, 'Get behind me, Satan! You are a stumbling block to me'"** (Matthew 16:21-23).

Peter and the gang wanted something more like King David, who slew Philistines, or King Solomon, who was stupendously wealthy. They were hoping for John Wayne, Chuck Norris, or Rambo. Instead they got someone who was planning to surrender to his bitterest enemies.

Later on the Spirit helped them to realize that it was that very meekness that would keep them out of hell. Jesus came not to kill his enemies but to let them kill him. Forgiveness of sins could be bought and given only by a Lamb, not a lion. Atonement could not be made by the blood of God's enemies but by the blood of God himself.

By the way, all those who wish to follow Jesus are invited to pick up their own crosses.

_____

_____

_____

_____

APRIL 2
Mutual submission

If you are not a believer in Christ, you probably won't get this one at all. In the marketplace, you have to demand your rights or you will get walked over. You have to make your demands and expectations explicit. In Christ's world, though, you enter marriage the way he entered planet Earth: as a servant.

Does this sound like fun? **"Submit to one another out of reverence for Christ"** (Ephesians 5:21). On the face of it, I suppose not. It sounds like a lot of work. It sounds risky—won't your spouse just take advantage of you? What if nobody takes care of *your* needs?

Mutual submission is actually one of the great secrets of a "happily ever after" marriage. If I make demands of my wife, then I'm just another drain on her capacity. On the other hand, if I serve her, I will take pressure off her. I will add energy to her spirit. I will inspire her heart to want to serve me back.

You know what downward spirals are, right? When two people's negativity feeds off each other and drives the relationship into the ground. Mutual submission ignites the reverse—an upward spiral. Talk about win/win—you honor Christ and your life gets better.

_____

_____

_____

_____

_____

APRIL 3

A to Z

Normally I don't like people to tell me how a movie turns out. I may want to see it and don't want the plot given away. I appreciate it when magazine movie reviews announce "spoiler alert" early on; if I have even a half interest in seeing the movie, I will skip the review.

I'll tell you, though, that in one major aspect of my life I don't mind at all hearing the outcome in advance. Jesus our Savior was present at creation, will live into a grand eternal future, and has seen everything in between. He is the Be-All and End-All, the Alpha to Omega, the A to Z—not only in the Greek alphabet but every alphabet.

Anytime he wants to he can tell me about my wonderful personal future: **"I am the Alpha and the Omega, the First and the Last, the Beginning and the End"** (Revelation 22:13). Unlike all the crystal ball gazers and fakers and psychics here on earth, he can describe what lies ahead for the believers because he's already been there. My life has had enough disappointment and bitterness, enough frustration and unfulfilled longing, that I don't mind one bit if he risks a spoiler alert and tells me about the new world he's going to create.

He likes it. We're going to like it too.

_____

_____

_____

_____

_____

Work ethic

Todd Rundgren got it right. There is a sound track running in most guys' brains (and probably a lot of women's too), and it goes like this: "I don't want to work. I just want to bang on the drum all day."

When children are babies, their parents are their servants, even slaves, because they are so helpless. Teenagers kind of want it to stay that way—they easily grow fond of someone else washing dishes, clothes, and cars. Teaching my own children to work willingly has proven to be one of the hardest aspects of my parenting (and it brings back faint memories of my own resistance to my father). I didn't really want to work, and as teenagers my kids didn't either.

Teaching your children how to work, and how to love working, is harder than it looks. I think Satan himself wears a feed cap that says, "Take this job and shove it." Let us pray for God's help and strength and guidance so that this generation of adults does not fail to pass on God's mind-set to the next. **"Discipline your son, for in that there is hope; do not be a willing party to his death"** (Proverbs 19:18).

Hey, kid—take this job and love it.

_____

_____

_____

_____

_____

The power of one

When you read the Bible a lot, certain patterns emerge. One that has come to surprise me is the strategy that God keeps going back to over and over, especially when a major crisis looms. That strategy is to save the day by sending one guy. In the 9th century B.C., at a time of terrible spiritual weakness and even worse spiritual leadership, God's Plan A was to send Elijah to rebuke an evil king (sounds like a death sentence, doesn't it?) and to encourage the few faithful believers.

Elijah was sent to oppose the spiritual ruination being brought about by Ahab and his miserably idolatrous wife Jezebel. They developed a reputation for simply having their opponents killed.

Elijah was God's agent in bringing about a punitive drought and famine, but also in bringing about the merciful rainfall that ended them. **"Elijah was a man just like us. He prayed earnestly that it would not rain, and it did not rain on the land for three and a half years. Again he prayed, and the heavens gave rain"** (James 5:17,18).

When you are in tune with God's agenda, your prayers have the power of dynamite. Don't ever say, "I'm just one." From God's point of view, one is plenty.

APRIL 6
No cheating

Making money is a fine thing. Taking money is not. It is amazing how fertile the human brain can be in devising schemes to separate other people from their money. Have you gotten e-mails from Africa claiming that you are a trustee of a fortune? Or gotten e-mails from a "bank" that just needs your own checking account's routing numbers to fix something?

Some people define morality as whatever they can get away with. If there is no one in the forest to hear the tree fall, did it really make a noise? If I never get caught, is it really wrong?

Circus entrepreneur P. T. Barnum remarked famously that a sucker was born every minute. Do you share Barnum's sharp eye for taking advantage of people? You know how you hate being hustled and cheated. When you are selling something to somebody, are you driven by what's good for you or what's good for that person?

Remember that Someone is watching how you acquire your money. Satan owns the short term, but only the Lord can give lasting satisfaction, and his favor and blessing are worth far more than money. **"Food gained by fraud tastes sweet to a man, but he ends up with a mouth full of gravel"** (Proverbs 20:17).

_____

_____

_____

_____

_____

Less me, more Jesus

His conception and birth were swathed in drama and miracles. He burst onto the scene at age 30, just like his famous relative Jesus, and attracted huge crowds to hear him speak. He brilliantly fulfilled his God-given mission to prepare the way for the public revelation of the world's Savior. And then, after a ministry of maybe a year and a half, he was arrested and thrown into a dungeon.

"When John heard in prison what Christ was doing, he sent his disciples to ask him, 'Are you the one who was to come, or should we expect someone else?'" Does that question sound as though John's faith was collapsing? Jesus didn't think him weak or unworthy. He replied, **"I tell you the truth: Among those born of women there has not risen anyone greater than John the Baptist"** (Matthew 11:2,3,11).

John is a hero to me because he humbly accepted God's verdict that a ministry of a mere 18 months was enough. How he must have groaned in his prison cell. How shocked he must have been on the death walk to the place of his beheading.

John was content to fade out. "I must decrease," he said. "He must increase. Look—the Lamb of God, who takes away the sin of the world."

_____

_____

_____

_____

_____

APRIL 8
My brother is sinning

What do you do when someone you're close to is living what you know from God's Word to be a sinful lifestyle? A grandparent says, "My grandson moved in with his girlfriend. How can I talk about this without driving him away?"

You do this by remembering that you have two messages. One is a message of unconditional love, a love that is not based on the person's performance but on your decision to love. The second is to pass on God's truth from his Word. These messages might seem to contradict each other, but they simply reflect the very nature of God himself. At Moses' request, God on one occasion moved past him and solemnly explained who he was: **"He passed in front of Moses, proclaiming, 'The Lord, the Lord, the compassionate and gracious God, slow to anger, abounding in love and faithfulness, maintaining love to thousands, and forgiving wickedness, rebellion and sin. Yet he does not leave the guilty unpunished'"** (Exodus 34:6,7).

Does that sound like a contradiction? Forgiving sin *and* punishing sin? Only in Christ does it make sense. Our message to loved ones who are sinning is that same double message: God loves you and I love you, but God does not approve of your choices right now and will not bless your life.

_____

_____

_____

_____

_____

APRIL 9
I'm a winner no matter what

The Bible is full of stories about how Christ, the prophets, and the apostles used God's miraculous power to heal diseases, restore those with paralyzed and withered limbs, and drive out demons. But some people weren't cured; they lived out their lives with illness and disabilities, and some had lives drastically shortened because of them.

God may have miraculous healing for your physical brokenness. Or he may have "ordinary" medical solutions (i.e., modern-day miracles) for you. Or he may allow you to give him glory and advance his agenda by allowing you to struggle a lifetime with your weakness, as St. Paul struggled year after year with his "thorn in the flesh."

But you win no matter what. Even when you succumb to your final illness, when your weary body rests in the bosom of the earth, you will bolt from your grave when the archangel Michael sounds the trumpet. Your disabilities are temporary; your complete physical restoration will be eternal. **"Then will the eyes of the blind be opened and the ears of the deaf unstopped. Then will the lame leap like a deer, and the mute tongue shout for joy"** (Isaiah 35:5,6).

You are a winner no matter what. You will experience new health, perhaps now, certainly later. In heaven, absolutely every weakness of body and mind will vanish. Fear not!

_____
_____
_____
_____
_____

APRIL 10
Wake-up call

When I'm on the road and need to be up at a certain time, I will set an alarm clock. When it's really important, I will ask the hotel clerk to give me a wake-up call to blast me out of my slumber. Long ago God invented roosters for a number of different functions, but the job of which they are proudest is to set the barnyard into life with their raucous pre-daybreak crowing.

Churches have traditionally crowned their steeples with crosses, but a few chose to place a copper rooster up there—a wake-up call to their members and the community to rouse from spiritual sleep and get ready for Christ's soon return. Jesus used that very metaphor to warn his foolishly proud and careless disciple Peter on the night in which Jesus was arrested, convicted, and sentenced to be crucified.

Jesus predicted to him that the predawn crowing would mark a miserable collapse in Peter's personal faith-witness. Sadly it came true: **"Peter replied, 'Man, I don't know what you're talking about!' Just as he was speaking, the rooster crowed"** (Luke 22:60).

The sign of the rooster forever after reminds us Christians to stay alert and vigilant, repentant of our sins and grateful for Christ's daily forgiveness. But it is also a comforting image, for it was also at daybreak that a rooster would have signaled the empty tomb of the risen Christ.

I'm so confused

American society during the Truman presidency reinforced Christian values to a much greater extent than it does today. Heather didn't have two mommies in 1950. Marriage was to last until death us do part. You had to prove infidelity to get a divorce. Abortion was illegal and considered immoral. Living together without marriage was called "shacking up" and was not what nice people did. There was no such thing as a publicly gay legislator or pastor.

How do you figure out right and wrong today? Is there such a thing as immorality? Are there no absolutes? Is everybody's opinion just as valid as anybody else's? Is Christianity merely one of many interesting and equally valid religious philosophies?

I don't blame you if you feel that our culture is built on quicksand. People seem to think they have the right to invent their own morality. Or lack thereof. **"When the foundations are being destroyed, what can the righteous do?"** (Psalm 11:3).

Here's one source of information and authority that is never obsolete. In a world of confusion, contradiction, corruption, and change, there is a source of steady light to get you safely home. **"Your word is a lamp to my feet and a light for my path"** (Psalm 119:105). Read. Then you'll know.

_____

_____

_____

_____

_____

APRIL 12
Respect those in authority

In the summer of A.D. 64, a terrible fire in the city of Rome burned for six days and seven nights, consuming a quarter of the city and badly damaging another 50%. Fearing that he would be blamed, the emperor Nero accused the Christians of arson. He arrested many believers and tortured them until they gave the names of other believers. The historian Tacitus wrote, "Besides being put to death they were made to serve as objects of amusement; they were clothed in the hides of beasts and torn to death by dogs. Some were crucified, others set on fire to serve to illuminate the night when daylight failed."

That same emperor later issued St. Paul's death penalty. Does it surprise you that Paul would write the following about his government? **"Every person should obey the government in power. No government would exist if it hadn't been established by God. The governments which exist have been put in place by God"** (Romans 13:1).

Respecting government doesn't mean that you endorse all of its actions. It means that you respect God and his authority over your life.

In God's view, corruption in government may be bad but chaos and anarchy are worse. As Jesus himself was being condemned by his own Jewish government, he reminded the councilors that he would in turn hold them accountable on judgment day.

_____

_____

_____

_____

Be real

In the world in which Christ and the apostles lived and worked, slavery was not merely tolerated but widely used. In the great cities where Christianity was planted, there would have been hundreds of thousands of slaves, and many of them were found among the earliest believers.

Paul wrote to them to gain their freedom if they could but to learn to accept their lives and make the most of their situation. If you truly believe that you are a prince of heaven and a spiritual billionaire, you don't have to feel as though you have to get it all *right now.*

There's nothing basically wrong with wanting to be somebody. We all long for importance. Where that desire becomes sick is when we run out of patience. I know too many people who spend themselves into debt they can't handle trying to be somebody they're not.

There is a great freedom in choosing to like your life right now and in accepting your present situation. **"Better to be a nobody and yet have a servant than pretend to be somebody and have no food"** (Proverbs 12:9).

_____

_____

_____

_____

_____

I don't know if I'm up to the pressure

Lord, why does everything have to happen at once?

I don't mean to whine, but I don't know if I'm up to everything you are throwing at me right now. I know you say you will never load on us more than we can handle, but I'm not this good. I'm not this big. I'm not this strong. Many people depend on me, and some days I feel that I can barely take care of myself.

I guess you have a reason for everything you send and allow in my life, but—can I be honest?—I don't see it right now. Lord, when I am on empty, you have to fill me with yourself. Do it!

Give me some restful sleep tonight. I am going to surrender everything, I mean everything, into your capable and loving hands. I have no more to give today. I look forward to tomorrow, for you already live there. You already have solutions worked out to all my problems. Could you share one of them with me tomorrow? Your mercies are new every morning—let's start over. I can't wait to see what you will bring me tomorrow. **"Let the morning bring me word of your unfailing love, for I have put my trust in you. Show me the way I should go, for to you I lift up my soul"** (Psalm 143:8).

_____

_____

_____

_____

_____

The glory of the Lord—then

Indiana Jones and the Raiders of the Lost Ark was pure fantasy (and, of course, great fun), but the movie did do you one favor from a biblical point of view—its representation of what the ark of the covenant must have looked like was probably pretty close.

It was above the atonement cover (the ark's lid), between the cherubim wings, that the bright glory-cloud came to rest. **"Behind the second curtain was a room called the Most Holy Place, which had the golden altar of incense and the gold-covered ark of the covenant. . . . Above the ark were the cherubim of the Glory, overshadowing the atonement cover"** (Hebrews 9:3-5).

It was the most sacred object in the Old Covenant—about the size of a hope chest, covered in hammered gold sheets, with a pair of golden angels on the lid with their wings touching. Too holy to be touched, it could be moved only by four priests, carrying it on golden poles. Too holy even to be seen, it was set in the Most Holy Place of the tabernacle/temple where only the high priest could go once a year. Even at that, he could enter only with clouds of incense, eyes averted, and the sprinkling of blood.

The message was unmistakable: God was close, but you dared not go too close. Don't touch. He dwells on his earthly throne in holy solitude.

_____

_____

_____

_____

_____

The glory of the Lord—now

Where is the ark of the covenant now? Nobody has the slightest idea. The original ark was taken off to Babylon when Jerusalem fell in 586 B.C. When the temple was rebuilt in 520 B.C., another ark presumably was fabricated. The Romans would have plundered or destroyed it in A.D. 70. There has never been another temple.

God doesn't need one. The glory-cloud no longer lives on earth. When Christ was crucified, God tore the huge temple curtain of separation from top to bottom (Luke 23:45). The reason? Christ triumphant has opened up heaven to all believers. The reason? Christ triumphant *is* the glory of the Lord. **"For God, who said, 'Let light shine out of darkness,' made his light shine in our hearts to give us the light of the knowledge of the glory of God in the face of Christ"** (2 Corinthians 4:6).

You now encounter the glory of the Lord as you see and hear Christ in the Scriptures. You are clothed with his holiness and righteousness when you are baptized. In the Holy Supper you bond with him as you take into yourself the very body and blood given and poured out for you for the forgiveness of your sins.

One final step remains: to see Christ face-to-face. St. John tells us that when he appears, we will be like him, for we will see him as he is. Hang on. Believe. The Glory awaits you.

_____

_____

_____

_____

_____

I don't want to be pregnant anymore

What do you do when a woman confides in you that she's pregnant but doesn't want the baby? It could be any combination of 50 reasons—her boyfriend is threatening to leave her, she can't afford to raise a child, it will interfere with her career, this wasn't the time in her life when she had planned for a child, whatever—but the fact is she is confiding in you before she seeks an abortion because she wants to know what you think.

That is your moment to speak not only for the unborn child within her but for God himself. While you feel compassion for the terrible tension in her life situation, it is even more important to pay attention to God's point of view. God thinks that it is he who creates all human life; that a child is a person already in the womb; and that each child, born and unborn, is a masterpiece of his design and biomedical engineering. **"You created my inmost being; you knit me together in my mother's womb. . . . When I was woven together in the depths of the earth, your eyes saw my unformed body"** (Psalm 139:13-16).

Explore non-abortive options and talk them through with her. Identify pro-life counseling opportunities and go along. Pray for her and with her. Above all, claim God's promise that when we do what is right, he will send the resources.

APRIL 18
Fasting

Most of the outward features of worship life in the Old Testament have passed away (like the blood sacrifices of animals, burning up of the first fruits of farm produce, and the turban and ephod of a high priest). One aspect has persisted somewhat, and that is the custom of fasting.

In the New Testament era, it is just that—a custom, not a law or rule. Denial of food to oneself for a brief period of time can be used as a spiritual aid, to practice the urgently important skill of self-denial and to bring focus to God's agenda instead of your stomach's.

Jesus fasted from time to time; so did the early church leaders in Antioch as they prepared to send off Paul and Barnabas on their first mission journey. Paul did, too, as he chose and ordained congregational elders in Galatia.

Fasting should not be done if it makes you feel self-righteous or if you are trying to impress other believers with the passion and loftiness of your spirituality. Jesus said, **"When you fast, put oil on your head and wash your face, so that it will not be obvious to men that you are fasting, but only to your Father, who is unseen; and your Father, who sees what is done in secret, will reward you"** (Matthew 6:17,18).

It's good now and then to be really hungry. It's even better to be hungry for Christ.

_____

_____

_____

_____

_____

Think long term—really long term

Children don't think much about the future—there is only the Now. The Right Now. They need their parents to teach them about deferred gratification, that slogging through math problems now will help them get a good job in 15 years . . . that keeping an orderly bedroom will build habits of mental organization . . . that steadily saving a few dollars instead of blowing them on junk food will grow them over time.

Are you in love with your great-grandchildren? How happy is your life! I on the other hand, though no spring chicken, am still some years from great-grandchildren and may never hold one in my arms. But God wants me to think about them and love them right now. How?

"He decreed statutes for Jacob and established the law in Israel, which he commanded our forefathers to teach their children, so the next generation would know them, *even the children yet to be born,* **and they in turn would tell their children"** (Psalm 78:5,6). Did you grasp that key point? The spiritual condition of your grandchildren and great-grandchildren, human beings who haven't even been born yet, rides on how you are modeling and teaching and transmitting your faith today.

I am a believer now because of faithful Christians going back into the 1800s and even farther. You and I are important players in the spiritual condition of our descendants in the 22nd century.

_____

_____

_____

_____

Jesus' resurrection guarantees mine

The physical resurrection of Jesus Christ from the dead changes everything. And I mean absolutely everything.

It means first of all that his Father accepted his innocent life and death as worthy and completely substitutionary sacrifices on behalf of the sinful world. It means that whoever trusts and believes in Christ has peace with God now and forever. It means that all who trust and believe in Christ will rise from death just as he did, at a time of God's choosing.

Listen to the words of Job, a man bitterly familiar with attending funerals of people close to him, a man now chronically ill, living in daily pain, and sure that his own day of death is not far off: **"I know that my Redeemer lives, and that in the end he will stand upon the earth. And after my skin has been destroyed, yet in my flesh I will see God; I myself will see him with my own eyes—I, and not another. How my heart yearns within me!"** (Job 19:25-27).

A happy future is guaranteed to all believers. It is only the present that is hard. All the fear is removed from the dying process, because we know we are not heading into disaster but paradise. And it means that we don't "lose" our loved ones in Christ who pass away. We are simply investing them, confident that we will get them back with interest.

How our hearts yearn for that great day! Fear not!

_____

_____

_____

_____

_____

What a friend!

Joseph Scriven was an Irishman with a life of bitter disappointments. Poor health cut short his career as a military officer; his fiancée drowned in a terrible accident the night before their wedding day; and after moving to Canada, he suffered the sudden death of a second fiancée. His poem of faith and confidence in the power of prayer has encouraged many generations of Christians:

What a friend we have in Jesus, all our sins and griefs to bear!

What a privilege to carry everything to God in prayer!

Oh, what peace we often forfeit,

Oh, what needless pain we bear,

All because we do not carry everything to God in prayer!

As Jesus prepared his sad and frightened disciples for his coming death, resurrection, and ascension, he wanted them to live joyful and fearless lives. He promised them that he would be with them always, every day, and that he would personally guarantee that all their prayers were favorably received at the Father's throne in heaven. **"Until now you have not asked for anything in my name. Ask and you will receive, and your joy will be complete"** (John 16:24).

Don't hold back. Pray like crazy! Pray with complete and childlike confidence that everything you tell God is important and that through your Savior Jesus everything will be answered in the perfect way at the perfect time.

_____

_____

APRIL 22
Earth Day

It started out as an environmental celebration in the spring of 1970. Fueled by outrage over a huge oil spill off the coast of Santa Barbara, Earth Day has become a worldwide phenomenon. Each year April 22 provides an opportunity for people to rededicate themselves to learning about and caring for the earth.

It's good to clean up what has become polluted, recycle what can be used again, avoid waste, and live modestly. It's good to find ways to harness the energy of wind, water, and sun so that our fossil fuels will last longer.

"The earth is the Lord's, and everything in it, the world, and all who live in it" (Psalm 24:1). These wise words help Christians to steer between two extremes when it comes to environmental stewardship. Psalm 24 reminds us of Genesis chapters 1 and 2, where the Creator entrusts Adam and Eve with care of the earth. We are accountable to God for how we treat *his* world. He commissioned us to rule it, not rape it. Who more than Christians should care about clean air and water and have respect for animal habitats?

It's possible, however, to love the earth too much. Some Greens and public television science shows are not bashful about identifying cause and effect as "Mother Nature." Paganism is making a comeback.

The world is not your Mother; it's your Father's.

I feel like a loser

When you see somebody roll past you in a new BMW or Escalade, do you want to congratulate the person or curse your own junker transportation? Do other people's fabulous clothes make you want to praise them or hate your thrift-store wardrobe?

It seems that no matter how hard you struggle to get ahead, somebody is always already way past you. Maybe they were born to wealth; maybe they got lucky; maybe they married up; maybe they stole it. Does other people's wealth make you feel like a pauper? Does other people's success make you feel like a loser?

How are you keeping score in your life? Comparing clothes? jewelry? ride? If you judge others and yourself by material possessions, you may miss out on what God thinks is the biggest treasure anybody could have. The Bible says in 2 Corinthians 8:9, **"You know the grace of our Lord Jesus Christ, that though he was rich, yet for your sakes he became poor, so that you through his poverty might become rich."**

Nobody is a loser who enjoys God's favor. You will always have enough. You know you are precious to your Father, purchased by the blood of his Son. You know you are guarded by angels. You know your immortality in heaven is guaranteed.

You are loved.

_____

_____

_____

_____

The sons of thunder

If you've ever had your car or house broken into, I wouldn't be surprised if you harbored some revenge fantasies for a few weeks. That feeling of being violated makes us so angry that we would love to bring payback down on the perps' heads.

"Cursing" is not just foul language but the actual belief that righteous people can call down God's wrath on others. It's probably a good thing that people's cursing "gun" isn't loaded—we understand far too little about what's really going on to be trusted with the red button of God's nuclear strikes.

Jesus was not interested in James and John's plans to hasten judgment day: **"He sent messengers on ahead, who went into a Samaritan village to get things ready for him; but the people there did not welcome him, because he was heading for Jerusalem. When the disciples James and John saw this, they asked, 'Lord, do you want us to call fire down from heaven to destroy them?' But Jesus turned and rebuked them"** (Luke 9:52-55).

It's not our job to dish out vengeance, administer punishments, or organize retaliation. God says that he will take care of repaying evildoers. Our job is humbly to recognize our own evil thoughts, words, and deeds; be grateful for the Lord's mercy on us; and share good news of that mercy with the other fools and sinners around us.

_____

_____

_____

_____

_____

Be prepared

Generally it's a good idea to leave interventions to professionals. If somebody is brandishing a gun, call the police. If somebody is going into cardiac arrest, call the paramedics. If someone is in agony with impacted wisdom teeth, get her to an oral surgeon.

However, when you want to bring someone back to the faith, don't walk away because you're not a religious professional. When God calls you into his family as his child, he is simultaneously drafting you into his spiritual armed forces as a medic. God trusts you and has equipped you to go after the lost and straying.

Here are two things to do to get ready for that high calling: **"In your hearts set apart Christ as Lord. Always be prepared to give an answer to everyone who asks you to give the reason for the hope that you have"** (1 Peter 3:15). In other words, worship Jesus Christ as your Creator, Redeemer, and Helper and take the time to get into your Bible enough so that you can give a coherent account of what you believe and why.

I love being a pastor, and I dearly hope that people appreciate our work. But may I say that I believe that the most compelling testimonies of faith may come from people who are not being paid to say those things?

_____

_____

_____

_____

_____

APRIL 26
God and my enemies

Believers have to endure and overcome threats of various kinds. King David faced deadly violence for decades, first from wild animals, then from murderous King Saul, and then in all the military campaigns that he led. He left behind eloquent and passionate psalms that prayed both for his deliverance and for God to get rid of all who opposed his divine will.

Here are words when you fear for your life: **"He reached down from on high and took hold of me; he drew me out of deep waters. He rescued me from my powerful enemy, from my foes, who were too strong for me"** (Psalm 18:16,17).

Philistines and Amalekites no longer pose much of a threat to you. So who are "enemies" today? If you are a police officer, you may face deadly peril every time you clip on your badge and step onto the street. If you wear the uniform of our country, you become a target for all who hate America.

All of God's children do well to remember that the deadliest enemies of all come from hell. Satan and his demons would like to rip you apart, body and soul. Without divine and angelic protection, we would be shredded.

Lord Jesus, protect me this night from every evil power and watch over all who belong to you.

_____

_____

_____

_____

_____

Can people fall from faith?

Does it really matter if you live and practice the Christian faith outwardly as long as you still know and believe the basics in your heart? A little girl says, "Dad, why doesn't your brother go to church anymore?" If you were a believer once, can you lose your faith and salvation?

You most certainly can. If that happens, it is no fault of God's, who loves all people equally, distributes his grace and mercy unconditionally, and desires in his Fatherly heart that *all* should be saved. The sad truth is that just as some people weary of life and, in spite of many blessings, choose to end it through suicide, some people weary of their faith lives and flirt with spiritual suicide.

This warning is for real: **"Do not throw away your confidence; it will be richly rewarded. You need to persevere so that when you have done the will of God, you will receive what he has promised. For in just a very little while, 'He who is coming will come and will not delay'"** (Hebrews 10:35-37).

When people disconnect from God's Word and the sacraments, their faith begins to die. Some people actually *throw away their confidence,* i.e., their faith in the Savior's forgiveness and promise of immortality. You can't control people's decisions. But you can be God's words and hands of welcome, calling people to come in off the ledge.

_____

_____

_____

_____

_____

You will catch me when I die

Some people die before they've ever really given it much thought. It caught them by surprise, and they were spiritually unprepared. Others who have been Christians their whole lives have been singing hymns about their death, have had catechism training about it, heard many sermons about it, and attended many Christian funerals where it was the chief topic of conversation.

And yet when death comes, it will always be something of a shock, and Satan will try to mess with our minds to sow doubt and disrupt faith at the last hour. Today would be a good day, and right now would be a great moment, to script the dialogue that you will have with God at that time. Here is the conversation Jesus had with his Father when he faced death (written by King David in prophecy): **"My heart is glad and my tongue rejoices; my body also will rest secure, because you will not abandon me to the grave. . . . You have made known to me the path of life"** (Psalm 16:9-11).

At your last hour remember that you will be judged not on the basis of your great holiness or stack of good deeds. You can come with empty hands, pleading for mercy for Jesus' sake, and confident that no one who believes the gospel of Jesus' forgiveness will ever be turned away.

Your heart really can be glad.

Your tongue really can rejoice.

_____

_____

_____

_____

_____

APRIL 29

Devoted to serving together

People in the world are absolutely starved for love, acceptance, and significance. All they know is the dog-eat-dog competition to survive. They do a frantic dance to try to get it all before they die—and they hope nobody steals their stuff while they're here.

God has so much more to give us, and a happy, healthy Christian church can provide a culture and environment where he can guide us with his Word and where people take care of each other. One of the best aspects of our Christian faith is that we know we're immortal. Since we're going to live forever, we don't have to cheat and steal to get it all now. Instead, we can live out the words of Galatians 5:13: **"You, my brothers, were called to be free. But do not use your freedom to indulge the sinful nature; rather, serve one another in love."**

You never have to worry about being generous with others because you know that God has been and will always be generous with you. When you know you are a royal and immortal priest of God, destined for eternity in heaven, you can freely serve and give yourself away right now. In fact, selfless service is an unmistakable sign of authentic faith.

It is an unmistakable sign of the power of Christ living in you.

_____

_____

_____

_____

_____

I feel broken

Perhaps you know some people who are very sure of themselves—self-confident, brash, even arrogant. If you haven't noticed how great they are, they will help you figure it out. But there are probably just as many people with the opposite mind-set, broken in heart and spirit, constantly critical of themselves, feeling like failures pretty much every day. Know anybody like that? Is that you?

These people may seem to be just fine—they dress okay, still go to work and go through the motions, but their spirits are dead. They may trust you with a peek inside their bleak souls, hoping that you have something positive to say.

Maybe what they hope to hear are words like this from Jesus, the crucified and risen One: **"Come to me, all you who are weary and burdened, and I will give you rest. Take my yoke upon you and learn from me, for I am gentle and humble in heart, and you will find rest for your souls"** (Matthew 11:28,29). You can't really forgive yourself until you know that you are forgiven by Christ. If you're having trouble liking yourself, you will be refreshed by contact with the One who has defined unconditional love.

Jesus' message: "You're precious to me. I want you to live in my heavenly home forever. I would like you to make me the center of your life right now."

_____

_____

_____

_____

_____

May

Praise be to the God and Father
of our Lord Jesus Christ!
In his great mercy he has given us new birth
into a living hope through the resurrection
of Jesus Christ from the dead.

1 Peter 1:3

One way, one truth, one life

The Bible is either all true or it's a great big crock. There's no middle ground.

When Jesus walked the earth, he was awash in as many different political and religious philosophies as you and I are right now. And Jesus looked at them all and said, **"I am *the* way and *the* truth and *the* life"** (John 14:6).

He didn't say that whatever you believe is fine. He didn't say there were many paths to one God. He didn't say that all that matters is sincerity and love. He didn't say that if you were good enough, you'd get to heaven on your own.

No, he made it pretty clear where he stands. He is *the* truth—not one of many interesting "truths." He is *the* way— he alone gives you the forgiveness of sins and righteousness with God. He is *the* life—he's the only human being who lay down in a grave and got up on his own accord. Life comes only through him.

Jesus himself says, "It's me or nothing." This message is for everyone, whether you live in Belgrade or Brooklyn, Mumbai or Minneapolis. There is no other way to get a happy verdict on the day of judgment but through him. Wake the neighbors. Make some noise.

_____

_____

_____

_____

_____

MAY 2
Am I really a wretch?

Many years ago I heard the broadcast of a concert by folksinger Judy Collins. She led a closing sing-along of the famous gospel hymn "Amazing Grace," but she wanted people to refer to themselves as "souls." "You aren't wretches," she cried.

John Newton, the poem's author, would have disagreed strenuously. He had been the captain of a slave-trading ship and after coming to faith in Christ bitterly regretted the cruelties of his past life. He meant every word of what he wrote:

> Amazing grace—how sweet the sound—
> That saved a wretch like me!
> I once was lost but now am found,
> Was blind but now I see.

St. Paul's gratitude for God's grace and mercy also arose from his deep personal shame. He knew that he needed a Savior and was mighty glad to have found one in Christ. **"For that very reason I was shown mercy so that in me, the worst of sinners, Christ Jesus might display his unlimited patience as an example for those who would believe on him and receive eternal life"** (1 Timothy 1:16). The forgiveness of his many and grievous sins gave him peace in his heart and hope for his future.

So tell me—are you a wretch too?

_____

_____

Have you noticed how a declining stock market feeds on itself? As people see their share values go down, they feel the urge to sell. When the herd is selling, prices decline further. The same is true of marriage attitudes. As more children are born into unwed homes, fewer children have a working marriage model to imitate. *Normal* is redefined.

The Pharisees at Jesus' time (as well as Jesus' own disciples!) were convinced that lifelong marriage was too heavy an expectation and advocated for quick and easy divorce. They were shocked by Jesus' strong reaction: **"Haven't you read,"** he replied, **"that at the beginning the Creator 'made them male and female,' and said, 'For this reason a man will leave his father and mother and be united to his wife, and the two will become one flesh'? So they are no longer two, but one"** (Matthew 19:4-6).

In other words, marriage doesn't belong to people to experiment and play with. It belongs to God. It is his invention, designed during creation week itself.

Jesus said that couples are *joined together*. The phrase in its original Greek means "stuck like glue." Marriage superglues you to your partner; you are no longer "me" but "we." In God's marriage math, one plus one equals one. Are you disappointed or thrilled to hear that?

A human High Priest

Have you ever noticed how casually we sling around the words *die* and *death*? Like, "That tiramisu is to die for" or "That kid will be the death of me" or "I just died from embarrassment."

Jesus didn't die from embarrassment. He died from being crucified. But unlike the suicide bombers of today, he didn't throw away his life in a cruel and hate-filled act of terrorism. He allowed his life to be tortured and taken so that he could give life to the dying people of this world.

"For this reason he had to be made like his brothers in every way, in order that he might become a merciful and faithful high priest in service to God, and that he might make atonement for the sins of the people" (Hebrews 2:17).

Jesus humbly took on a body so that he could give it for us. He assumed our blood so that he could give it for us. He was both the priestly offerer and the Lamb offering, in order that all of God's wrath would be put on him and all of God's favor put on us. His *atonement* is now yours, i.e., you and God are no longer at odds but *at one.*

Sweet.

_____

_____

_____

_____

_____

Cinco de Mayo

The 5th of May has always been a big deal to people who trace their ancestry to Mexico. Now it's attracting the notice of Anglos as well, but generally only as an excuse to party with nachos, guacamole, margaritas, and Mexican beer.

Whether or not you choose to go to a party today, I hope that you will take just a little time to learn something about Hispanic culture. People from the majority culture often notice and remember only the worst aspects of other peoples. There is far more to the Latin world than gangs and tequila. There is amazing art, music, dance, literature, and food. There are amazing stories of resilience and overcoming as the Hispanic countries gained independence from their colonial overlords.

There is a strong Christian story too. God cares deeply about the Spanish people, and so did Paul, who had serious plans to bring the gospel there: **"After I have completed this task and have made sure that they have received this fruit, I will go to Spain and visit you on the way"** (Romans 15:28). Courageous Spanish missionaries brought the Christian faith to much of the New World.

God still loves Spanish-speaking people and still has important plans to use them to share the faith and grow his kingdom. *¡Viva México!*

Get these kids out of here

You understand, don't you, why Jesus' disciples wanted to get rid of the children? The six monthers screech, the toddlers talk and babble and blow out their diapers at inopportune times, the kindergarteners just fool around with their toys, the primary kids ask too many dumb questions, and the middle schoolers just roll their eyes and act bored. **"People were also bringing babies to Jesus to have him touch them. When the disciples saw this, they rebuked them. But Jesus called the children to him"** (Luke 18:15,16).

It wasn't just that Jesus thought the infants were cute and wanted to play with them (although both those things may have been true). The greater truth is that Jesus knew that these little ones needed him. They were sinners too—born with the fatal poison of sin already in their veins, already beginning to die even before they were full grown.

Children can believe as well as adults; in fact, Jesus said that adults needed to believe like children or they would never be saved. Children need forgiveness of their sins too, and the only place to get it is through Jesus. Shame on Christian parents who don't bring their kids to church; shame on fussy church members who don't want kids in the sanctuary.

Jesus said, **"The kingdom of God belongs to such as these."** Seriously.

_____

_____

_____

_____

_____

He entrusted me with a fortune!

When you play *Monopoly*, everybody starts out with the same amount of money—$1,500. Not in God's world. He loves diversity in his children, and it pleases him to make them all different. Nobody has everything and nobody has nothing. Everyone is gifted.

"To one he gave five talents of money, to another two talents, and to another one talent, each according to his ability" (Matthew 25:15).

In the monetary system of the Greek-speaking eastern Mediterranean world, a *talenton* weighed 75 pounds. That's 1,200 ounces! Do the math. If Jesus had a silver talent in mind, it would be worth more than $10,000 in today's money. If it was a gold talent, it would be worth more than half a million. The point: the wealthy traveler was entrusting his staff with a serious amount of money. He trusted them— both their honesty and their business aptitude.

God trusts you too. You have been given time, skills and abilities, and money to manage. The Giver watches you earnestly to see what you are going to do with these loans. He gives you an astonishing amount of leeway in what you do with it all, hoping that you use it for his agenda. Say it with me: I have a lot. It's all his. He trusts me.

_____

_____

_____

_____

_____

Mr. Encouragement

Young men can be pretty rude in the nicknames they choose for their friends. It would not be appropriate for me to put some of the nicknames of the guys in my college dorm in a devotional book. That was not a problem for Joseph of Cyprus (one of the big Mediterranean islands). He had developed such a reputation for being kind and generous, such a willing help to his friends, that they called him "Mr. Encouragement." **"Joseph, a Levite from Cyprus, whom the apostles called Barnabas (which means Son of Encouragement), sold a field he owned and brought the money and put it at the apostles' feet"** (Acts 4:36,37).

If you've heard of this wonderful man, you will probably remember him as Barnabas. We admire him not only for his generosity in liquidating some real estate that he owned and investing the proceeds in God's kingdom work. He also accompanied Paul on his first mission journey, an extended loop through Asia Minor (today's country of Turkey). He took John Mark with him on another evangelistic tour, helping people on Cyprus realize that the Messiah had come.

People who are kind and helpful to others will never lack friends. We love being around people like that. Encouragers like Barnabas know how to make people feel important.

_____

_____

_____

_____

_____

Why is my life so hard?

"Doesn't God say he'll bless us? Then why did I get let go from my job?" You have heard that question and its many variations before, have you not? If God loves me, why does he let me struggle like this?

Probably for the same reason that you don't do your kids' math problems for them. They will never learn quadratic equations until they have struggled with them, failed a few times, and learned to overcome. **"My son, do not make light of the Lord's discipline, and do not lose heart when he rebukes you, because the Lord disciplines those he loves, and he punishes everyone he accepts as a son"** (Hebrews 12:5,6).

It is a feature of human life that growth and change come only with challenge and pressure. Muscles don't come from donuts, and speed doesn't come from watching TV. When God lets us experience conflict or loss, it's not because he doesn't care *but because he does.* He wants to grow and develop us into something different and something better. His greatest desire for our lives is not our pleasure and comfort. It is that we survive this world with our faith in Christ intact.

Here's the beautiful promise: when you are an unbeliever, your sufferings have no meaning. When you are connected to Christ, your Father will make all hardships work for you. And for him.

_____

_____

_____

_____

_____

God's sweet breath

One of the surprising discoveries of parenthood is how much you like "baby smell," even the smell of your baby's breath. Did you know that God's breath is sweet too?

"Then the Lord God formed the man from the dust of the earth and blew the breath of life into his nostrils. The man became a living being" (Genesis 2:7). When God created animals, he simply formed them and they started living. For people, he did something special. He took dust and shaped it, and then God injected life into Adam *right through the nose!* From that moment on, humans walked around with the breath of the living God inside them.

When Jesus was preparing to return to heaven, he knew that his disciples would be terrified of being left alone. To reassure them that they weren't being abandoned, **"Jesus said to them again, 'Peace be with you! As the Father has sent me, so I am sending you.' After he had said this, he breathed on the disciples and said, 'Receive the Holy Spirit'"** (John 20:21,22).

The first time God breathed into a person, life began. The next time God breathed on a person, the power and wisdom of the Holy Spirit was given to us.

Love that smell!

_____

_____

_____

_____

_____

It's my wife

"Husbands, love your wives as Christ loved the church" is St. Paul's charge and commission to all Christian husbands of all time. Love them as Christ loves us, that is, unconditionally and freely, permanently and patiently.

That means you keep loving them even if they fall away from their faith and seem to become a boat anchor on yours. True love, Christ-love, doesn't fluctuate like feelings. Christ-love originates not in the glands but in the head. It is a choice. It is a decision that you make.

"Love always protects, always trusts, always hopes, always perseveres" (1 Corinthians 13:7). Christ-love is irresistible. Husbands, as you are fueled up by Christ's love for you, you will have love to give her. Protect her (she was designed to respond to your strength). Trust her (you can't believe for her). Never give up hope (the age of miracles isn't over). Persevere (a man's strength is not only in his muscles).

_____

_____

_____

_____

_____

MAY 12
Burial

Burial is a big deal in every culture. In ours you will see caskets with locking screws, a long parade of cars with high beams on, concrete vaults with rubber gaskets, plastic flowers at gravesites, green carpeting around the hole as mourners gather, polished granite markers with names and two very important four-digit numbers.

The whole scene is solemn, respectful, and a little creepy. As hard as we try to prettify the death business, we know there's a lot of pretending going on. Our loved one is not just taking a nap in an expensive steel or mahogany bed. Cemeteries are not merely lovely picnic sites. Graves hold the casualties of mankind's war with God. Whether the people died of illness or injury or old age, they are still paying the ultimate price for the wages of sin.

Only God has a solution. But wow—what a solution! He is going to undo it all: **"On this mountain** [the Lord] **will destroy the shroud that enfolds all peoples, the sheet that covers all nations; he will swallow up death forever"** (Isaiah 25:7,8).

Did you get that? Faith in Jesus Christ makes you immortal in soul and body. Death itself will die when Jesus comes back, never to intimidate you again. Funeral directors will need to find new work in heaven.

_____

_____

_____

_____

_____

Why, God?

It is a great comfort to know that God oversees all things; controls and directs the affairs of angels, stars, and mankind; and has a plan for each of our lives. Except when it isn't. It's fun to praise God when you get a promotion, find a great new boyfriend, inherit a chunk of money, or close on a new house. But do you still feel blessed when you get laid off, hear a chilling diagnosis from your spouse's doctor, or stand next to the casket of somebody you really, really loved and needed?

"Why, God?" is the aching cry from believers who really want to believe but just can't understand how a wise, powerful, and loving God would let something this bad happen. **"Who has understood the mind of the LORD, or instructed him as his counselor?"** (Isaiah 40:13). Is any of that song playing in your head right now?

Two things: first, you will understand more as you get older. One of the compensations for your diminished vertical leap and sprinter speed is a sense of perspective. If you live long enough, you will start to see that God blesses us not only through treats but through hardships as well.

Second, it's okay that there are some things you will never understand this side of the grave. The One who thought you worthwhile enough to sacrifice his Son can be trusted to guide your life. He'll explain later.

_____

_____

_____

_____

_____

I feel so depressed

Everybody feels down now and then. Everybody gets the blues. But that's not depression. Depression is a daily prison of self-hatred, a life with long stretches of wretched darkness.

The darkest place of all for a Christian is to fear that it was God who sent the misery. Has God now become my enemy? How could I possibly ever succeed in my life if the Power behind everything is against me? Have you ever thought something like this: **"You have put me in the lowest pit, in the darkest depths"** (Psalm 88:6)?

People cannot be argued out of depression. They cannot be shamed, scolded, or tricked out of it. The light in your darkest places must come from the cross of Christ. Since God punished him for all of your sins, then there is no wrath left for you. If God did not spare his Son to win you back, then you must be valuable indeed.

"If you, O Lord, kept a record of sins, O Lord, who could stand? But with you there is forgiveness" (Psalm 130:3,4). If I have forgiveness, I have hope. God is working for me. Tomorrow will be better.

_____

_____

_____

_____

_____

I have trouble being happy

As life goes on, sometimes it drags on, doesn't it? Our gait slows, our heads droop. Saggy faces see only the ground, the dust, the litter, and garbage. When we look and think only about our own little worlds, the ones we've constructed, our lives can seem small and cramped and brittle. Things break. People let us down. Things we've woven unravel. Things we've built soften and erode like sand castles at the beach.

"Lift up your heads," the Bible tells us. See things from God's point of view, God's intent, God's design. See where you fit in both in this world and the next: **"[God] has made everything beautiful in its time. He has also set eternity in the hearts of men; yet they cannot fathom what God has done from beginning to end"** (Ecclesiastes 3:11).

The poorest person in the world can enjoy a fiery sunset for free—how long has it been since you sat still and just gawked at God's celestial paintbrush? or got out of town and stood in silent wonder beneath the stars on a cloudless night? or watched the surf ceaselessly smash into a rocky coastline?

Even better—how long has it been since you savored the Bible's descriptions of how beautiful heaven will be? God put eternity in your heart for a reason.

_____

_____

_____

_____

_____

You're talking with a woman!

Jesus' disciples were steeped in a male-only religious environment where women's input was neither needed nor wanted. One day they returned from a trip into town for provisions to find a sight that amazed and disturbed them. They **"were surprised to find [Jesus] talking with a woman"** (John 4:27).

God's creative design for humanity was to create male and female in his image. Adam was made from dirt, and Eve was made from Adam. Men and women are gifted, both are equally valuable and important to God's master plan, and both have unique roles. The male/female polarity of our lives creates a wonderful buzz and makes the journey much more interesting. We are made from each other and for each other.

But of course why would Satan ever tolerate peaceful and happy relationships between genders? He hates happy homes and happy churches and tries to plant dissension to make them more like his sulfurous habitat. He likes it better when men refuse to lead, women refuse to follow, and both fear and resent the other in an endless power struggle.

The better way is to treat each other as precious and gifted partners in Christ's mission, fellow heirs of eternal life.

_____

_____

_____

_____

_____

I'm tired

Why do you suppose so many people run away from God and try their best to avoid going to church? My guess is that a lot of people are afraid of getting hustled. They assume that the church just wants to *take* from them. They assume that Christianity is basically a load of rules that will just add to their life's burdens.

Would it surprise you to know that God's basic message to you is what he wants to *give* you, that God's first desire for you is to lighten your load rather than increase it? The Lord Jesus says in Matthew 11:28, **"Come to me, all you who are weary and burdened, and I will give you rest."**

Some perhaps well-meaning religious people have tried to portray the church as a country club, where membership brings exclusivity and insiders-only benefits. Some portray it as a gym, where you submit to discipline and work out until you look better.

In fact, God wants his church to be a M.A.S.H. unit out in the world where medics can bring in wounded people to be restored in Jesus, where exhausted souls can be refreshed, and where joy is restored to people's lives.

_____

_____

_____

_____

_____

So many prodigals

A mother groans, "What did we do wrong? Why is our daughter seeing another woman?" Parents in every generation since the fall have seen their children reject the value system they were given. You can transfer financial wealth to the next generation, but you can't believe for them. You can't simply transplant faith from your heart to theirs.

As great a man as the prophet Samuel was, he must have felt like a terrible failure as a father. **"When Samuel grew old, he appointed his sons as judges for Israel. The name of the firstborn was Joel and the name of the second was Abijah, and they served at Beersheba. But his sons did not walk in his ways. They turned aside after dishonest gain and accepted bribes and perverted justice"** (1 Samuel 8:1-3).

What to do? First, love unconditionally. Your approval of his or her lifestyle may be conditional, but your love is not. Second, do your homework in the Bible and simply speak the truth. It is God's truth after all, not just your (outmoded) opinion. If your kids reject what you say, their real issue is with God, not you. Make sure your disapproval is based on God's Word, not just fashion or style. Third, give 'em time. Perhaps your faith life at age 22 was no great shakes either.

Fourth, pray for them every day and give God what you can't control.

_____

_____

_____

_____

_____

Small faith

Somebody observed once that you can tell how big a person's God is by how big his or her prayers are. Do you get the point? Do you agree? Whom really do you worship? Is he omnipotent or semi-omnipotent? Is he the King and Lord of all or just the duke or earl of all? Is he the Master of the universe or merely a middle manager? Has Satan really been dealt a mortal blow or is it just a flesh wound?

Jesus' disciples were once in a little boat during a mammoth storm. The boat was taking on water, and their God seemed small and remote. "Don't you care if we drown?" At just the right time Jesus looked at the waves and reminded them that they worked for him. "Be still!" He rebuked the furious winds, "Quiet!"

To the stunned disciples Jesus commented sadly, **"Why are you so afraid? Do you still have no faith?"** (Mark 4:40). The upside is that experiences like this one helped their faith to mature and grow. Their memory of such extraordinary events served them well later in life when they were called on to risk their lives for the gospel.

How big is your faith? How big is your God? How big do you dare to pray?

_____

_____

_____

_____

_____

Inheriting

There are legal and moral ways to acquire money other than by working. One of them is by inheriting. It is a beautiful thing when people make estate plans and actually leave a bequest to friends and relatives.

Aye, but here's the rub—inheritances are often not expected (and thus not planned for), and as such can lead people to sudden extravagant spending. **"An inheritance quickly gained at the beginning will not be blessed at the end"** (Proverbs 20:21).

What on earth does that mean? Well, it is a sad feature of human life that we tend not to respect money that we didn't first have to work for. Money gained too quickly leads people to acquire appetites and habits that they can't sustain. You can readily imagine praying that God would bless your job and regular income. I bet you never prayed that God would bless an inheritance you just received so that it would be a blessing to you and not a curse.

You know about setting aside a percentage of your regular income as a gift to thank the Giver. When you receive an inheritance, would it occur to you to set aside for God a percentage of those funds as well?

_____

_____

_____

_____

_____

Everybody but me has it together

Okay, Lord, time for some honesty. When I look at the people around me, the people I'm related to, work with, and live near, they all seem to be doing better than I am. I want to be happy for them, but to tell the truth, inside I envy and resent how successful they seem.

Why did you ordain such a hard road for me? Did I do it to myself? Or am I the victim of the neglect of others? Why do the people around me seem well organized, have perfect clothes, kids, and happy homes? How did they find those perfect jobs? When is it my turn for some prosperity and smooth sailing?

I probably sound materialistic and ungrateful when I talk like this, but I'm being honest. Can you help me see more clearly how richly I have been blessed? Can you help me see how I fit into your plans? Can you help me get a better perspective of how you can use me and my life in your kingdom? Am I missing something? Am I blind to the good things you've enabled me to do?

Help me want the right things and be happy for other people. **"Turn my heart toward your statutes and not toward selfish gain. Turn my eyes away from worthless things; preserve my life according to your word"** (Psalm 119:36,37).

_____

_____

_____

_____

_____

I don't have any friends

It isn't too hard to acquire relatives, classmates, and coworkers. It is much harder to gain friends, real friends, people who love and accept you, flaws and all. Perhaps you've heard the cry of the heart from a kid to his mom, "I don't have any friends." Perhaps he had been betrayed by people he thought liked him, people who later mocked him publicly or used him to get something they wanted.

Do you fear sometimes that you don't have any true friends? If so, you may have noticed that waiting around for people to notice you and come to you probably isn't working as a strategy. The writer to the Hebrews has a better idea: **"Let us not give up meeting together, as some are in the habit of doing, but let us encourage one another—and all the more as you see the Day approaching"** (Hebrews 10:25).

Your congregation is a great place to build relationships that matter. In that sacred space we all come as starving beggars, lost and foolish sinners, desperately in need of God's mercy. There we are welcomed by Jesus, Friend of sinners, whose unconditional love warms our cold hearts and makes them beat again.

There we find meaning for our lives by helping and serving other people. And it is in that blessed work that God will send people into your life to fill the hole in your heart.

_____

_____

_____

_____

_____

God and my guilt

"Out, damned spot! Out, I say!" muttered the sleepwalking Lady Macbeth, restlessly rubbing her hands as though to wash away the guilt of her conspiracy to murder. What invisible stains are on your hands? What have they stolen? What have they damaged? Whom have they hurt? What good things have they omitted doing?

People try all sorts of behaviors to stop feeling their guilt. They stay obsessively busy. They distract themselves with constant amusements. They try to work it off with good deeds. They rationalize away responsibility. They blame other people. They sedate themselves with drugs or alcohol or food. But guess what? Nothing works.

Except this: accepting responsibility for your own sins against God, and this: embracing the gift of the forgiveness of your sins through the payment made by Jesus Christ on his cross of Calvary. A great sinner named David gave you words to say in prayer: **"Have mercy on me, O God, according to your unfailing love; according to your great compassion blot out my transgressions. Wash away all my iniquity and cleanse me from my sin"** (Psalm 51:1,2).

What guilt are you dragging around right now? Want to be rid of it? Admit your responsibility, let Jesus have it, and serve him anew with a clear conscience.

_____

_____

_____

_____

_____

Worship in Jerusalem then

For 15 centuries the Israelite people exhibited a remarkable geographical cohesion. After their miraculous liberation from slavery and exodus from a country no longer hospitable to them, they settled in Canaan and stayed put. Each of the tribes was assigned a territory. The whole country was chosen by God partly for its compactness—it averaged only about 60 miles in width and about 100 miles from north to south.

That compactness made centralization possible. God wanted all family leaders to present themselves before the tabernacle (also called the tent of meeting) and later the temple not just once or twice, but **"three times a year all the men are to appear before the Sovereign Lord"** (Exodus 23:17). The feasts of Passover, Weeks, and Tabernacles had mandatory attendance.

Jesus himself observed all of the ceremonial regulations of the Old Covenant. Though they were northerners, living in Galilee, his parents took him to Jerusalem for his circumcision, naming, and presentation. They took him again at age 12 for his bar mitzvah. As an adult he presented himself at each of the three "pilgrim" festivals.

How ironic that as he came to Jerusalem to celebrate the Passover, he became the ultimate Passover Lamb.

Worship in spirit and truth now

The New Covenant is no longer place specific. You may enjoy a visit to the land of Israel and the ancient holy city of Jerusalem, and I hope you can someday, for you will understand the events of the Bible so much better. But it is not mandatory for you to make this pilgrimage.

Jesus himself explained this to a Samaritan woman who seemed to want to start an argument over which site in the ancient Middle East was the true place for worship. Jesus replied, **"A time is coming when you will worship the Father neither on this mountain** [i.e., Mt. Gerizim in Samaria] **nor in Jerusalem. . . . God is spirit, and his worshipers must worship in spirit and in truth"** (John 4:21,24).

God no longer localizes his presence through a bright glory-cloud. You can meet him anywhere on this planet. He comes to people and touches their lives in three ways: through his mighty Word, through the splash of baptismal water, and through the sacred Supper of Christ's body and blood.

The Day of Pentecost described in Acts chapter 2 reverses the covenant direction. Instead of "Come to Jerusalem," the New Testament church's mandate and commission is "Go!" **"*Go* and make disciples"** (Matthew 28:19).

_____

_____

_____

_____

_____

Gravestones

Have you ever visited a military cemetery? All burial places are holy and a little spooky, but veterans' cemeteries are profoundly moving: row upon row of identical, small, white stone markers, each with a terse legend of the person's name, dates, and military unit.

Some of the bodies lying there were shot up badly; many of the dead died of disease; some graves contain only fragments. All those stones mark the final resting places of fallen warriors; all are heroes to their countrymen. All of those deaths left behind sad and grieving families.

Would you be willing to take a little bit of time to do two things? One is to thank God for the successful outcomes of the sacrifices that these graves represent. Our country is a free and blessed place, and our freedom was bought at a terrible price.

Second, will you rededicate yourself to sharing the good news of Jesus so that as many people as possible will be rejoicing on resurrection day? As you think about cemeteries, realize that God has the last word: **"Multitudes who sleep in the dust of the earth will awake: some to everlasting life, others to shame and everlasting contempt"** (Daniel 12:2). All Christian warriors will awake soon to new life.

Go public

You've heard of secret relationships, right? When a married man is having an affair, the woman he is seeing on the side is his "mistress." Nobody can know because it's a secret. He can never take her anywhere, never say anything publicly about her, never mention her name in his regular world.

I wonder if sometimes God feels like a mistress. People want a personal relationship with him, but they're not proud of him in public. Nobody else knows they're Christians.

The Bible encourages us to be proud of our God and to go public with it. The church is good for public worship, by which I mean acknowledging your love for the Lord, your appreciation for the Lord, your gratitude to the Lord *with an audience*! When you worship and praise God in front of your friends, they know how you feel and they also see that you are proud enough of your God to claim him.

Here are a few words of inspiration from Psalm 96:7,8: **"Ascribe to the Lord, O families of nations, ascribe to the Lord glory and strength. Ascribe to the Lord the glory due his name; bring an offering and come into his courts."**

In other words, get off your chair. Get out of your living room. Get out on the street. Go public and show the world that you are proud of your God and grateful to him for what he's done for you.

_____

_____

_____

_____

_____

Does God cry too?

How do you imagine God from day to day? All-powerful? Serene in majesty? Imperturbable and calm, always in control?

Does it surprise you to hear that the Bible tells us that God does not always get what he wants? That he is often frustrated, unable to understand the destructive behaviors of his children, upon whom he has lavished education, love, and resources? That God gets sad too?

Sad enough to cry. **"When Jesus saw her weeping, and the Jews who had come along with her also weeping, he was deeply moved in spirit and troubled. 'Where have you laid him,' he asked. 'Come and see, Lord,' they replied. Jesus wept"** (John 11:33-35). God takes no pleasure in human death. When the reaper cuts down his children, God cries as would any parent. Jesus Christ, God in human flesh, came to the burial site of his friend Lazarus and felt the full weight of what we all feel at the death of someone we love. God himself wept at the tomb.

But then God spoke, and death was forced to release its grip. Lazarus lived again, thanks to the One who by his death defeated death. Jesus will reenact that same resurrection command on the Last Day, and you and I will emerge from our graves. And you know what? He will be smiling.

_____

_____

_____

_____

_____

When we dare to speak out and reach out to people who seem to be sliding away, we don't have to put pressure on them to clean themselves up first. Undoubtedly they will be caught in some sins private or public, but that's not where the change process starts. It doesn't start in the individual.

It starts with simply telling some good news about God, about who he is and what he has done. **"I, even I, am he who blots out your transgressions, for my own sake, and remembers your sins no more"** (Isaiah 43:25). Did you catch that? *"For my own sake,"* God said. That is, *"I* take the initiative. Your forgiveness comes from *me,* from the gracious goodness in my heart."

You can't reignite faith in someone else with threats, rules, laws, pressure, fear, or bribes. It is God who restarts a spiritually dead heart, using the message of the priceless gift of the forgiveness of sins, a gift he alone can give.

Scripture is full of stories of human foolishness and frailties, of human wickedness and rebellion. Scripture is also full of stories of lives changed by the gospel of God's forgiveness. When you undertake to bring a lost soul back to the Savior, start with the story of the tender heart of God.

_____

_____

_____

_____

_____

I'm afraid of being alone

God made us to be social creatures—we were not made to exist alone. We were all made to communicate and love. But what do you do when "alone" is where life put you, when there is no one in your house to love and communicate with? Not all those who want to be married find a spouse whom they can trust. In spite of the best intentions, divorce happens. Children all move away. Far away. Widowhood happens.

Do you know any people who are terrified to be alone? Do you feel that way? Do these words come from your heart? **"I am lonely and afflicted. The troubles of my heart have multiplied; free me from anguish. Look upon my affliction and my distress"** (Psalm 25:16-18).

Where do you go to fill that vast emptiness in your life? There are plenty of social groups where lonely people get involved, but the best of all solutions is to give your needs to your heavenly Father and watch for his way of answering. The Bible tells us, **"A father to the fatherless, a defender of widows, is God in his holy dwelling. God sets the lonely in families"** (Psalm 68:5,6).

Pray with me: Lord, I need you to keep that promise. I'm afraid of being alone. Please put some kind people in my life.

_____

_____

_____

_____

_____

MAY 31
We're exhausted

Have you ever noticed that when God is about to do something extraordinary, he first lets the believers exhaust themselves trying to do it on their own? He made Abraham and Sarah wait until he was 99 and she 89 before she conceived the child promised a quarter century earlier.

And when Jesus was going to use a mammoth fish catch as the platform for re-calling his disciples, he first let them exhaust themselves in the boat all night. Their results: nada. **"'I'm going out to fish,' Simon Peter told them, and they said, 'We'll go with you.' So they went out and got into the boat, but that night they caught nothing. Early in the morning, Jesus stood on the shore, but the disciples did not realize that it was Jesus. He called out to them, 'Friends, haven't you any fish?' 'No,' they answered"** (John 21:3-5).

Jesus told them to try the right side of the boat (like that would make a difference), but they followed his instructions and immediately hit on a load of fish so great they couldn't haul it into the boat. That was the God who called them into full-time service; that was the God who promoted them to the rank of apostle; that was the God who commissioned them to go to the ends of the earth with the Good News.

June

May the God of hope
fill you with all joy and peace
as you trust in him,
so that you may overflow with hope
by the power of the Holy Spirit.

Romans 15:13

I'm ashamed of my past

'Tis a sad thing that the past cannot be changed. Even the great St. Paul had some permanent and painful memories of violent and unbelieving things he had done as a young man. I certainly am ashamed of time and money wasted on stupid things in my own youth.

That's why we so resonate with Jesus' parable of the prodigal son: **"The younger son got together all he had, set off for a distant country and there squandered his wealth in wild living"** (Luke 15:13). We know that feeling. Shame persists long after the deeds. Embarrassing memories of squandered resources contribute mightily to our feelings of self-hatred.

But 'tis a great thing that the past cannot be changed. Jesus' triumphant death and resurrection cannot be changed. God's not guilty verdict on us cannot be changed. And that means that the Father's love for his sometimes lost and wayward children is always there for us. Wear his ring! Dine on his fatted calf!

The gospel tells us, with great tenderness and sincerity, that God is more interested in building our future than beating on us for our past. Your past failures and waste have already been freely forgiven. Hey—look through your windshield, not the rearview.

JUNE 2
From creation

One of the crucially important roles that families are supposed to play is to socialize the next generation, that is, hand down instruction about social behaviors that are appropriate, constructive, polite, and functional. Kids are not born knowing how to finish a job, keep a promise, or hold their tempers.

Or build a lasting, happy marriage. Here is where God's Word really helps. Marriage is not a business contract that two corporate attorneys hammer out. Marriage is not a somewhat outdated social arrangement that an ever-evolving humanity came up with millennia ago and is now moving beyond as it comes up with new arrangements. God made people fully developed. He also made marriage fully developed. He made it *immediately* after making people— Eve was only minutes old when she was led to God's "altar."

Jesus did not say a lot about marriage, but when he did, it was intense. In Matthew chapter 19 we hear Jesus explaining God's beautiful plan and intent. Jesus wants you to know that "happily ever after" begins with recognizing where marriage came from in the first place: **"Haven't you read . . . that at the beginning the *Creator* 'made them male and female'?"** (verse 4).

Are you engaged or married? Just think—you are privileged to participate in a grand divine drama that goes clear back to the Garden of Eden.

_____

_____

_____

_____

I don't know what to do

For a book whose last chapter was completed roughly two thousand years ago, the Bible is an astonishingly comprehensive and contemporary resource. It lays out who God is, what he has done in human history, how he would like to be treated, and how he would like us to treat one another. Want to know how to act? **"Should not a people inquire of their God?"** (Isaiah 8:19). The more of the Word you know, the clearer your mind.

But it does not answer every question we may have about God's ways, nor does it provide guidance to every specific life decision we have to make. A man says, "If I take this job, I would have to uproot my whole family. What does God want me to do?" Have you had similar life dilemmas? Many decisions we have to make don't have morally right or wrong choices. They are judgment calls, and God lets us exercise our judgment to grow us up as his servants and leaders.

When you face a tough choice, (1) find the Bible's teachings on the subject, (2) pray for inspiration and guidance, (3) draw your family and friends into the issues and ask for advice, (4) make a list with two columns and weigh the pros and cons.

My personal advice when you can't decide? If a logical analysis leaves you deadlocked, go with your gut. Your insides are usually right.

_____

_____

_____

_____

_____

Money or God?

God has a lot of competition in the category of what people most desire. Jesus had been watching human behavior for many millennia and saw a sad pattern emerge. He saw it in the materialistic heart of one of his closest friends, one of his own chosen disciples, Judas. He saw how easily money could become an idol, a substitute god that ruled in people's hearts.

He said once, **"No one can serve two masters. Either he will hate the one and love the other, or he will be devoted to the one and despise the other. You cannot serve both God and Money"** (Matthew 6:24).

How can you tell whom you're serving? If you serve Money, you will find justification for lying and cheating to get it. If you serve Money, you will find justification for stealing it, hoarding it, and flaunting it.

If you serve God, you will acknowledge that it all belongs to God. You will see yourself only as a temporary manager who is accountable to the great King. You will find greater joy in using money to accomplish God's agenda than in acquiring possessions or experiences for yourself. If you serve God, you will enjoy being generous with others, since you know with absolute certainty that God will soon replace all that and give you more.

_____

_____

_____

_____

_____

Noah believed and obeyed

Noah wasn't the first or the only believer to whom God gave difficult instructions. But he surely had the biggest task—the construction of a gigantic floating barge, big enough for all the animals that God was going to send him. Not only did he have no heavy construction machinery or electricity, but he wasn't a pharaoh and couldn't command an army of thousands of construction slaves. He and presumably his boys were the work crew, plugging away at their gigantic task month after month.

Not only did they have to overcome formidable engineering problems, but they also had to bear the brunt of community mockery. The construction site was probably nowhere near a major body of water. Noah didn't need to build the ark in a shipyard because the huge craft wouldn't need to be launched. Noah also had to face down his own fears and keep his family focused on God's words. He persevered: **"Noah did everything just as God commanded him"** (Genesis 6:22).

His barge was watertight—all people and animals survived their 12-month-plus ordeal. He had witnessed the greatest unleashing of the fury of God ever to come upon humankind. He also experienced the mercy and promises of God like no other.

Every time you see a rainbow, I hope you think of a God who means business and the grateful man who believed and obeyed him.

_____

_____

_____

_____

Time to listen to your teachers

One of the things I've learned the hard way in life is that I need people. It's good to be independent and self-reliant. But you can't invent the wheel in absolutely every aspect of your life. Listening to a teacher gets you farther faster.

I could be a much better mandolin player if I had taken some lessons and had a master nudge me and guide me along. I could have been a far better woodworker with a mentor. I could be a much better golfer if I had sought instruction years ago.

That's true of your faith life as well. The Bible is a vast and complicated book. You will absorb its marvelous content much better and faster if you choose to learn from the people God sent to help you along in your spiritual growth. He gave some people a special ability to communicate, to make God's truths plain and simple. These people don't just happen into your life; God sends them to you and reminds you to **"remember your leaders, who spoke the word of God to you. Consider the outcome of their way of life and imitate their faith"** (Hebrews 13:7).

It's one of the benefits of organized religion, you know.

_____

_____

_____

_____

_____

First the cross, then the crown

The Christian faith is one of paradoxes, isn't it? God has designed a set of opposite principles that at first seem to contradict and nullify each other. He says he is a God who condemns sin *and* forgives sin. Jesus Christ is fully God *and* fully human. He is a King who made himself a slave. We are saved by *grace* (inclusive—given freely to all) through *faith* (exclusive—only some believe).

Here's another: we are simultaneously mortal and immortal. Our bodies grow older and frailer each day, and yet we will spend eternity in these very bodies. Death is simultaneously an enemy that stalks us every day but also the blessed gateway through which we inherit the kingdom prepared for us ever since the world was begun.

The aged apostle John, by now in his 90s, shared his confidence with the Christians of the church in Smyrna: **"Be faithful, even to the point of death, and I will give you the crown of life"** (Revelation 2:10). It is our honor and destiny to follow in the footsteps of Jesus. First the hardships, then the joy. First the war, then the peace. First the cross, then the crown.

You will receive a personal heavenly welcome from the royal Monarch who still has nail marks in his hands.

_____

_____

_____

_____

_____

Spirit power

One of the things I appreciate about the Bible is its honesty about its heroes and main characters. Noah, Moses, Aaron, David, and Solomon were great men but also sometimes great fools. The four gospels that tell the life of Christ are also brutally honest about the foolish things Jesus' disciples said and did during their three-year training course.

But they learned, matured, and grew up. It is the Holy Spirit's job to take the message about Christ's person and work, bring it to people one by one, and patiently plant and grow faith where there had been confusion and unbelief and doubt.

Jesus promised his disciples a great outpouring of the Holy Spirit: **"All this I have spoken while still with you. But the Counselor, the Holy Spirit, whom the Father will send in my name, will teach you all things and will remind you of everything I have said to you"** (John 14:25,26).

With the Spirit's help and coaching and power, Jesus' teachings finally made sense to them. With the Spirit's encouragement, they shed their doubts and fear and became bold witnesses to the truth. With the Spirit's guidance, they carried out Jesus' commission to bring good news of forgiveness and immortality to the ends of the earth. That same Spirit works in you too—to give you clarity of mind, courage of heart, and boldness of vision.

Go!

_____

_____

_____

_____

I need proof

Biblical Christians are sometimes accused of being anti-scientific because they can't accept the theories of evolution and natural selection. Actually the reverse is true. Christians make great scientists—after all, there is only one truth, God's truth. God himself loves science—his natural universe is full of order, design, rules, and laws. All its intricacies that we humans discover bit by bit were placed there by him long ago.

Some features of the Christian faith, however, will forever be beyond the reach of scientific inquiry. The resurrection of the body, for instance, is something we will witness only in the future. Jesus' disciple Thomas, however, refused to believe what he couldn't examine and touch: **"Unless I see the nail marks in his hands and put my finger where the nails were, and put my hand into his side, I will not believe it"** (John 20:25).

You can't discover God's forgiveness of our sins through empirical research. You can't determine the existence of angels by studying electromagnetic fields. The only way you will know anything at all about God's grace, God's angels, and God's raising of the dead is by letting him tell you all about it in his Word. If you refuse to believe it until you can see it, it will be too late.

Believe it now.

_____

_____

_____

_____

_____

Care for the weak

A strange paradox takes place when people become caregivers to special needs people. If you didn't know the families, you would think that a child with Down syndrome or spina bifida or cerebral palsy would be a terrible burden. You'd think that it would be a terrible curse to be stuck with years, even decades, of the enormous responsibility of that level of care.

Actually the reverse occurs. The family is ennobled and lifted up by learning how to be servants. Family members find that the joy of helping someone, especially someone who is weaker, provides much more lasting satisfaction than playing video games and watching TV. The family develops a huge friend network because they need so much help. The very pain and struggle in their lives provides a platform for authentic sharing of the gospel with the multitude of professionals and aides with whom they interact.

"Religion that God our Father accepts as pure and faultless is this: to look after orphans and widows in their distress" (James 1:27). We all crave significance. What could be more significant than living our lives the way Jesus lived his—using our gifts, our time, our energy, our passion and love, bringing benefit to the lives of other people who need us.

_____

_____

_____

_____

_____

I gotta tell somebody

When we're pleased with a product or service, nobody has to nag us to share our experience. When we finally find a good auto mechanic, hairdresser, cabernet sauvignon, laundry detergent, or thrift store, we will happily tell everybody who will listen.

Do you get animated when talking about your faith? Are you excited about what you've found? **"Andrew, Simon Peter's brother, was one of the two who heard what John had said and who had followed Jesus. The first thing Andrew did was to find his brother Simon and tell him, 'We have found the Messiah'"** (John 1:40,41).

Pastors love talking about the gospel, but you know what's even more powerful? When laypeople share the Word. Pastors get paid for what they do, and skeptics will assume that they are just performing for the money, building the business from which they derive their income. When regular people talk about Jesus, it can be much more powerful and believable because they are doing it for free. They don't get commissions. Their words don't need to be fancy or elegant, full of Greek and Hebrew words and theological terms. Simple talk from the heart is the best.

Do you believe in the power of word-of-mouth evangelism? God's Word from your mouth?

_____

_____

_____

_____

_____

Fly like an eagle

Michael Joncas, priest and church musician, was only 27 when he wrote the words to "On Eagle's Wings," without a doubt one of the most popular Christian hymns today. Had he already known major suffering, despair, and a feeling of hopelessness in his short life? Had he personally experienced the tremendous lift that comes from God's chosen time of rescue? Millions of struggling believers have rejoiced to sing with him:

> He will raise you up on eagles' wings,
> Bear you on the breath of dawn,
> Make you to shine like the sun,
> And hold you in the palm of his hand.

His inspiration, of course, came from the experiences of the nation of Israel, just set free from Egyptian slavery and now gathered at Mt. Sinai. They were about to feel terrible earthquakes, see God's lightning from the summit, and hear the thunder and trumpet blasts and roar of God's own solemn voice as he spoke his holy law. But Moses brought a tender and thrilling message as well from God: **"You yourselves have seen what I did to Egypt, and how I carried you on eagles' wings and brought you to myself"** (Exodus 19:4).

Whether 27 or 87, you will experience God's mighty hand lifting you up when you need it most. Let him pick the moment. Let him hear your praise when he does.

_____

_____

The Word

I think I know why so many people underestimate the power of the Bible. Jesus Christ himself, the Son of God, came to earth "disguised" as one of us, walked in humility, took a lot of abuse, and died in shame. And yet it is through his wounds that we are healed.

In the same way, the Bible seems like a lot of not much. It's just words on a page. Talk, as we all know, is cheap. The Bible appears to have a string of human authors; on the surface it looks not like God's Word but like a collection of human opinions.

Jesus taught that God supervised all its content, from Genesis to Revelation, and guarantees its message. God supercharged its words with the very presence and power of the Holy Spirit. Thus to read or hear the Bible is to hear *the voice of God himself.* Jesus thinks it's enough to get the job done.

In Jesus' famous parable, a sinner in hell pleaded with Abraham in heaven, **"'Then I beg you, father, send Lazarus to my father's house, for I have five brothers. Let him warn them, so that they will not also come to this place of torment.' Abraham replied, 'They have Moses and the Prophets; let them listen to them'"** (Luke 16:27-29).

In Jesus' view, if the Word doesn't bring people to faith, nothing will.

Flag Day

People are intensely proud of their national flags. That simple piece of colored cloth evokes powerful feelings. Brits love their Union Jack, Canadians love their maple leaf, and Americans love their star-spangled banner. Flags give people a sense of history, of belonging, of place, of identity.

The message of salvation won for us by Jesus Christ is central to Christianity, and the symbol of the cross elegantly sums up his blood-purchase on our behalf. The most important message we have, and the most important concept to lift up high for the world to see, is the powerful image of Christ victorious over sin, Satan, death, and hell.

"In that day the Root of Jesse will stand as a banner for the peoples; the nations will rally to him. . . . [The Lord] will raise a banner for the nations and gather the exiles of Israel; he will assemble the scattered people of Judah from the four quarters of the earth" (Isaiah 11:10,12). Jesse was King David's father. When the royal line of Israelite kings was ended in 586 B.C., the great tree of David's dynasty became a stump.

Jesus Christ is a blood descendant of David and reestablished the kingship once and for all eternity. His royal banner now goes forth, calling one and all to repentance, faith, forgiveness, and immortality. The image of the cross, once an instrument of torture, has now become beautiful enough for our King's flag.

_____

_____

_____

_____

It's my husband

How hard it must be to have an unbelieving husband — to have to pray alone, go to church alone, read your Bible alone, and receive no spiritual support. How hard it must be to feel like a widow or divorcee in church. What would make it seem even worse is a situation in which the husband once was an active believer but fell away.

Is that your life? Don't give up — maybe just change your strategy. Not all witnessing for your faith is verbal. Sometimes the fallen-away husband knows all the words but just can't believe them. That's where nonverbal witnessing comes in: **"Wives, in the same way be submissive to your husbands so that, if any of them do not believe the word, they may be won over without words by the behavior of their wives, when they see the purity and reverence of your lives"** (1 Peter 3:1,2).

Love professed can be blown off. Love demonstrated is much more powerful. Any man who feels despised by his wife will die inside and will close himself off to her. A man who has rejected his wife's beliefs but still feels respected and supported may be moved to change his mind.

_____

_____

_____

_____

_____

One man, one woman

It is our duty and destiny to live in an age in which people think they have the right to define marriage as they please. Gay rights activists have already succeeded in gaining recognition for homosexual civil unions. Worse, they have persuaded a growing number of states to sanction marriage between two men or two women.

The debate in our country is focused on *rights,* and it draws on the grievances and successes of the racial civil rights struggle. Gay advocates portray themselves as an injured and oppressed minority.

People who believe the Bible, who respect God's will as expressed in Romans chapter 1, see the debate not in terms of rights but of design and blessing. How can God bless an ongoing legal sexual arrangement that defies and contradicts what he designed? Jesus himself said, **"For this reason a man will leave his father and mother and be united to his wife"** (Matthew 19:5).

If marriage itself is subject to human revision according to the desires of those who see themselves as a persecuted and oppressed minority, where will it end? Will we live to see a day where marriages of three people become legal? Will polygamy make a comeback?

Just because something is legal does not make it right in the eyes of God.

JUNE 17
God's power

"Talk is cheap." You've heard that before. What are words? Ink on paper; air waves moving from lips, tongue, and throat. Human talk is indeed often cheap and insubstantial. But when God speaks, there is power.

When God spoke at the beginning of time, matter erupted out of nothing. When God spoke, light shattered the darkness. When God spoke, the globe's entire water system rearranged itself, vegetation exploded into existence, stars and solar systems leaped into the sky, and air and sea and land welcomed millions of animals. When God spoke, lifeless dirt became Adam and a rib became Eve.

When God the Son said from his cross, "It is finished," sin, death, the grave, and Satan himself were finished. **"'Is not my word like fire,' declares the LORD, 'and like a hammer that breaks a rock in pieces?'"** (Jeremiah 23:29).

When God speaks to a human heart, his hammer breaks down walls of sin and his fire reignites saving faith in the one Savior. When you speak God's words, therefore, *his* power comes out of *your* mouth. Really.

_____

_____

_____

_____

_____

I'm afraid for my children

A young couple says, "This world is unsafe. Is it a good idea to have children?" I'm sure part of you resonates with that statement. Our streets are dangerous indeed. Adult temptations come at children at earlier and earlier ages, usually far before they are ready to deal with them. It seems that no place is safe from armed, angry, and violent people—schools, theaters, malls, even army bases.

Sad to say, things have always been that way. The world the Israelites lived in could be just as violent as ours, and God still invited couples to bring forth new people. He promises to limit the damage Satan and his demons can do, promises to give us no more than we can handle, and promises to give us strength to stand up on evil days.

David was a shepherd, courtier, fugitive, king, and warrior. Violence was never far from his life. He found great comfort in simply surrendering his life and those he led to the guidance and care of the Lord: **"I trust in you, O LORD; I say, 'You are my God.' My times are in your hands"** (Psalm 31:14,15).

Life without risk does not exist. But people committed to God can live joyfully and without fear, knowing that their lives are serving God's great saving purpose and that their place in heaven is safe and secure.

_____

_____

_____

_____

_____

A God of abundance

Human beings have some pretty ironclad limitations. We can be in only one place at a time. We are locked into one little moving dot on the time line of history; the past is hazy and fuzzy, and the future is completely unknown. And we all know that there are only limited resources for solving big problems.

Except when God steps in. When he chooses, God can bust loose from all the restraints of the laws of physics. Whether it involves Jesus walking on water, restoration of atrophied legs and muscles with a word, or defying gravity by rising off the ground, our God is a God of abundance, whose power and compassion know no limits.

A great crowd of people had been listening to Jesus. They were past hungry—they were in danger of collapse from lack of sustenance. **"When Jesus looked up and saw a great crowd coming toward him, he said to Philip, 'Where shall we buy bread for these people to eat?' He asked this only to test him, for he already had in mind what he was going to do. Philip answered him, 'Eight months' wages would not buy enough bread for each one to have a bite!'"** (John 6:5-7).

Philip could not imagine that there was a solution to the food problem. How he must have been dazzled by what Jesus did with five loaves of bread and two fish! Are you dazzled too? Does your God have limits?

_____

_____

_____

_____

_____

Making money God's way

One of the things that everybody knows for sure about money is that it is the root of all evil, right? Well, er, no. The Bible says that it is the *love* of money that is a root of all kinds of evil. Can you see the difference?

Money is just a tool—it's portable power. It's a convenient way to turn labor into goods and the need for goods into labor. Money is a far better way to store wealth than livestock.

If you are poor, God most certainly loves you, and he will help you survive. And yes, materialism and cash idolatry are deadly sins indeed. But it is certainly not God's *desire* that his people should all be poor. He *approves* of your making money, and he would like you to build wealth for your family's needs, for community investment, and for generosity in spreading the gospel. **"Lazy hands make a man poor, but diligent hands bring wealth"** (Proverbs 10:4).

Did you catch that? God not only allows you to pursue building wealth; he actually promises to bless your hard work with a decent financial return. Don't love the wealth, but love the one who allows you to earn it.

_____

_____

_____

_____

_____

Misplaced priorities

One of my persistent weaknesses is that I want to author my own play, the play of my life, in which I am the star, for which I would like to write the script. I can pretty much do fine on my own for a while, and then when I encounter a problem too big for me, I holler for God to show up on "my" stage, on my cue. He generally does not oblige me at such times. *Hmm.* Wonder why.

In the middle of his Sermon on the Mount, Jesus helped his disciples to see how the universe really operates. The more you grasp for material things, the more in love you are with yourself and your agenda, the less you will achieve and the less satisfaction you will feel.

Here is a better way: **"Seek first his** [i.e., God's] **kingdom and his righteousness, and all these things will be given to you as well"** (Matthew 6:33). Seeking God's kingdom means seeing yourself as God's creation, placed here on earth for a mission, *his* mission. You are in *his* play, and he will let you know the role he needs you to play for him.

Seeking God's righteousness means choosing to value your forgiveness of sins through the blood of Jesus as your most precious possession. When you have that, everything else that God thinks you need will come flowing into your life.

On his cue.

_____

_____

_____

_____

_____

Am I doomed to become my father?

The statistics are sobering—children of abusive parents are likely to become abusers themselves. Children from divorced parents are less likely to be able to build a lasting marriage. A woman sighs, "My parents were so critical of me, and now I hear myself talking like that to my children." Are we doomed to become our parents?

Tempted? Yes. Doomed? No. You are not destined to any sort of sinful behaviors. Forgiven by Christ and renewed by the Holy Spirit, you now have power from God to choose your behaviors. King Saul hated the young upstart David, who had been anointed as the next king. Saul wanted his son Jonathan, the crown prince, to hate David too: **"Saul's anger flared up at Jonathan and he said to him, 'You son of a perverse and rebellious woman! Don't I know that you have sided with the son of Jesse to your own shame and to the shame of the mother who bore you? As long as the son of Jesse lives on this earth, neither you nor your kingdom will be established'"** (1 Samuel 20:30,31).

But Jonathan refused to imitate his father's paranoia and cruelty. He saw God's hand in David's anointing and threw his support behind him, risking his life to help David flee.

God's Spirit has freed you to be you.

_____

_____

_____

_____

_____

JUNE 23
I can't seem to control my tongue

Why do I do it? Lord, I am so sorry for what I said. If only I could put those words back behind my teeth and swallow them back down. But they're out. Why is my tongue so loose? Why do lies come out when I know I should tell the truth? Why does gossip come out so easily when I know I should be building other people up? Why do I sound bitter so often when I know I have been richly blessed by you? Why has my anger hurt so many people, especially my family?

I need help! **"Set a guard over my mouth, O Lord; keep watch over the door of my lips. Let not my heart be drawn to what is evil, to take part in wicked deeds"** (Psalm 141:3,4). I know that it's not literally my tongue that's at fault. My tongue is only a wet muscle operated by my brain. It's my mind and feelings and thoughts that need work.

Help me think twice before speaking once. Help me praise twice before criticizing. Help me tell the truth always and trust that you will bless me even if the truth makes me look bad. Help me be mindful at all times that I am your beloved and gifted child, representing you in all I do. May my words, all of them, honor you.

_____

_____

_____

_____

_____

JUNE 24
Is you is or is you ain't?

That's the name of a tune from the swing era by Louis
Jordan, who earnestly desired to know if his beloved was
interested in a long-term relationship or not. Louis had
learned that a relationship cannot be sustained if only one
party is putting energy into it.

Does it surprise you to know that God has the same
question for his believers? He created us, designed and
executed a fabulously successful plan of salvation after our
rebellion, brought his Word to us, and even implanted faith
in our hearts through the Spirit. Now he seeks a response,
and he better not find a yawn and eye rolls from us.

**"These are the words of the Amen, the faithful and true
witness, the ruler of God's creation. I know your deeds,
that you are neither cold nor hot. I wish you were either
one or the other! So, because you are lukewarm—neither
hot nor cold—I am about to spit you out of my mouth"**
(Revelation 3:14-16).

Our faith-relationship with God is life or death; our eternity
rides on what we do with the gospel message of Christ. Let
your response to God's declaration of love be as passionate
and intense as his. Let God know today, right now, how
precious his presence, forgiveness, and gifts are to you.

_____

_____

_____

_____

_____

I feel so sad

As you have figured out by now, life is not a sprint. It is a marathon. And just as our bodies physically don't bounce back as quickly from exertion or illness as they used to, I think our spirits lose some elasticity as the years roll on too.

Persistent disappointments sometimes make people violent or abusive or bitter. Sometimes they just make us sad. They grind down our optimism and cheerfulness to the point where even bits of good news don't cheer us up.

Here's where God can help. He is not only going to restore us completely in *heaven*—his restoration work is going on *right now.* If you have an ocean of sadness inside, don't give up. God hasn't! **"You turned my wailing into dancing; you removed my sackcloth and clothed me with joy"** (Psalm 30:11).

If you're thinking that you no longer have the strength to make your sad heart smile, you might be right. So give God a chance to do what you can't do on your own. Review the amazing stories in his Word in which he reversed people's downward slides and made things happen for them. Trust his kindly intent and limitless power. Give him your hopes and fears, your brokenness and needs. Dance with him!

_____

_____

_____

_____

_____

Christian funeral confidence

Poor Martha has gotten a bum rap over the centuries. She is remembered primarily for one weak moment when she snapped at her sister for not helping more in lunch preparation; Mary is remembered forever after as the good girl who attended Bible study with Jesus.

But Martha was no spiritual slouch; in fact, her powerful faith and confident testimony at the time of her brother's funeral and burial is one of the most inspirational speeches in the entire Bible. **"'Lord,' Martha said to Jesus, 'if you had been here, my brother would not have died. But I know that even now God will give you whatever you ask.' Jesus said to her, 'Your brother will rise again.' Martha answered, 'I know he will rise again in the resurrection at the last day'"** (John 11:21-24).

Imagine that! Not only did she believe that Jesus could have healed her terminally ill brother, which would have taken considerable faith. But she was also able, in her misery and grief, to see ahead, past the grave and burial, to her brother's resurrection and new life.

Jesus confirmed and built up that great faith into an even greater faith. He told her that he himself was the resurrection and the life. Then he called Lazarus out of his grave, a demo version of what he intends to do on a global scale when he comes back.

Remember Martha at your next funeral.

_____

_____

_____

_____

JUNE 27

Control your anger

"Born to Be Wild" is more than just a song (Steppenwolf, ca. 1968). It is a summary of the basic human state of mind when untouched by the gospel. There is a beast inside each of us, and we love to let him out of his cage. Come on— admit it. Throwing off restraint is exhilarating.

So is losing your temper. There was a time when I thought that angry people were unhappy. Actually it's worse than that. Blowing up and "going off" on someone actually releases a blast of adrenaline that many people find exciting. There's a thrill to telling somebody off. Have you felt it?

The problem is that anger is pure emotion, and emotion is usually irrational. Anger outbursts rarely solve any problems or do any good. They more often destroy things and people. Here is some of God's wisdom: **"He who guards his lips guards his life, but he who speaks rashly will come to ruin"** (Proverbs 13:3). You can spend years of your life trying to fix what you wrecked in three minutes.

If you've lost your temper, let Jesus help you find it again. As you savor the sweet forgiveness given so freely to you, find the joy of extending that forgiveness to others, *even when you know you're right.* And if you must be wild, take a ride on a Harley.

God and my mission

Have you ever wondered why you're still here? I mean, if God has saved you, if you are now guaranteed eternal life through Jesus, why doesn't he just whisk you away to heaven?

The reason is that you are far too valuable to his plan. He has a mission for you. Just as other people helped you to hear and understand the Bible's message, so you are part of the communication network that other people need so that they can become believers too. When you speak of what God has done, it's as though God were telling the story himself. When you speak God's words of instruction for godly living, it's as though God himself were speaking directly and personally to them.

Look first within your own family, especially to the younger ones. **"We will tell the next generation the praiseworthy deeds of the Lord, his power, and the wonders he has done . . . which he commanded our forefathers to teach their children, so the next generation would know them, even the children yet to be born, and they in turn would tell their children"** (Psalm 78:4-6).

Who are the three individuals in your life who most helped you to hear Jesus' voice? Can you think of three people in your life who need to hear about Jesus?

_____

_____

_____

_____

_____

May I have this dance?

When you're on a dance floor and it's a "modern" dance, people don't have to pay the slightest bit of attention to what their partners are doing. You don't have to coordinate anything. You can just bust your moves.

Being happily married, however, is more like a waltz or a tango. You have to hold each other carefully, move in sync with each other, pay attention to your partner, and mind your feet. In both marriage and ballroom dancing, someone has to lead and someone has to be willing to be led. You have to communicate so that you can move gracefully together.

Do you think that the cosmic designer and engineer of gender, sexuality, and marriage might know how this dance works best? **"Husbands, . . . be considerate as you live with your wives, and treat them with respect"** (1 Peter 3:7).

This means that men need to step up and accept responsibility for leadership, leading like Jesus. He led like a servant, willing to give up his life for the people he loved. This means that women need to surrender some of their independence and cheerfully place themselves under the leadership of their husbands, whom God expects to represent Jesus in the home.

Do you trust the divine dance instructor enough to let him teach you his moves?

JUNE 30
You can expect God's blessings

People get down when they feel that all their efforts are wasted and pointless. They get cynical and say things like, "Virtue is its own punishment" and "No good deed ever goes unpunished." Earth seems like a desert drear pretty much all the time. We think we know too many stories about how cheaters prosper and the violent always win.

That's just bitter talk. Blind too. The Bible says that the Lord **"blesses the home of the righteous. . . . You will go on your way in safety. . . . When you lie down, your sleep will be sweet"** (Proverbs 3:33,23,24). Those who believe in Jesus as their Savior exchange their sinful rags for righteous robes. Through faith, all of Jesus' holiness is transferred to your account. The Lord pays attention. He remembers. And then he acts.

The word *bless* means that God intervenes in our lives to make them better. He accepted the obligation of fatherhood when we were washed with water and the Word. Since he loves you even more than you love your children, he derives great pleasure from making you happy, seeing you grow, and helping you to live a successful life.

When you claim Christ's righteousness as yours, your sleep is sweet indeed.

_____

_____

_____

_____

_____

July

**Cast all your anxiety
on him because
he cares for you.**
1 Peter 5:7

JULY 1
The agony and the ecstasy

The cross and crown. No, that's not the name of an English pub; it's a pair of biblical symbols that is often used in church architecture and design, the one overlaid upon the other. It describes the two phases of the saving work of Jesus Christ—that he suffered death on a cross so that he might receive the crown of heaven as King of kings and Lord of lords.

Those two symbols are also metaphors for two phases of *your* life. Jesus invites all of his followers to pick up their own crosses and follow him, but he promises a place in his throne room to all who hold fast to him in faith and refuse to let sin, Satan, hardship, or loss induce them to throw away their treasure: **"I am coming soon. Hold on to what you have, so that no one will take your crown. Those who overcome I will make pillars in the temple of my God"** (Revelation 3:11,12).

What is your cross? Anything you suffer or give up or have taken from you because you are a Christian. Anything it costs you to follow Jesus—friends, money, position, perks, rank, status, or advantages. What is the crown Jesus promises? His holiness upon your head like an aura; status as prince or princess in the heavenly courts; a position at his side as he judges and rules the world; an everlasting relationship with him and all the saints.

_____

_____

_____

_____

_____

God and my needs

What are you afraid of?

When men hear a question like that, they go into John Wayne mode: "I ain't afraid o' nuthin', ma'am." Well, baloney. We all have fears, whether we admit it or not. Men are afraid of being seen as weak. They fear losing respect, losing their jobs, losing their place. Women fear for their personal safety and the safety of those they love. Women fear for their family's health and wellness. Children have a thousand fears, of which the terror of abandonment is near the top.

All of us fear death and the dying process. And I think if we're honest, we would admit to being vulnerable to Satan's whisperings that our faith is a fraud and that there is no God and no help as we struggle to survive.

Here is God's solemn promise to you: **"'Because he loves me,' says the Lord, 'I will rescue him; I will protect him, for he acknowledges my name. He will call upon me, and I will answer him; I will be with him in trouble, I will deliver him and honor him'"** (Psalm 91:14,15).

God sees you. He cares about you. He knows what you need and when. He acts, always right on time.

_____

_____

_____

_____

_____

Clay pots

Everybody's got 'em. The commonest and cheapest flowerpots are all the same color—orange. People aren't that interested in the pot—they want to spend their money on the flowers after all. The pots are brittle—one drop and they shatter into a bazillion pieces. It's the glory of the flowers that matters.

Christians are messengers for Jesus. We carry around good news of forgiveness and immortality—the glory of God that shines on us through Jesus Christ. But we are as fragile as flowerpots. **"God . . . made his light shine in our hearts to give us the light of the knowledge of the glory of God in the face of Christ. But we have this treasure in jars of clay to show that this all-surpassing power is from God"** (2 Corinthians 4:6,7).

The truth of your message to another sinner isn't spoiled by your personal weaknesses. God's truth is true no matter who speaks it. Your own moral failings don't diminish the power of the gospel message—that Jesus Christ lived for you and died for you to transform you from God's enemy into God's child.

Our sins do not disqualify us from sharing a message of full and free forgiveness. Our mortality does not disqualify us from sharing a message of immortality. You're a jar of clay—relax! What matters is the treasure within.

_____

_____

_____

_____

_____

JULY 4
Freedom in Christ

This week you just might hear these Lee Greenwood lyrics somewhere: "I'm proud to be an American, where at least I know I'm free." People who live in the United States are proud of their revolution, their freedoms, and their rights as listed in the first ten amendments to the Constitution. It is worth noting that there is no corresponding "Bill of Responsibilities" to go with the Bill of Rights.

A powerful theme running through the epistles of St. Paul is our freedom in Christ. Through faith in his suffering, death, and resurrection we are forgiven of all sins and given the precious promise of eternal life. Our Christian identity, however, does indeed come with a Bill of Responsibilities. We are simultaneously free men and women and servants to others. **"Though I am free and belong to no man, I make myself a slave to everyone, to win as many as possible"** (1 Corinthians 9:19).

Our spiritual freedom from sin, death, and hell gives us a great message to share with others who are still trapped in guilt and fear. As Jesus Christ, Lord of all, made himself a servant to all, we are called to that same paradoxical mind-set.

America's political revolution was a great leap forward in the development of democracy. As Christians speak and live the gospel of Christ, we can help to bring about an even greater form of government—the lordship of Jesus Christ.

JULY 5
Too young to die

People were saying, "His grandkids really needed him, especially as a Christian example, since the parents didn't do it. Why did he die now? I don't get it. Those kids are going to suffer because he's gone." Has anybody in your family died too young, leaving behind minor children, a load of debts, or a business that couldn't survive without him?

Sometimes God's ways just make no sense. John the Baptist was just getting started with his nationwide wake-up call to take notice that the Messiah had arrived. He was drawing huge crowds and having a massive impact. First God let him become imprisoned, and his fiery sermons ceased. Then God allowed him to be executed. **"The king** [Herod Antipas] **was greatly distressed, but because of his oaths and dinner guests, he did not want to refuse her** [his stepdaughter Salome]. **So he immediately sent an executioner with orders to bring John's head"** (Mark 6:26,27).

John must have thought till the very last second that there would be a miraculous angelic escape and he would be able to resume his ministry. What a shock when he woke up in heaven. God had decided that his mission on earth was accomplished. So it is when God allows people to die that we thought were "too young." Now other people have an important mission.

_____

_____

_____

_____

_____

I'm so dumb

"Well, here's another nice mess you've gotten me into." Oliver Hardy made a career out of scolding Stan Laurel on stage and screen. The audience members always laughed because they did it too. The first stage of response when things go wrong is to look for others to blame. Second, you can always blame God for sending or allowing trouble.

The darkest phase is when you realize how many of your wounds are self-inflicted.

Nobody made me down all those drinks or chase after that woman. Nobody made me make those worthless investments or argue with the boss. Nobody made me keep pulling that slot machine handle. Nobody made me flirt with that married man. Why don't I know when to shut up? Why am I crabby all the time? Why did I take that money when I didn't even need it?

What to do? Talk to God and tell him the truth. **"You know my folly, O God; my guilt is not hidden from you"** (Psalm 69:5). Humbling ourselves is good. The proud and arrogant don't think they need him. God can help the humble. And the humbler our spirit, the more likely it is that we will listen to God's words, words of forgiveness, affection, and instruction.

_____

_____

_____

_____

_____

I lost a lot of money

Money slips away bit by bit from all of us. Inflation drains the buying power of our dollars. Withholding taxes silently subtracts a piece from every paycheck.

But have you ever suffered a big financial loss? Maybe it was through your own stupid weakness for gambling. Maybe it was a major illness that ate up your savings and left you with debts. Maybe a nasty divorce ruined your retirement plans. Maybe some of your major investments suffered a serious loss in value. Or someone you trusted ripped you off.

An Old Testament hero named Job knows your pain. **"While he was still speaking, another messenger came and said, 'The Chaldeans formed three raiding parties and swept down on your camels and carried them off. They put the servants to the sword, and I am the only one who has escaped to tell you!'"** (Job 1:17). His financial losses were staggering.

What do you do when you're in a financial hole? First, listen anew to the messages of love and commitment from your God. He doesn't stop being your Father when you're broke. Don't be too proud to ask for his help, and watch for doors and windows opening. Second, don't be too proud to ask for help from the people in your life whom God has given you. They may bring solutions.

Wait with patience. And remember that your real treasure is in heaven.

Free to be a slave

Frederick Douglass and Harriet Tubman are American national heroes. They escaped from slavery and became passionate abolitionists.

Slavery was also widespread in the Roman Empire of New Testament times; many of the first Christians were slaves. One of them, a man named Onesimus, ran away and found the apostle Paul, certain that someone who proclaimed freedom in Christ would provide refuge.

To Onesimus' great chagrin, Paul asked him to go back to his master. **"I am sending him—who is my very heart—back to you. I would have liked to keep him with me so that he could take your place in helping me while I am in chains for the gospel. . . . He is very dear to me but even dearer to you, both as a man and as a brother in the Lord"** (Philemon 12,16). The letter that Paul wrote asked sacrifices of both, but the greater sacrifice was that of the ex-slave who had to decide whether or not to give up his freedom.

Would I have given up my freedom for Jesus? I don't know, but I do know I admire Onesimus' courage and trust in Paul's judgment. And get this—50 years later Bishop Ignatius of Smyrna wrote a letter referring to a certain Bishop Onesimus of Ephesus. *Hmm* . . . Do you think this was God's way of rewarding a faithful slave?

_____

_____

_____

_____

_____

Nobody appreciates me

I'm tired of doing all the grunt work. There. I've said it. I'm not proud of complaining like this, Lord, but that's how I feel right now. It's not so much that I resent the beautiful people who are out front. I just wish that my humbler contributions would get noticed once in a while. Is that too much to ask? Why am I so invisible? Doesn't anybody see any value in my work?

It's not that I'm not willing to work. It's not that I'm lazy—you see that, right? It's not even that I think I'm too good to do humble chores. I just feel like I'm being taken advantage of. Lord, could you please let people notice me a little bit? I don't have to be the star, but couldn't I at least be made to feel like part of the team?

In the meantime, I want you to know that I get a great deal of comfort from knowing that your eyes are everywhere. I know that even when nobody notices me, you do. You told me that once: **"The eyes of the Lord are on the righteous"** (Psalm 34:15).

Lord, maybe I will get noticed and thanked today, and maybe I won't. But ultimately I care more for your approval than other people's. It is enough for me that *you* see me and smile.

_____

_____

_____

_____

_____

How great thou art

When was the last time you were overcome by the greatness of God and the majesty of his works in creation? Was it when you gazed into the sky on a clear night with no streetlights to dim the twinkling billions of night-lights? When you drove through the Rocky Mountain passes, feeling very small next to those immense peaks? Peered out the windows as a blizzard raged all around your house? Jumped at the crash of thunder on a summer night? Say it with me: **"O Lord, our Lord, how majestic is your name in all the earth!"** (Psalm 8:1).

A Swedish pastor named Carl Boberg felt those very things and wrote a poem to express his worship. It came into English through Stuart Hine and has become a well-loved song—"How Great Thou Art." Pick up your closest hymnbook and read the stanzas. They tell of the author's "awesome wonder" as he considers God's creation, his might and power, and his wonderful works.

Made famous through the Billy Graham crusades, that song would be a wonderful soundtrack for your day today. In the midst of the mess of human life, with its pains, wounds, disappointments, failures, betrayals, and brokenness, we can lift up our eyes to the heavenly One whose power, passion, and purpose for us will never change. We are safe in his arms.

No shortcuts

When my children were young, each day they showed me what I must have been like to my parents when I was growing up. Some days were good; some were not pretty. I occasionally had flashbacks, when I could hear my father's voice in my own as I was scolding the troops.

It is part of our sinful inheritance to want the harvest without the work. Satan is a liar and cheater, and so we shouldn't be surprised to see such a strong inclination to shortcuts in ourselves and others. Fantasizing about hitting a jackpot through gambling will always sound like more fun than working. Cheating and stealing always seem to go so much faster and easier than working.

Satan owns the short term. Sin always provides that short burst of excitement. **"Food gained by fraud tastes sweet to a man, but he ends up with a mouth full of gravel"** (Proverbs 20:17). God alone owns the long term. There are no shortcuts to satisfaction and true peace of mind. You really won't like the taste of gravel.

_____

_____

_____

_____

_____

The gateway to mortality

"You must not eat from the tree of the knowledge of good and evil, for when you eat of it you will surely die," God told Adam. "You will not surely die," Satan told Eve. They ate. Satan lied. In a flash, immortal Adam and Eve became mortal. *Mortal* is a polite word to describe the process whereby cell death begins to creep through our tissues and veins.

Physical death is part of the curse of sin. Death is not natural or beautiful or normal. It is a sick, violent intruder into God's paradise. Death is not just part of Mufasa's lovely "circle of life" in *The Lion King*. It is Part 2 of God's severe punishment upon his traitorous, mutinous creatures.

"The time came when the beggar died and the angels carried him to Abraham's side. The rich man also died and was buried" (Luke 16:22).

We're all afraid of death. That's why we have so many jokes about it. That's why we spend such staggering amounts of money staving it off. That's why Jesus' hearers leaned closer when he told the story of the rich man and Lazarus—because he was describing the fate that awaits us all, rich and poor alike.

That's why Jesus' incarnation was necessary. He became fully human in order to have a body that could die like ours, that could die for us. His mortality becomes the gateway to our immortality, where we can be reunited with him and Abraham and all believers.

_____

_____

_____

_____

Good fire

Distressingly many things in our lives, really too many, are violently combustible. My house is filled with items that would dearly love to combine with oxygen, if only the temperature could be raised a little more. The 130-year-old framing timbers of the house itself would gladly join in a blaze if they just got a little start. A cupful of gasoline and one match would turn everything into a blackened shell and piles of ash. I am mighty glad that there's a firehouse two blocks away.

Some fire burns brightly but does not destroy. It signals the presence of God when he is up to something big in the development of his plan of salvation. A burning bush once called Moses to leadership; a pillar of fire led and protected the Israelite nation after the exodus.

And Pentecost flames appeared above the heads of a handful of believers as God turned them from cowards into champions. **"Suddenly a sound like the blowing of a violent wind came from heaven and filled the whole house where they were sitting. They saw what seemed to be tongues of fire that separated and came to rest on each of them"** (Acts 2:2,3).

The Spirit's flame has become a cherished Christian symbol. It's a reminder that God himself is in our midst, that his power is formidable, but that he has come to save and bless and guide.

_____

_____

_____

_____

Storm the Bastille

For those connected to French culture, the middle of July brings the annual remembrance of the French revolution. The storming of the Bastille, a massive old fort converted into a prison, has become a symbol of France's chaotic and bloody transition from a totalitarian monarchy into the democracy of today.

Concentrating power into the hands of only a few powerful sinners usually doesn't work out well for the masses. Samuel had some words of warning for the Israelites who were longing to be governed by a king: **"This is what the king who will reign over you will do: He will take your sons and make them serve with his chariots and horses. . . . He will take your daughters to be perfumers and cooks and bakers. He will take a tenth of your grain and of your vintage and give it to his officials and attendants. When that day comes, you will cry out for relief from the king you have chosen"** (1 Samuel 8:11,13,15,18).

God has been gathering people into his holy family steadily over the centuries, whether they live free or as slaves, well-governed or poorly governed, whether their leaders seized power in a coup or were elected or descended from a royal dynasty. If you, like the French, live in a democracy and enjoy freedom of worship, you might just want to offer special thanks to God today.

_____

_____

_____

_____

_____

JULY 15
I'm so lonely

"Eleanor Rigby died in the church and was buried along with her name; nobody came. . . . All the lonely people, where do they all come from?" Have you ever felt as though that Beatles anthem to loneliness was written for your life?

Loneliness has nothing to do with how many other people are passing through your life. In fact, some of the deepest pangs of loneliness come when you feel totally disconnected, unnoticed, and "uncared for" by the many people who happen to be around. Seeing other people enjoying happy relationships only intensifies the fear of being alone.

Conquering that fear starts with getting reacquainted with your Creator, your heavenly Father, and with his Son, the heavenly Bridegroom, whose greatest desire is to love you and be loved by you forever. Have you read his love letters to you lately? **"Those who know your name will trust in you, for you, Lord, have never forsaken those who seek you"** (Psalm 9:10).

When you are confident of God's love, you can look up from the ground and might just notice some of the kind people whom God is sending into your life.

_____

_____

_____

_____

_____

JULY 16
My life is a mess

The meaning of life, the wasted years of life, the poor choices of life. God answers the mess of life with one word: grace.
—Max Lucado

In Jesus' parable of the prodigal son, with whom do you identify? The prodigal? The judgmental brother? The forgiving father? At one time or another in your life you will probably have been all three. **"The son said to him, 'Father, I have sinned against heaven and against you. I am no longer worthy to be called your son.' But the father said to his servants, 'Quick! Bring the best robe and put it on him. Put a ring on his finger and sandals on his feet. Bring the fattened calf'"** (Luke 15:21-23).

What a great story to teach the Bible's central truth that God's grace is the force that transforms our lives—it changes his righteous anger into mercy toward us, changes our unbelief into faith, and changes our lives from selfishness to service. Grace is God's unconditional love for those *who don't deserve it.*

Just when you think there is no hope for you, his grace touches your heart. Just when words of judgment on another sinner start rising up your throat, his grace leads you to choke them off before you utter them. And when someone in your life says, "I'm sorry," quick!—get a ring, a robe, and a calf.

_____

_____

_____

_____

Avoidance

Thanks to Jesus' famous parable in Luke chapter 10 about highway bandits and an amazing rescue, the word *Samaritan* today always connotes compassion and generosity. The term has become a compliment.

Ironically in Jesus' time, it was the opposite. To call someone a Samaritan was to insult him. The Jews viewed their "middle neighbors" as racial half-breeds and renegades to their religious tradition. They showed their disapproval and fear by avoidance: **"Jews do not associate with Samaritans"** (John 4:9). When riding or walking from Judea in the south to Galilee in the north, Jewish travelers preferred to cross the Jordan and go the long way 'round in order to minimize any contact with "those" people.

Not much has changed human nature in two thousand years. There is a strong urge in us all to avoid people not like us and to associate only with people who share our race or tribe or social or economic level. Satan grins at all racial and cultural firewalls. Keeping people apart minimizes movement of the gospel. It also increases the chances that the isolated "avoiders" group will grow stagnant.

It takes no brains or courage to avoid people. It takes Christ, and Christ-inspired believers, to create a culture that sees people movements not as threats but as opportunities to share the Word of Life.

_____

_____

_____

_____

_____

Treat her right

"If Mama ain't happy, ain't nobody happy." That phrase rings so true that it sounds like it must be taken from the Bible . . . maybe 2 Hezekiah, or was it the Epistle to the Mesopotamians?

Okay, maybe not. But, husbands, let's be honest. There is no misery like that of being handcuffed to a miserable woman. Do you agree? Women may be a little physically weaker than their husbands, but their emotions and state of mind are powerful enough to dominate the whole house.

The key is how the man in her life treats her. The apostle Paul wrote, **"In this same way, husbands ought to love their wives as their own bodies. He who loves his wife loves himself"** (Ephesians 5:28). Christian women love Jesus—he listens to their pain and sorrows, feels their pain and sorrows, and even *carries* their pain and sorrows. A woman who has a man whom she can depend on, who loves her the way Jesus loves her, who will open his heart and let her share her frustrations, is a woman at peace.

Guys, when you serve her and meet her needs, your life will get a lot better. When Mama's happy, everybody's happy.

_____

_____

_____

_____

_____

Treat him right

Married behaviors are learned behaviors. Newlyweds assume that their partner's needs are identical to theirs, and they are not. That's why God gives different instructions. Women may think that their husbands crave love most of all. But it's not the main thing. Here's the secret: your man's greatest need is respect.

Love is nice, but respect is oxygen for a man's soul. We may have bigger bodies and be physically stronger than our wives. Still, every woman has the ability to cut a man down to the ground. Just with words, you can make us feel stupid and small. Instead, we need your help to grow into the leaders God wants us to be. **"The wife must respect her husband"** (Ephesians 5:33).

Do you want the man in your home to lead, provide, and take responsibility? The way you talk will establish the environment. Sarcasm and belittling can crush his spirit. No man can lead unless the woman is willing to take the risk of being willing to follow.

A man who feels like a midget in his home will find excuses to stay away. A man who feels like a king will run home each day to take care of and protect his queen and the royal family.

_____

_____

_____

_____

_____

Don't stop praying

To be a Christian without prayer is no more possible than to be alive without breathing. —Martin Luther

Only someone could say that who knew exhaustion, pain, guilt, and the relentless attacks of Satan. Praying is not something that we need to be nagged into doing. You don't need to be nagged to breathe. It is not a performance requirement. Prayer is simply God's oxygen for the lungs of our faith.

"Be joyful always; pray continually; give thanks in all circumstances, for this is God's will for you in Christ Jesus" (1 Thessalonians 5:16-18). Prayer is a communication privilege that only Christians can enjoy, for access to God's throne comes only through Jesus Christ. Through Jesus Christ, the Father guarantees that he will hear, decide, and act on everything we bring him.

And what a gift it is! Prayer guarantees God's interaction with your life, no matter how small and unworthy you feel. God intentionally waits with the full measure of his blessings until you ask, in order that you might notice his working in your life. Prayer gives you a way to benefit the lives of other people, even when they are thousands of miles away or even if you don't know their names. Prayer demonstrates to God that you are proud to identify yourself as his child.

What's on your mind? Tell God. Ask God. Pray right now! Don't stop!

_____

_____

Whose money is it anyway?

If you talk to people who dislike church (a.k.a. "organized religion"), high on the list of most-hated features is what they see as institutional money hustling. While most ministries authentically seek to reach out to people's souls, sometimes all that visitors see (or choose to see) is the church reaching out for their wallets.

The real reason why Christian ministries gather offerings of money from worshipers and members is not because God is broke and needs our contributions. **"I have no need of a bull from your stall or of goats from your pens, for every animal of the forest is mine, and the cattle on a thousand hills. . . . The world is mine, and all that is in it"** (Psalm 50:9,10,12).

The real reason is that giving money (and our time and skills) is an act of worship by which we assert over and over, to the world and to God and to ourselves, that we are thrilled to be allowed to be managers and stewards of money that actually doesn't belong to us. We love to give gifts back to God because he first loved us so much.

_____

_____

_____

_____

_____

God and my work

Most of us struggle with inadequate vision—we forget we are immortal through Christ, forget our time on this earth is fleeting, and fall in love with things.

But the reverse is just as bad—to be so heaven-focused that we ignore the significance of our mission and work right now. Your baptism was also your commissioning into God's workforce. He calls you royal priests, not just irrelevant placeholders. He calls you to work for him, not just kill time waiting for St. Michael's trumpet.

What you do for him, great or small, really matters! The example you set, the love you demonstrate, the mercy you show, the values you embrace, the priorities you set, the words you say all really matter! Many people in your world have not yet encountered the true Jesus—you are the first bit of Jesus they may see. Many people once loved Jesus but have fallen away. Your integrity and joy in your faith might be the tipping point to inspire someone to believe again.

The work you and your fellow Christians do is of crucial importance in sharing the water of life with thirsty and dying travelers. Moses helps you pray for God's blessings so that your labors for him can have maximum impact: **"May the favor of the Lord our God rest upon us; establish the work of our hands for us—yes, establish the work of our hands"** (Psalm 90:17).

Love is the better way

I have decided to stick with love.
Hate is too great a burden to bear.
—Dr. Martin Luther King, Jr.

Dr. King is uniquely qualified to teach us about the futility of revenge and the ultimate triumph of love. He was unjustly imprisoned, his home was firebombed, and he was assassinated in the prime of life. He had various teachers and mentors in the area of nonviolent protest, but the greatest of them was Christ himself, who triumphed over evil by first bearing its wrath.

Revenge seems sweet and right; it is the plot line in a thousand movies and TV shows. But revenge only provokes the next act of vengeance from the other side. Hating cannot bring peace. **"Do not take revenge, my friends, but leave room for God's wrath, for it is written 'It is mine to avenge; I will repay,' says the Lord. On the contrary: 'If your enemy is hungry, feed him'"** (Romans 12:19,20). You don't need to anoint yourself the avenger; God will take care of business in his time.

Choosing to love your enemies is not easy, and it doesn't always yield visible results right away, but it is the main reason that people of color were finally treated with dignity in our land. It is also the gift given to the human race by the Savior who forgave his enemies from the cross.

Who needs your mercy today?

_____

_____

JULY 24
He gets the last word

One of the girls in my sixth-grade class loved to see naughty boys get caught by the teacher. "Cheaters never prosper," she would cackle.

Ah, if only she were right. Alas, my sad life experience is that cheaters seem to do very well. Everything's a hustle. Everything's for sale. Them that's got shall get.

Do you ever feel as though you are wasting your time trying to get ahead through honesty and hard work? Do you ever fantasize about taking shortcuts to prosperity like everyone else? King David knew that feeling. In Psalm 12:1,2 he wrote, **"Help, Lord, for the godly are no more; the faithful have vanished. . . . Everyone lies to his neighbor."**

But the planet is not out of God's control, and your life isn't either. He sees *everything* going on around you, cares about you, and acts at just the right time. That same psalm says, **"'Because of the oppression of the weak and the groaning of the needy, I will now arise,' says the Lord. 'I will protect them'"** (verse 5).

God always gets the last word, and his last word is "I love you."

Eat kosher then

Believing Israelites had important dietary restrictions, not because there was anything sinful or unhygienic about certain foods but as a form of self-denial. The kosher laws emphasized Israel's distinctiveness. If you couldn't eat in a Gentile's home, you would be more likely to stick together with other Israelites and not lose your culture *and belief system.*

Leviticus itemized strict dietary laws for Israel: **"These are the regulations concerning animals, birds, every living thing that moves in the water and every creature that moves about on the ground. You must distinguish between the unclean and the clean, between living creatures that may be eaten and those that may not be eaten"** (Leviticus 11:46,47).

Pork and shellfish were off limits, not because God has anything against those two delicious foods but to keep Israel aware of its separateness. Complex dietary rules were intended to keep Israelites thinking about purity. Elaborate rules about how to butcher animals were intended to keep Israel thinking about the blood of the covenant, not because there is anything essentially unclean about grilling meat that hasn't been totally and thoroughly drained of all its blood.

The strategy of keeping Israel separate worked. Now a greater mission is to reach out and connect with the world to share the good news. Eating together is a great way to get close to people.

_____

_____

_____

_____

_____

Now eat whatever God created

Quite a few world religions, including some Christian groups, have food rules and restrictions today. Judaism still resolutely mandates kosher diet for its adherents.

Acts chapter 10 has an amazing story about the lifting of kosher food restrictions. A Jewish fisherman and a Gentile military officer discovered that they were brothers and could eat together. "[Peter] **fell into a trance. He saw heaven opened and something like a large sheet being let down to earth by its four corners. It contained all kinds of four-footed animals, as well as reptiles of the earth and birds of the air. Then a voice told him, 'Get up, Peter. Kill and eat.' 'Surely not, Lord!' Peter replied. 'I have never eaten anything impure or unclean.' The voice spoke to him a second time, 'Do not call anything impure that God has made clean'"** (Acts 10:10-15).

The fact that God allows you to eat all things does not mean that he commands it. You may choose to omit things from your diet, like alcohol or red meat or any meat, for that matter. God loves vegans too. Just don't use a religious rationale to impose your food choices on others. And remember to use moderation as you exercise your Christian freedom. You are not free to eat yourself obese or drink yourself drunk. When you eat and drink, do it to the glory of God (1 Corinthians 10:31).

_____

_____

_____

_____

_____

Whose agenda drives you?

The forgiveness of your sins costs you nothing. It is free and full, God's gift to you through faith in Jesus Christ. Grace is always free and complete, 100% God's doing. But though free to you, it cost Jesus his life. As he received it back through his resurrection, he gives you yours back too.

And invites you to give it to him. We were designed to live with God, live for God. We can't find fulfillment, happiness, or satisfaction unless we are dialed into his agenda. Our faith changes how we relate to God. Instead of defiance—worship. Instead of fear—confidence. Instead of guilt—joy.

Our faith will also change how we relate to other people. Let the prophet Micah explain God's agenda: **"He has shown you, O man, what is good. And what does the Lord require of you? To act justly and to love mercy and to walk humbly with your God"** (Micah 6:8). You do these mighty works of faith not in order to become saved, but because you are saved.

Act justly, i.e., your personal morality is drawn from God's Word. *Love mercy,* i.e., show the same patience and forgiveness to the fools and sinners around you that God has shown to you. *Walk humbly.* Everything good in your life is God's gift of love to you.

_____

_____

_____

_____

_____

I'm afraid of rejection

A couple of the girls I asked out back in my college years said no. Why can I still remember those occasions so clearly? Why does that embarrassment and self-doubt persist after all these years? Rejection hurts.

I don't even have to ask. You've been stung by rejection too, haven't you? Were you the last chosen for a team on the playground? Have your kids rejected your belief and value system? Has a loved one or spouse walked out on you? Have you been fired from a job?

You know what's an even worse nightmare? Fearing that God has no more use for you. We have all given God more than enough reasons to turn away in disgust and to be done with us. **"Zion said, 'The Lord has forsaken me, the Lord has forgotten me'"** (Isaiah 49:14).

That's what you'd expect. That's what you deserve. The reality, however, is that your relationship with God is based not on your performance but on Christ's. It's based not on your conclusions but on Christ's sacrifice. It's based not on your fears but on God's love.

Born under the law

When an accused person first appears in court, it is called an arraignment. It is there that the formal accusations are brought forth.

The Bible teaches repeatedly that every human being who ever lived stands arraigned before God the Judge. Without divine intervention, every case would turn out the same. The Judge, who is also the Maker of all, has pure and holy expectations of all. His law, his will, was made known to all. All have sinned against it. All are guilty.

The incarnation of Jesus made possible a divine substitute for all of us. He entered the "game" like all of us, subject to the law's commands and curses. **"When the time had fully come, God sent his Son, born of a woman, born under law, to redeem those under law"** (Galatians 4:4,5).

What a gracious act of humility! The Co-Creator of the universe submitted to the rules of others for the sole purpose of giving you his perfect record. By faith you may claim his holiness as if it were your own. Through faith it now *is* your own!

_____

_____

_____

_____

_____

Mother Ann Lee, the founder of the peculiar American religious sect called the Shakers, was terribly afraid of the corrupting power of sexuality. She kept the men and women in her communities largely separate. Dating and marriage were forbidden.

That fear of sex's power to destabilize the brain may have been part of the church's motivation for many centuries to hold forth life in a monastery as superior to and holier than marriage and family life.

In God's view, there is nothing inherently dirty about human sexuality. He made it for us to enjoy. The Song of Songs in the Bible is essentially the libretto to a romantic musical (alas, the original music was not able to be preserved) that describes the longing and ecstasy of human emotional and physical love.

The "Lover" and the "Beloved" express their rapture and delight in their love: **"Let him kiss me with the kisses of his mouth—for your love is more delightful than wine"** (Song of Songs 1:2).

The romantic and physical magnetism that you feel toward the opposite sex is God's gift. Enjoy it.

_____

_____

_____

_____

_____

We've already won

I can't blame you if you've concluded that the world is going to hell and Satan won after all. Any cop could tell you that most days things look pretty bleak. The human race is not evolving into better people. The last century was the bloodiest in history. Increases in technology only mean that people can rob and kill on a bigger scale.

People who feel defeated probably don't feel like praying much. What's the use? Everything's going downhill. I'm doomed. Nothing is working for me. When gloomy thoughts like that overtake your mind, recall Jesus' words: **"In this world you will have trouble. But take heart! I have overcome the world"** (John 16:33).

The American/Philippine retreat and defeat at Bataan and Corregidor during World War II was a miserable time for the Allies, but it would have been much more bearable if they could have seen just three years into the future—the Japanese surrender on the battleship *Missouri* in Tokyo Bay.

Jesus' prophecy came true. His disciples did indeed have trouble—persecution, imprisonment, death. But their faith in Jesus' ultimate victory sustained them. Now they wear a crown of glory, and you will too. Take heart!

August

God is our refuge and strength,
an ever-present help in trouble.

Psalm 46:1

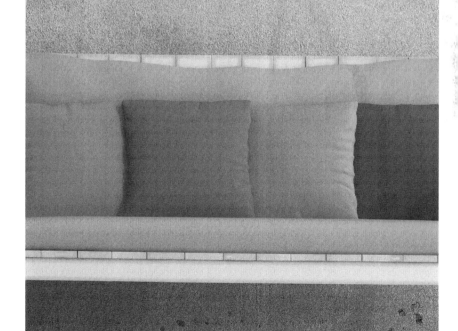

I'm your handiwork

Some of God's best work is invisible.

Men and women are allowed to assist God in the process of conception, but God takes over completely from that point. The mother is only a vessel for that divine artistry; she eats, sleeps, walks, and works, but all of the brilliant design work and engineering that grows a fully formed baby from a zygote is accomplished by the word and will of God. **"You created my inmost being; you knit me together in my mother's womb"** (Psalm 139:13).

Each child is a masterpiece; each is known in heaven with a unique DNA. Each is precious to a heavenly Father; each is a little sinner who needs to be converted through Word and water. Each deserves a chance to live out her life, his time of grace.

We will never be a healthy society as long as people are allowed legally to invade the womb and cut, vacuum, scrape, or poison the little person there. Let your heart be broken for the missing children of the world. Speak for those who cannot speak for themselves.

Thank your mother for thinking you worth having. Help women with crisis pregnancies to choose life.

_____

_____

_____

_____

_____

Imperfect heroes

Can I make a personal confession? The heroes I most look up to are not the perfect ones, the superheroes, but rather people who achieved great things even though they themselves were deeply flawed. King David did extraordinary things for the Lord, but his miserable sins are also laid out there for all to read in the Bible.

David is the chief author of the psalms—at least half of them were written by him. His psalms are real; they are authentic and true to life. He tells it just like it is. Even this mighty warrior, slayer of the giant Goliath, could write things like: **"Have mercy on me, O God, according to your unfailing love"** (Psalm 51:1).

David knew that his approval with his God rested not on his own performance but with God's saving mercy. He prayed for forgiveness, for help with his problems, for protection from those who wished him harm, and for glory to God for his great and mighty acts.

I am happy if God has found a use for me during my time on earth. Truly it is a joy to serve him. But I am happier still that I have forgiveness for my sins. I crave God's mercy far more than God's praise. I think David did too.

_____

_____

_____

_____

_____

Make peace

Here's a riddle for you: why are newspapers and playground bullies similar? Answer: because they both love a fight. Television and print editors gravitate to covering violence ("if it bleeds, it leads"). Voyeuristic spectators get a thrill out of others in combat: "Fight!"

Anyone can start a fight. Anyone can continue a fight long after it should have been over. It is a trademark of Jesus' followers to make peace. **"Better a dry crust with peace and quiet than a house full of feasting with strife"** (Proverbs 17:1).

Our hero is the Prince of peace, who turned God's withering judgment upon himself so that he could turn God's forgiveness and mercy upon us. Are you willing to trust God that there is far greater satisfaction in ending a quarrel than in starting or continuing one?

Are there two people in conflict in your life whom you could bring together today?

AUGUST 4
Am I generous enough?

My uncle says, "I feel like I should be giving more to God. Jesus told the rich young ruler to sell all his possessions, give the money to the poor, and follow him. There are people who do give up everything for Jesus, but I own a house and two cars. Does that make me a weak and shallow Christian?"

Perhaps you have had moments of guilt flashes like that. Remember that Jesus' instructions to that wealthy young man were specific to his situation, not universal commands to every believer. True enough, Jesus and his disciples lived off the charity of others, but somebody had to labor for and pay for their daily food.

Jesus' words were a strong warning against making an idol of your wealth, not a condemnation of wealth accumulation per se. If significant numbers of people don't earn more than they spend and have money to give, Christian congregations and schools would collapse.

Here's my counsel: earn as much as you can; pay off your debts as fast as you can; save as much as you can; and with that money follow Jesus by investing generously in ministries that serve people's spiritual and physical needs. **"Each one should give what he has decided in his heart to give, not reluctantly or under compulsion, for God loves a cheerful giver"** (2 Corinthians 9:7).

_____

_____

_____

_____

_____

AUGUST 5
No do-overs

Our culture is based on the concept of second chances. After all, is not America itself based on the dream so eloquently articulated by Emma Lazarus' poem on the base of the Statue of Liberty: "Give me your tired, your poor, your huddled masses yearning to breathe free, the wretched refuse of your teeming shore"? Millions of immigrants came here to start over.

Students always pester their teachers for bonus points, test retakes, and extra credit. My own mediocre golf scores would be even worse if I didn't persuade the other guys in my foursome to let me have a couple mulligans per 18 holes.

There are no do-overs after God has made his decisions. There will be no court of appeals. No hung juries. No mistrials. No stays of execution. It will be too late for petitions for executive clemency.

Abraham replied to the rich man who was in hell, **"Between us and you a great chasm has been fixed, so that those who want to go from here to you cannot, nor can anyone cross over from there to us"** (Luke 16:26).

As you believe, so you will live. As you live, so you will be judged. As you are judged, so you will be placed. As you are placed, so you will remain.

_____

_____

_____

_____

_____

AUGUST 6
A Roman and a Jew

Occupied nations have always hated their invaders, and the occupiers have usually despised their subject peoples. Only with deliberate cruelty can the invaders keep the outer parts of their empire under control.

The Jews hated their Roman occupiers, not only for their military presence and heavy taxation but because of their pagan religion. The Romans despised the Jews as uncivilized barbarians. Until one day . . . **"At Caesarea there was a man named Cornelius, a centurion in what was known as the Italian Regiment"** (Acts 10:1). This amazing chapter tells one of the stories of how the gospel was bursting out of its first generation Jewish culture into the wider Mediterranean world.

Cornelius is a hero of mine. The Spirit's power led him to overcome his cultural snobbery and superiority and see in Peter, a humble Jewish fisherman, his brother in faith. In the presence of his relatives and close friends, the Italian military officer allowed the uneducated peasant to teach him about God as though he were a child. And he loved it.

On that magical day the kingdom of God took a significant leap forward in God's passionate plan to bring the good news of a Savior from its Jewish homeland to the ends of the earth. You and I today are still enjoying the energy waves from that evangelistic explosion.

Be still

It's not so very hard to be brave when you have weapons and superior field position. It is another thing entirely to be brave when you are essentially unarmed, trying to take care of a massive civilian population, have your back to water, and are facing massed Egyptian infantry with six hundred chariots.

Here is one reason why Moses is such a hero. At age 80 he encouraged the terrified Israelites not to believe their eyes but to believe the words of God. **"Moses answered the people, 'Do not be afraid. Stand firm and you will see the deliverance the Lord will bring you today. The Egyptians you see today you will never see again. The Lord will fight for you; you need only to *be still*'"** (Exodus 14:13,14).

He was right. God simply arranged for the drowning of their foes as they watched.

Any fool can be confident after a victory. God does his best work in building our faith during our times of waiting, testing, and suffering. When God calls us to action, we need to move. But sometimes, when faced by huge obstacles, we need only to listen to God's words and be still.

_____

_____

_____

_____

_____

Sometimes anchors are good

Ever been called a "boat anchor," i.e., a dead weight that's holding back someone else's dreams? There's always somebody in every organization who is a buzzkill, a complainer and foot-dragger, forever draining energy from the group. In that sense *anchor* means "nuisance," a hindrance to progress. Anchors in and of themselves are basically good though. They keep your fishing boat from drifting into the weeds, and they keep seagoing vessels away from sandbars and dangerous reefs when they need to maintain their offshore position as they load and unload when a deep-draft dock is not available.

A ship's anchor is a familiar Christian symbol that you will see in paint, mosaic, or stained glass in churches. It is a reminder that one of God's chosen writers used that metaphor to show how secure we can be when our hopes of forgiveness, acceptance, and eternal life are guaranteed by God himself. **"We have this hope as an anchor for the soul, firm and secure"** (Hebrews 6:19).

Our lives are sometimes blown about by terrible winds—financial losses, illnesses, family breakups, quarrels, spiritual breakdowns, job layoffs, and worse. But God's words, backed up by his solemn oath, guarantee that we are loved and forgiven now, acquitted in heaven's court, and heirs of a joyful eternity. You are not strong enough to be the anchor of your life. God's Word is.

_____

_____

_____

_____

I'm tired

Some days I'm riding high. Things just work. They click. They go my way.

But some days, Lord, I can almost see the devil hindering me, laughing at me, breaking what I try to build, attacking me, lying to me, weakening me. He mocks my hopes, makes me doubt, urges me to ignore you, and makes despair look like my only option.

I don't know how long I can go on like this. Lord, I'm so tired. **"The enemy pursues me, he crushes me to the ground; he makes me dwell in darkness like those long dead. So my spirit grows faint within me; my heart within me is dismayed"** (Psalm 143:3,4).

Where can I go but to you? When my body is giving out, I must have strength from you. When my mind is confused, I must get clarity from your Word. When my path is nothing but fog, I must get directions from you. When my spirit sags, I must get courage from you.

May I be bold to remind you that I am your child? May I point out that my baptism has sealed me in the Spirit and that you have accepted responsibility for my well-being? Remember that I am part of the body of your Son. Pour out your Spirit upon me, Lord, and give me courage to live joyfully and confidently. Can we start today?

_____

_____

_____

_____

_____

News about friends

One of my dearest friends loves to yak on the phone, and she is a never-ending source of information about people we know. "But it's not gossip," she says. "It's just news about friends."

How can you tell the difference? Gossip damages people's reputations. Gossip passes on rumors as though they were truth. Gossips enjoy other people's difficulties. Gossips try to make themselves taller by stepping on other people. Gossips use behind-the-back talk as a form of revenge.

Gossip hurts not only the gossipee but the gossiper as well. **"The words of a gossip are like choice morsels; they go down to a man's inward parts"** (Proverbs 18:8). Get the point? Swapping juicy bits of information can taste like chocolate in the mouth, but as you swallow it you poison and corrupt your soul.

God has a better way. Use your tongue to build up.

_____

_____

_____

_____

_____

Prophet with the blues

What could be better than a direct information line straight from God? Wouldn't it make life wonderful if you could see ahead into the future?

Well, maybe not. The Old Testament prophet Jeremiah did have that ability, but it brought him a great deal of pain, so much pain, in fact, that Jeremiah's nickname is the "weeping prophet." God let him see what was coming for Israel, and he saw military disaster, plundering armies, burning cities, and national captivity. **"Oh, that my head were a spring of water and my eyes a fountain of tears!"** he said (Jeremiah 9:1). But Jeremiah was allowed also to foresee the return from captivity and the successful arrival of the Messiah, Jesus Christ, who became the fulfillment of God's original covenant promises to the nation he loved.

Be glad you can't see too far ahead in your own life. There are probably enough hardships and bitter blows coming to make you weep like a fountain too. Content yourself with knowing that the Lord is already living in your future, has seen it all, and guarantees your safe arrival in heaven. Rejoice to know that your sins of past, present, and future are already forgiven in Christ; that God's grace will be sufficient each day to help you survive and thrive and live out the full measure of life that God has ordained; and that through his grace you will complete your mission.

Sleep well tonight.

_____

_____

_____

_____

I'm dying

We sling around the words *die* and *death* very casually in day-to-day conversation. "I could have just died from embarrassment." "I'm dying for some chocolate right now." "That cheesecake is to die for." "That kid's going to be the death of me."

Some of us will die instantly—in a car accident, aneurysm, or massive heart attack. But insurance actuaries will tell you that the majority of people will die slowly enough to be aware of death's approach. Are you ready for that time? Does death terrify you? Does the dying process terrify you?

One of the most comforting aspects of Christ's work for us is that he has gone through pain, dying, and death in advance of us. He didn't eliminate it from the human experience. He *transformed* it into our Homecoming. The transition now holds no terror, no sting. Our last moment on earth is instantly transformed into our first moment with Jesus.

Here are words from the One who thought you valuable enough to die for: **"God will redeem my life from the grave; he will surely take me to himself"** (Psalm 49:15).

_____

_____

_____

_____

_____

God will give me strength to love

One of the sweet features of Christianity is that God never calls us to his way of living without also giving us the wisdom we need and the power and strength to carry it out.

He knows all about how hard it is to choose to love someone who is treating you poorly. God often compared himself in the Bible to a husband with an unfaithful wife (a metaphor for his often backsliding believers). He even instructed his prophet Hosea to marry an immoral woman as an ongoing visual aid: **"The Lord said to me, 'Go, show your love to your wife again, though she is loved by another and is an adulteress. Love her as the Lord loves the Israelites, though they turn to other gods'"** (Hosea 3:1).

True enough—some marriages can't be saved. But as we reflect on God's unconditional love and forgiveness for us, we are strengthened to love difficult people. As we reflect on God's tremendous patience with us, we find strength to be patient with the sinners around us. As we reflect on his optimism and hope in our future, we will find strength to stay positive as a sacrifice of praise to him.

To all who fear that their marriage has become loveless, know this: only the gospel changes hearts. Nagging, retaliation, and the silent treatment only make the angry angrier. Only love can create love.

_____

_____

_____

_____

_____

God can be trusted with my secrets

God's omniscience and omnipresence can be a terrifying thought. Someone can read my mind? Someone has watched all that I have ever done? Even believers in their weaker moments dread the realization that their thoughts and lives are an open book to the God who reads all and sees all. Does he despise me? Will he punish me? Will he see to it that all the dirt comes out?

It was just for this very purpose that the Son of God needed to come to earth in person. He came as a true human being, as human as you and I, but without the sin. His stainless life and innocent death were offered to God as the perfect substitute for our soiled lives. Through faith in him you are forgiven of everything—the obvious sins and the secret sins, the ones that show and the ones you are hiding.

King David wrote, **"Who can discern his errors? Forgive my hidden faults. Keep your servant also from willful sins; may they not rule over me"** (Psalm 19:12,13). David nailed it. We can trust God for the forgiveness of our rotten past and imperfect present, and we can trust him to give us strength to overcome our sinful weaknesses.

Isn't it sweet that your heavenly Father is more interested in building you up than in condemning you?

Teach them respect

Want to see someone's blood boil? Ask a veteran teacher about the increasing levels of student violence, specifically assaults on teachers. Our American obsessions with freedom and the right to personal expression, coupled with weakening family structure, are eroding people's trust and respect for institutions like government and schools. Angry, violent children are the result.

Satan laughs. What he knows, and not enough parents realize, is that there is a beast inside each of us that wants to be let loose, that wants to be wild. One of the greatest tasks that our society rightly expects from parents is that they teach their children self-control, that they learn to restrain their inner beasts.

Showing respect is learned behavior. It needs to be taught and modeled. It was needed as badly two thousand years ago as it is today. Jesus is our hero—though persecuted by both the religious establishment and Roman government, he always showed respect to both. Peter wrote, **"Show proper respect to everyone: Love the brotherhood of believers, fear God, honor the king"** (1 Peter 2:17). Our children need to know that you don't build your own self-esteem by tearing down others. They need to believe that you don't grow any more liberated by trying to destroy the authority around you.

And you're just the one to teach them.

Small prayers

Do you save prayer energy only for "big asks," i.e., major crises? Do you hate to bother God with trivia? Is it appropriate to pray over basketball games and business deals? the health of a pet? a successful family gathering?

If God were human like us, he would have little interest in or capacity for the smaller things in our lives. But he is God—unlimited mental ability, unlimited interest in our lives, unlimited resources, unlimited power, unlimited love for us. He uses all the events in our lives, big and small, to change us and grow us and make us more like him and more useful to his agenda.

Jesus himself once attended a lengthy wedding reception and perceived that the bridal couple and their family were about to suffer the embarrassment of running out of wine. Jesus chose that moment to utilize his almighty power for something as "small" as banquet supplies. Out of ordinary water he made 120 gallons of '47 Château Margaux, astonishing the maitre d'. **"This, the first of his miraculous signs, Jesus performed in Cana of Galilee. He thus revealed his glory, and his disciples put their faith in him"** (John 2:11).

Small things on your mind? Bring them to the Lord. Let him decide how to bless you, discipline you, grow you, toughen you, and use you for his agenda, and in the process reveal his glory in your life.

_____

_____

_____

_____

A great many people are terrified that sometime soon the earth will run out of petroleum deposits. In that view, fossil fuels are a zero-sum game—there is a strict, finite limit on how much oil exists underground, and when that oil is all pumped out, our cars will all wheeze to a halt.

That fear is behind the push for renewable resources, that is, drawing energy from theoretically infinite sources such as the sun, wind, and falling water. More and more we see solar panels and giant wind turbines sprouting up. More and more ethanol plants are being built that derive their energy output from plants.

Do you see giving money back to God as a zero-sum game (if he gets more of my money, then I get less; soon I'll have nothing)? Did you know that God solemnly guarantees to be an endlessly renewable resource for cheerful givers? Here is his promise: **"Now he who supplies seed to the sower and bread for food will also supply and increase your store of seed and will enlarge the harvest of your righteousness. You will be made rich in every way so that you can be generous on every occasion, and through us your generosity will result in thanksgiving to God"** (2 Corinthians 9:10,11).

That's a pretty big promise. Do you believe it?

_____

_____

_____

_____

_____

Showing kindness

Have you ever noticed that when people are believers in Christ, God treats them like spiritual adults (whether or not they've deserved it)? He doesn't call us fools, criminals, disappointments, or failures, though in many ways we have earned all of those labels. No. He treats us better than we deserve.

"As God's chosen people, holy and dearly loved, clothe yourselves with . . . kindness" (Colossians 3:12). You are *chosen*—that means that he cared enough for you to come and find you. You are *holy*—washed in the blood of Jesus, you are now considered to be as pure and holy as Christ himself. You are *dearly loved*—how valuable he thinks you are!

As he has treated us better than we deserve, he now invites you to put on the marriage garment of kindness. You can speak words that don't cut your husband down but build him up. You can go first in doing things for her, being extra nice when she's crabby. You can always assume the best possible explanation when he says or does something you don't understand, rather than leaping to the worst possible conclusion.

Are you afraid that you don't have it in you to be that nice? You probably don't. Draw energy and inspiration from Christ and the way in which he treats you.

_____

_____

_____

_____

_____

God's persuasive power

When God commissioned Moses to represent him to the pharaoh of Egypt, Moses' courage failed. He was afraid to speak up because he knew that in and of himself he could never change the mind and attitudes of the most powerful man on the planet.

You might have that same apprehension about speaking up to bring someone back to the faith. Perhaps you wish you knew more about the Bible. Perhaps you are rusty at witnessing for your faith. Perhaps you are not a good public speaker or don't do well under stress.

Relax. It's not your power of persuasion that will do it. **"It is God who works in you to will and to act according to his good purpose"** (Philippians 2:13). God heard Moses' fears and commissioned him anyway. He promised to put his own words into Moses' mouth.

You don't have to put a lot of pressure on yourself to be persuasive, forceful, poetic, or scholarly. Just tell the great things God has done. Tell of his great love even for foolish rebels. Let his persuasive power, not your power, go to work in someone's heart and mind.

_____

_____

_____

_____

_____

Loss of a loved one

There are no good funerals.

Even when a 95-year-old passes, even when the death brought an end to pain and suffering, the family still grieves a loss. How much more it hurts when the deceased was "too young to die." When the breadwinner dies, when a child dies, when there's been a terrible accident, where can you go with your grief? How can you survive?

The patriarch Jacob knows how you feel. He was told the news that his young son had been slaughtered by a wild animal. **"Then Jacob tore his clothes, put on sackcloth and mourned for his son many days. All his sons and daughters came to comfort him, but he refused to be comforted. 'No,' he said, 'in mourning will I go down to the grave to my son.' So his father wept for him"** (Genesis 37:34,35).

Jacob could see no comfort or relief anywhere. That's why he and all who are coping with a bitter loss need their loved ones and friends who are believers to surround them with gospel comfort. They need help to celebrate the significance of a life; they need someone to hug and share their sorrow; they need someone to assure them that in Christ we never die. We just transition to a new and better life.

We haven't *lost* those who die in the Lord. We know exactly where they are.

_____

_____

_____

_____

_____

The boss is going away

Somebody told me that the true test of a person's character is how he acts when he thinks nobody's watching. In the parable of the talents, Jesus gives us a peek into some of the mysteries of human existence. When he says "kingdom of heaven," Jesus means, "Here is how God interacts with people and his goals for our lives. Here is how the King gathers people into his kingdom."

The kingdom of heaven **"will be like a man going on a journey, who called his servants and entrusted his property to them"** (Matthew 25:14).

The wealthy man in the story is God. All believers in Christ, forgiven and restored, now work for him.

This verse presents two challenges to us sinners. First, everything we have—our money; our families; our jobs; our community; and especially our dearest treasure, the gospel of Christ—is a gift from God. How gratifying it is to our egos to suppose that we earned and built it ourselves. But how healthy it is to give the Creator and Giver our praise for the wealth we have.

The second challenge is to remember that God's "absence" in our world is not because he's weak, uninterested, or dead. The truth? It thrills him to entrust us with his stuff. He then deliberately steps back into the shadows to watch and see what we do with our lives. He is *intensely* interested in what we do.

_____

_____

_____

_____

No more tears

Bath time for small children is partly fun and partly an ordeal. There are plenty of giggles with the bubbles, but there will be angry shrieks when soap gets in their eyes. Some lab and marketing geniuses developed a "no more tears" children's shampoo that takes the crying out of the experience.

Don't you wish that you could shampoo your hair with some miracle substance in the morning that would guarantee that you wouldn't need to cry that day? The reality is that we have to live in a broken and sinful world. Stuff happens. We get hurt.

When you cry, God's heart aches too. His answer to your misery was to put his Son through hell on Calvary. That sacrifice opens up his pure and peaceful everlasting kingdom. I think we will like living there.

The Bible promises all believers in Revelation 21:4 that God **"will wipe every tear from their eyes. There will be no more death or mourning or crying or pain, for the old order of things has passed away."** Really. No more tears.

_____

_____

_____

_____

_____

AUGUST 23
Carry each other's burdens

Nobody has to tell a Marine platoon that soldiers need one another. From the first day of their basic training, recruits are trained to watch out for each other and depend on one another.

You know, a congregation is also a band of brothers (and sisters). Sometimes you will need to lean on somebody else—when there's a cancer diagnosis, job loss, or empty nest—and other times somebody will need to lean on you.

The Bible says, **"Carry each other's burdens, and in this way you will fulfill the law of Christ"** (Galatians 6:2). When you see somebody who's struggling and you provide help, you fulfill one of the reasons why God placed you on this earth. He designed you to be useful, to be kind, to reflect his love to the people in the world around you. That's why you're still here; that's why you're not in heaven already.

One of the things that hardship does for soldiers in training is that it helps them know what great things they're capable of.

_____

_____

_____

_____

_____

God and my past

I happen to know too many people who are haunted by their pasts.

Perhaps they can't shake the memories of their own moral breakdowns. Or maybe they suffered abuse from people they were powerless to resist. The stories emerge long after people have become adults, stories of sexual molestation and harsh abuse, and they just break your heart. They break God's too.

The great work of Jesus Christ brings forgiveness of sins and release of guilt from sinners, no matter how long ago the crimes. The great work of Jesus Christ also helps set people free from ancient prisons of hatred and long-ago humiliation, fear, and hurt. **"He lifted me out of the slimy pit, out of the mud and mire; he set my feet on a rock and gave me a firm place to stand. He put a new song in my mouth, a hymn of praise to our God"** (Psalm 40:2,3).

Jesus helps us even when we can't forget. He helps us let go, move on, and regain our joy. His gospel is always creating new things out of the old, keeping our eyes eagerly looking ahead through the windshield instead of obsessing over the rearview. He gives sad hearts a new song to sing.

The old rugged cross

St. Paul was not always a saint. In his younger years he was Sinner Saul, a violent persecutor of the Christian faith. By the mercy of God he was converted and gave his life to the proclamation of the gospel, but he always gave God all the credit. The cross of Christ was his personal life logo: **"God was pleased to have all his fullness dwell in him** (i.e., Jesus Christ), **and through him to reconcile to himself all things, whether things on earth or things in heaven, by making peace through his blood, shed on the cross"** (Colossians 1:19,20).

George Bennard had had a hard life, but his great passion, like Paul's, was to be an evangelist. In response to some mockery and ridicule received at a revival meeting one night, he began a poem that crystallized his faith. Joined to a stately waltz melody, his hymn became one of the most recorded gospel songs in history.

On a hill far away stood an old rugged cross,

The emblem of suffering and shame;

And I love that old cross where the dearest and best

For a world of lost sinners was slain.

So I'll cherish the old rugged cross,

Till my trophies at last I lay down;

I will cling to the old rugged cross,

And exchange it some day for a crown.

We will too.

One flesh

It is fashionable these days for women to keep their maiden names even after marriage. Two different surnames in a marriage makes it look to casual acquaintances as if the people aren't married at all, just cohabiting. Apparently, the idea is for the woman to make it clear that her identity isn't being subsumed into that of her husband.

Actually, losing some of your independence and being merged with your spouse is part of the thrill that God designed into marriage. Jesus had a striking term for it: **"The two will become one flesh. So they are no longer two, but one"** (Matthew 19:5,6).

"One flesh" alludes to the magic and mystery of sex, the closest way to share human intimacy. Bodies briefly are interconnected and physically one flesh.

But the term is perhaps even more significant in an emotional way. After years of happy marriage, couples begin to think alike, grow in mutual dependence, and bask in a sense of completeness that single people can never know. *Me* becomes *we. Mine* becomes *ours.*

Perhaps you know older married people who can finish each other's sentences and who complement each other. Perhaps you know widows or widowers who so miss their late spouses that they feel like half a person. They knew the joy of "one flesh."

My health is gone

You've heard the line before—"I don't care if I don't have much money as long as I have my health." Nice thought, except when it isn't. What happens in the lives of people who aren't healthy anymore? Is your life over? Is it proof that God's favor has been taken away from you?

"There is in Jerusalem near the Sheep Gate a pool, which in Aramaic is called Bethesda and which is surrounded by five covered colonnades. Here a great number of disabled people used to lie—the blind, the lame, the paralyzed. One who was there had been an invalid for thirty-eight years" (John 5:2-5). Living in biblical times didn't mean that your life would be way better than today. People still suffered; people still struggled with disabilities, and sometimes those disabilities lasted a long time.

A paralyzed man's atrophied legs became the platform for the grace of God to work one day next to Bethesda Pool. Jesus there gave a demonstration of healing power flowing from his voice and hands that will serve forever as a demo of what he will do on a grand scale when he returns.

In the meantime, every believing struggler is comforted with the certainty of God's love, the guarantee of free and full forgiveness, and the absolute guarantee that in heaven the lame will leap like a deer.

_____

_____

_____

_____

_____

His problem, my problem

So many people. So much sin. So many lost. So many fallen away. I must confess that my own outreach and restoration efforts sometimes bog down because I feel overwhelmed. You too?

So let's bring it down to just one. Look around you. Pick one person close to you who seems to have lost his or her faith. Care about that *one.* Maybe it's your brother. **"The Lord said to Cain, 'Where is your brother Abel?' 'I don't know,' he replied. 'Am I my brother's keeper?'"** (Genesis 4:9).

That phrase, uttered to cover up the first murder, has become a slogan to rationalize indifference to someone else's struggles. Cain thought the answer was an obvious one— No. God thinks the opposite. In fact, it's one of his chief reasons for inventing families and congregations—so that nobody slips between the cracks, unnoticed, uncared for, unlamented.

That's what *compassion* means—that we are willing to feel someone else's pain, help carry someone else's burden, care about someone else's eternal destiny.

_____

_____

_____

_____

_____

I fear the aging process

Here I am again, Lord. I feel kind of guilty about this: I know I'm supposed to age gracefully and gratefully, but right now my heart isn't in it. Can I be honest with you? I feel like my body is betraying me one piece at a time. How did I get so many wrinkles? Where did those brown spots on my skin come from? I didn't sign up for purple bags under my eyes. I have no stamina anymore. I eat less than I ever did, and I still gain weight. What's happening to my hair?

I ache for my lost youth, but I'm even more anxious about the further losses that lie ahead. I fear the loss of my independence, having my driver's license taken away, becoming dependent on one medication after another to regulate all of my bodily processes. I know I am losing vision clarity, and my hearing has been going for years. I fear being left out.

You alone have answers and hope for me as my body ages and declines. **"My flesh and my heart may fail, but God is the strength of my heart and my portion forever"** (Psalm 73:26). You will help me along my pathway and see to it that I am up to whatever you need me to do for you. Your agenda for now is more important than mine. I await with joy your promise of full restoration.

_____

_____

_____

_____

_____

Work hard

It is undeniable that the poor have a special place in God's heart. He promises over and over to look after the poor, the needy, widows, outcasts, and orphans. Perhaps you have survived some desperate times in your life through God's timely intervention. What a comfort it is to know that if we do suffer financial setbacks or stretches of unemployment, God will be there for us.

However—God's compassion for the poor doesn't mean that poverty is acceptable as a life goal for you and your children. Poverty sometimes must be suffered and endured but never settled for if God has given you opportunities to advance. **"A little sleep, a little slumber, a little folding of the hands to rest—and poverty will come on you like a bandit and scarcity like an armed man"** (Proverbs 6:10,11).

Jesus said once, "My Father works, and I work." Those of us who are fathers have a special obligation and commission to mentor and teach young people to grow out of their instinctive laziness and choose to love work.

Some of my greatest personal heroes are retired people who have never slowed down. They are now free to work for God according to their passion.

_____

_____

_____

_____

_____

Clear as a bell

When Christian lands fell to Muslim armies, the believers in Christ were not all killed, but they did become second-class citizens called *dhimmis*. They were allowed to gather in their churches but were forbidden to ring their bells, so powerful was the influence of that ringing perceived by the new masters. Still today church bells call the faithful to worship and announce the passage of time. I hope you can hear some wherever you may live.

If you would climb up to the bell tower of my church, you would find three bells. Those many hundreds of pounds of solid bronze send a beautiful musical message before every worship service. In raised letters on the middle-sized bell is the legend, **"O land, land, land, hear the word of the Lord!"** (Jeremiah 22:29). That bell announces to our community that it is of first importance that you listen to what God says so that he can tell you what he has done.

The music of church bells makes some important promises: here you will find a community of people washed in the cleansing of Holy Baptism, nourished by the Word of God, and strengthened by the sacred Supper. Here is a safe place to bring your brokenness and needs; here is a training school to help you develop your talents and gifts.

Bells, ring your invitation: "Come and be blessed. Go and serve."

_____

_____

_____

_____

_____

September

I have told you these things,
so that in me you may have peace.
In this world you will have trouble.
But take heart!
I have overcome the world.

John 16:33

You've heard of dual citizenship, in which a person actually carries two passports? Did you know that you hold dual family membership?

The Bible says that your baptism actually represents a moment in which God the Father publicly claimed you and accepted a lifelong obligation to do for you what good fathers do for children they love. I guess that makes your baptismal certificate your adoption papers: **"You are all sons of God through faith in Christ Jesus, for all of you who were baptized into Christ have clothed yourselves with Christ"** (Galatians 3:26,27).

This is great news, especially for people whose own earthly families are missing some pieces. If your biological father was missing in your life or is deceased, you are not fatherless anymore. If you are an only child, guess what? Your adopted family is huge, and you're connected to them all. If you are single and longing for a feeling of belonging and connection, Christ your Savior loves to compare himself to a bridegroom. You're engaged! The wedding feast is coming soon.

God is proud publicly to call you his daughter or his son. May I invite you to be just as proud to call him your Father?

_____

_____

_____

_____

_____

A second-grade girl stayed after school because she adored her teacher. She helped tidy up the room and did little tasks to prolong the time together. One day the teacher was busily writing on some papers and the girl asked her what she was doing. "Oh, filling out forms for my job," the teacher replied. "Where do you work?" the little girl asked.

It is the lot of teachers to be taken for granted.

This is a great time of year to pause and reflect on the wonderful people that will be caring for the kids in your life—your own children, grandchildren, nieces, nephews, and dear friends. It would be a great time to pray for them and thank God for them.

Thank God especially for the teachers who assist you in the task of passing on our faith. They are God's gifts to you and to his lambs. **"It was** [God] **who gave some to be . . . pastors and teachers, to prepare God's people for works of service, so that the body of Christ may be built up until we all reach unity in the faith and in the knowledge of the Son of God and become mature, attaining to the whole measure of the fullness of Christ"** (Ephesians 4:11-13).

A small army of Christian teachers made me who I am today. Next to your parents, who were the teachers that most shaped your character and personal philosophy?

_____

_____

_____

_____

_____

You're doing it for him

Everyday question #25: A friend says, "I know I should help out at church, and sometimes I do volunteer, but I'd really rather be doing something else. Anything else. How can I get my joy in service back when my selfish side would rather be playing video games?"

Well, this guy gets points for honesty. But it does indeed sound like it's time for a reality check. Pinch yourself, buddy. What you just pinched is sinful flesh. It's the reason why the Son of God had to become like you so that he could absorb in himself the punishment that your sins deserved (including the sin of viewing service to God as an annoying irritation instead of a sacred privilege).

Here's what Jesus' work accomplished for you: forgiveness for your many sins and a shine put on your life so dazzling that you will look like a saint on judgment day. Here is how your service appears to the King on that day: **"Then the King will say to those on his right, 'Come, you who are blessed by my Father; take your inheritance, the kingdom prepared for you since the creation of the world. . . . Whatever you did for one of the least of these brothers of mine, you did for me'"** (Matthew 25:34,40).

Serve the Lord with gladness. Everything you do for others in Jesus' name you are really doing for him.

_____

_____

_____

_____

_____

He is smiling at you

You can read a lot from people's faces, can't you? Without ever hearing a word, you can sense irritation, pleasure, doubt, worry, and fear. You can sense condemnation too. You can tell if someone is angry with you before a word is said. How good are you at forgiving people who have done you wrong? Not so hot? Do you hold grudges sometimes?

Sometimes we assume that that's how God looks at us— never really forgiving completely, still angry, still remembering our moral failures. If we try to imagine his face, we fear that he is frowning.

Our God eagerly desires a loving relationship with all of his lost and estranged children. That's why he arranged for our wrongs to be placed on the head of an innocent substitute, his own Son. That's why he instructed Moses to speak words of kindness to the believers and bless them like this: **"The Lord make his face shine upon you and be gracious to you"** (Numbers 6:25).

Visualize God's face right now. Visualize him smiling at you. He likes you, you know.

_____

_____

_____

_____

Who says?

Next to the content of your religious faith, the next most important question in your entire life is the *authority* behind your information. It is our curse to live in an age where truth is thought to be relative, i.e., variable from one person to the next. There are no absolutes, we're told. Everyone must set up his or her own guidelines for truth and morality.

God loves you more than that. Next to the gift of his Son, Jesus, his gift of his Word is the most valuable. In clear and eloquent language, the Bible tells you of God's mighty acts in human history, describes your origin, your purpose, your miserable dilemma, and his stunning rescue. You don't have to invent your own faith—you can just watch God work and listen to his voice tell you how you fit into his master plan.

Scripture speaks highly of the people in the Macedonian town of Berea because of the reception they gave Paul on his second mission journey: **"Now the Bereans were of more noble character than the Thessalonians, for they received the message with great eagerness and examined the Scriptures every day to see if what Paul said was true"** (Acts 17:11).

I hope you have come to trust your pastor, that he has earned your confidence. But be a Berean too—dig into your Scriptures to see for yourself if what he says is true.

_____

_____

_____

_____

_____

Why doesn't God just take me?

Have you ever heard a senior citizen, frail and full of years, bedridden and often in pain, groan, "Why doesn't God just take me? I hurt all the time; I'm no good to anyone. I've been ready to go for a long time. Why am I still here?" What can you say to someone you love whose life is full of sighs like this: **"Out of the depths I cry to you, O Lord; O Lord, hear my voice. Let your ears be attentive to my cry for mercy"** (Psalm 130:1,2).

Some countries have passed euthanasia laws that essentially allow people to commit legal suicide, assisted by a physician. Any biblical Christian would recoil in horror from that kind of "mercy killing," no matter how good a case could be made for ending a life of pain. But back to the main question: why doesn't God just take them?

Why indeed? The Almighty may have many reasons for allowing a sufferer to linger longer. Their words of hope, their courage and stamina, their patience in bearing their burden, and their serene confidence in eternal life through Christ may change the hearts of younger and healthier people around them. They may have a greater impact on others more in their illness than in wellness. St. Paul said, **"God chose the weak things of the world to shame the strong"** (1 Corinthians 1:27).

He will take us home when our mission is completed.

_____

_____

_____

_____

_____

SEPTEMBER 7

A powerful role

Timothy is a wonderful name for Christian parents to choose for a son. Besides referring to one of the heroes of the apostolic age, it has a beautiful meaning: "One who honors God." A woman named Eunice gave that name to her son, but the faith that was so effectively passed on to him came from his grandmother. St. Paul wrote to the man who was arguably his most trusted lieutenant: **"I have been reminded of your sincere faith, which first lived in your grandmother Lois"** (2 Timothy 1:5).

You might think about Grandma Lois on the first Sunday after Labor Day, which in the U.S. has loosely been recognized as Grandparents Day since 1978. Grandparents can play a powerful role in passing on the Christian faith. They serve as baptismal sponsors, frequent babysitters, and sometimes daily caregivers while the parents are at work. Did you know that about 7% of all children in the U.S. are in the formal custody of their grandparents?

Although our culture idolizes youth and tends to ignore those with gray hair, seniors bring enormous value to their churches, families, and communities. After surviving decades of the storms of life, they have grown wise about people and money. They don't rush around quite as fast and take the time to savor conversations and meals together.

They can make sure that little children feel important and that they know what Jesus did for them.

_____

_____

_____

_____

The hardest workers oughtta get more

One of the hardest tasks in running any business is determining salaries and benefits. Human resource committees and officials do a lot of research to figure out what the market is paying. Larger firms hire expensive consultants to help them get their compensation and benefit packages just right.

Generally, seniority with the company gets rewarded, right? Not in God's heavenly HR scheme. Read Jesus' parable of the workers in the vineyard. **"'These men who were hired last worked only one hour,' they said, 'and you have made them equal to us who have borne the burden of the work and the heat of the day'"** (Matthew 20:12).

Have you been a Christian for a long time? Do you feel twinges of resentment that people who are party animals and hell-raisers might come to the Christian faith late in life and be accepted to the same heaven where you are planning your everlasting retirement?

Might it help to remember that you have no right to set even your sinful big toe into God's holy presence? Your forgiveness, gifts, accomplishments, and immortality are all gifts of his grace, not rewards for your achievement. We must never take for granted the mercy shown us to the point where we resent that mercy being shown to someone else. Rejoice with the angels over even one bad boy who repents.

_____

_____

_____

_____

_____

Is personal ambition good? You bet. You need ambition to go looking for that first job while in high school, to enroll in a decent college, tough it through brutal courses in statistics and calculus, and hit the job market. You need ambition to sell yourself, rise up in the business world, and gain people's respect. But at what point does ambition get sick? When does ambition become greed, selfishness, manipulation of others, and nothing more than the satisfaction of your own appetites?

The apostle James is brutal on those whose desires and appetites consume them. **"What causes fights and quarrels among you? Don't they come from your desires that battle within you? You want something but don't get it. You kill and covet, but you cannot have what you want. You quarrel and fight. You do not have, because you do not ask God"** (James 4:1,2).

How can you make sure that your ambition stays in bounds? Listen to your family—they will tell you the truth if you've sold out. Listen to Christian friends—they will tell you if you're no fun to be with anymore. Most of all, listen to the Word of your God. Realize that every nickel you have is his investment in you and that true satisfaction comes only when you invest your money and yourself in his agenda.

_____

_____

_____

_____

_____

Transforming grace

Could there be a better example of God's transforming grace than Rahab of Jericho? She is usually identified as "Rahab the harlot," for at one time she apparently plied the ancient trade of prostitution. But our God uses all kinds of people to advance his plan of salvation. She listened to reports about the advancing Israelite nation and rightly concluded that Jericho was doomed because Israel's Lord was the true God of all.

She sheltered the scouts that Joshua had sent, explained her change of allegiance, and extracted a promise from them: **"When we heard of it** [the mighty exodus from Egypt], **our hearts melted and everyone's courage failed because of you, for the Lord your God is God in heaven above and on the earth below. Now then, please swear to me by the Lord that you will show kindness to my family, because I have shown kindness to you"** (Joshua 2:11,12).

She was indeed spared. But God had further plans. She must have been such an extraordinary woman that she caught the eye of the leader of the tribe of Judah, a man named Salmon. He married her, and their famous great-great-grandson David became king of Israel.

Not only does Matthew list her in the genealogy of Christ our Savior, but the writer to the Hebrews lists her in the catalog of heroes of faith in chapter 11. Truly God is not as interested in condemning us for our past as in using us right now for his human rescue plans.

_____

_____

_____

SEPTEMBER 11
Sex isn't a weapon

Marriage opens the door to a richness in life that single people don't experience. Marriage can also trap you in a world of pain. When you're dating and the relationship is getting unpleasant, you just don't call for a while. When you live together, there's nowhere to hide.

When you're married, you are totally vulnerable—open 24/7 to attack from your mate, who knows all your owies and buttons to push. There are many ways to "punish" your spouse and "teach him a lesson": verbal belittling, temper displays, or the silent treatment.

And then there's the nuclear option: Don't touch me. The Designer of marriage knew that under stress married people would reach too quickly for that weapon: **"The husband should fulfill his marital duty to his wife, and likewise the wife to her husband. The wife's body does not belong to her alone but also to her husband. In the same way, the husband's body does not belong to him alone but also to his wife. Do not deprive each other except by mutual consent and for a time, so that you may devote yourselves to prayer"** (1 Corinthians 7:3-5).

Well?

_____

_____

_____

_____

_____

SEPTEMBER 12
Abide with me

Two of the people in Jesus' wider circle of disciples had a miserable Sunday afternoon. Their long-awaited Passover festival had been completely ruined because of the sudden arrest, conviction, torture, and crucifixion of Jesus, their beloved Teacher. A mysterious stranger walked with them for a while on their road that Easter Sunday afternoon. He led them through a Bible study they would never forget, and somehow their hopes revived. As he explained things, forgiveness of sins and eternal life would be earned for the believers through the Messiah's suffering, death, and resurrection.

"As they approached the village to which they were going, Jesus acted as if he were going farther. But they urged him strongly, 'Stay with us, for it is nearly evening; the day is almost over'" (Luke 24:28,29). The stranger agreed. He stayed with them and shared their meal. Suddenly they recognized that their guest was Jesus himself, alive and triumphant. Their lives would never be the same.

A Church of England clergyman named Henry Lyte longed for Jesus' comforting and abiding presence just as much as they did, and the beautiful verses he penned have become known and loved by Christians for many generations:

Abide with me; fast falls the eventide.
The darkness deepens; Lord, with me abide.
When other helpers fail and comforts flee,
Help of the helpless, oh, abide with me!

I live with pain

I don't know why, Lord, but you have chosen to let me live with chronic pain. I have tried everything; nothing works. Is this my destiny for the rest of my life?

I've talked to you about it; I've pleaded and prayed, but my pain remains. I remember longingly the pain-free days of my youth—they seem gone forever. I pray for sleep, for at least I gain a temporary respite. You must have a plan, Lord. I will admit that I can't figure it out, but somehow my pain is being worked into your plans.

I need help. I fear my stamina is eroding. Help me wait cheerfully, confidently, and faithfully. Help me honor and worship and praise you even when I hurt. **"My soul waits for the Lord more than watchmen wait for the morning, more than watchmen wait for the morning. O Israel, put your hope in the Lord, for with the Lord is unfailing love and with him is full redemption"** (Psalm 130:6,7).

Lord, I wait and watch for you. None of my troubles is too great for you. Come to my relief. I take great comfort in your unfailing love. I eagerly await the full redemption I know is coming. Work all things together for my good. Refresh my spirit and my weary body. Please come now.

_____

_____

_____

_____

_____

My best for you, Lord

One of the terrible hazards of being famous for one particular thing is that for the rest of your life, and perhaps forever, you are known for *only* that one thing. Actors dread being typecast and wearily accept the risk. Jerry Mathers was "The Beaver" his entire adult life. Carrie Fisher could never shake her identity as Princess Leia. And Abel will forever be known as the victim of the first homicide.

Read a little more of Genesis chapter 4, however, and you will see that he was far more than just a nice guy who was hit on the head by his evil brother. Abel had come to know his Creator and Savior, and he found joy in giving back to the Giver serious gifts. Abel made his living by raising livestock, and what is even more noteworthy for posterity than his death was his life—he gave offerings that were the *best*. **"Abel brought fat portions from some of the firstborn of his flock. The Lord looked with favor on Abel and his offering."** (Genesis 4:4).

Abel's parents, Adam and Eve, undoubtedly told him stories of the Garden of Eden, their paradise lost. Even in our sin-damaged and broken world, there are still marvelous glimmers of that paradise, and also of the heavenly paradise still to come. Abel's gifts to the Lord expressed both his appreciation for the many blessings in his life and a joyful anticipation of paradise regained.

_____

_____

_____

_____

Circumcise all the males then

In some ways, mandatory religious circumcision seems like God's strangest commandment. **"This is my covenant with you and your descendants after you, the covenant you are to keep: Every male among you shall be circumcised"** (Genesis 17:10). From the time of Abraham until the time of Christ, this was God's will, and he was very serious.

What could possibly be the rationale for cutting a piece of skin off the male reproductive organ? It was to be done at whatever age the male came into the covenant family—as a baby (the usual age) or as an adult (ouch!). God had two powerful objectives. The first was to put his mark on his men to keep them conscious of their unique and separate status. For Israel to fulfill its destiny, the Israelites could not just blend into and assimilate into the Canaanite culture around them. They needed to stay distinct.

An even more urgent reason was that Israel's greatest purpose was to give the Savior to the world. God had invested his solemn honor in his promise to Abraham that in him all peoples on earth would be blessed (Genesis 12:1-3). It was through the reproductive act that one day there would be a Jewish woman named Mary who would give birth to the Savior.

When God began the writing of the New Testament (Matthew 1), what did he write about first? The bloodline from Abraham to Jesus' stepfather, Joseph. Mission accomplished.

_____

_____

_____

_____

Circumcise your hearts now

No doubt about it—people like to make rules. Religious leaders are sometimes the worst offenders—all too often we love to make rules and make other people obey them. On top of that, Satan loves to convince people that the way to approval with God is by *performance,* by our *doing* things to *work* for God's favor.

After the Savior was born, the special mark of circumcision on males of the covenant became unnecessary. Parents today can arrange for their newborn sons to be circumcised or not, but the procedure no longer has any religious significance in the New Covenant.

It took a while for Jewish Christians to stop mandating the practice. Paul warned them about imposing laws that God had abolished: **"It is for freedom that Christ has set us free. Stand firm, then, and do not let yourselves be burdened again by a yoke of slavery. . . . If you let yourselves be circumcised, Christ will be of no value to you at all . . . for in Christ Jesus neither circumcision nor uncircumcision has any value. The only thing that counts is faith expressing itself through love"** (Galatians 5:1-6).

If you want to cut something, he told them, metaphorically cut your hearts, i.e., repent of your sins, claim Christ's forgiveness, and dedicate yourself to living a new life of service to God and people.

_____

_____

_____

_____

_____

Promises, promises

Faith is believing what you do not see; the reward of this faith is seeing what you believe. —St. Augustine

It was Augustine's lot in life to serve God and the church in the waning days of the Roman Empire's authority and peace in North Africa in the early 400s A.D. The Visigoths had already sacked Rome in 410, and Augustine wrote his masterful book *The City of God* to console his fellow Christians as they saw earthly prosperity and peace disappear. Soon the Vandals would overrun his beloved Hippo.

Hebrews chapter 11 is a masterful list of heroes of faith—people who listened to God's astonishing promises and believed him, even though they died before they saw the glorious fulfillment. **"These were all commended for their faith, yet none of them received what had been promised. God had planned something better for us so that only together with us would they be made perfect"** (Hebrews 11:39,40).

You've been given a string of incredible promises from God, and many of them can't be detected by the naked eye. You've been washed of your sins in Baptism, and yet you are all too aware of your many sins. You are fed with Christ himself in Holy Communion, yet all you can see is bread and wine. God himself thunders from heaven, but you can only read about it in ink on paper. Just believe. Soon comes sight.

_____

_____

_____

_____

Time for you to find joy in serving

Everybody needs to feel safe. Everybody needs to feel needed. A happy and healthy congregation will provide both of those things. But it can also meet another significant need of yours—to help you feel significant by giving you a venue for serving other people.

The Bible uses the metaphor of the human body to help you get this critically important point. Believers all together form the "body of Christ." Each of the parts is unique; each is important; each needs the other parts to flourish and grow. **"Just as each of us has one body with many members, and these members do not all have the same function, so in Christ we who are many form one body, and each member belongs to all the others"** (Romans 12:4,5).

Does that statement scare you? Are you afraid of commitment and "belonging" to other people? Relax. It's how your Creator designed you. When you call a sick friend, send a card, congratulate an achiever, encourage a drooper, pursue a stray, or teach a child, you will feel a satisfaction in your heart that not even the devil can steal.

_____

_____

_____

_____

_____

You can't love both

A man I know who grew up in central Michigan told me once that you can't root for both Michigan State and Michigan. You have to pick one or the other. You can't love them both. It's either green and white or maize and blue.

Satan will present you with rationalizations to encourage you to make deals in your mind and play a variety of games. He tried to get Jesus himself to play it both ways. He promised that Jesus could avoid suffering and the cross and still accomplish his mission. **"Jesus said to him, 'Away from me, Satan! For it is written: "Worship the Lord your God, and serve him only"'"** (Matthew 4:10). It was the Father, not Satan, who defined Jesus' mission.

I will never forget the words of a recovering alcoholic who told me once that the bottle had become his god. Where do you go most often for a feeling of self-worth, for comfort, for your identity when you're stressed or afraid?

_____

_____

_____

_____

_____

Which comes first?

The Christian does not think God will love us because we are good, but that God will make us good because he loves us.
—C.S. Lewis

I used to have a pear tree in my backyard. It bore pears like crazy. I ate as many as I could, gave away as many as I could, composted as many as I had energy to pick up, and toward the end of summer just drove the lawn mower over the rest and fertilized the grass. That tree bore pears not in order to become a pear tree but because it *was* a pear tree. It couldn't help it. That's what God made it to be. That was its design, function, and purpose.

God designed you to be a good works machine—worshipful, kind, generous, and eager to share the gospel. And you do those good works not in order to *become* a child of God but because you *are* one. **"When the kindness and love of God our Savior appeared, he saved us, not because of righteous things we had done, but because of his mercy. He saved us through the washing of rebirth and renewal by the Holy Spirit"** (Titus 3:4,5).

God's promises and plans take away our fear. God's generosity to us takes away our excuses. God's Spirit in our hearts replaces the god of Self. So tell me—what fruit did you bear today?

_____

_____

_____

_____

SEPTEMBER 21
Devoted to prayer together

The apostle Peter was once sprung out of prison by an angel who infiltrated perimeter security, cut the chains right off Peter's wrists, and led him out. Did he go home after that? No. Where, then, did he go? He immediately went to find his friends. They had been so worried about Peter that they were gathered together praying. Seeing him come through the doors was a stunning and direct answer to their group intercessions.

God loves when you pray not only *for* other people but *with* other people, because it helps you pay attention to other people's needs. He says, **"If two of you on earth agree about anything you ask for, it will be done for you by my Father in heaven. For where two or three come together in my name, there am I with them"** (Matthew 18:19,20).

God loves to hear your solo prayers, but he promises even greater things when you bind your individual heart with other believers' hearts. When you pray together, your burdens become only half as heavy. When you pray together, your joys are doubled.

Nurses will tell you that patients who feel loved and connected to other people get better faster.

_____

_____

_____

_____

_____

A slave for others

Why are so many Christian congregations no longer growing and now in decline? It may be that the surrounding communities are unaware of any important resources there. It may be that the congregation is interested in gathering only people just like those already there.

The sad truth is that even though neighborhoods may change outwardly, the same desperate, inward human needs are still there—loneliness, depression, guilt, sickness, and fear. When there is a communication gap between Christians and their communities, guess who adapts? **"Though I am free and belong to no man, I make myself a slave to everyone, to win as many as possible"** (1 Corinthians 9:19).

Did you catch that? The one who knows God will adapt. The one who is stronger in faith will bend. The one more experienced in the Word will take the posture of the servant.

It is my belief and experience that when a congregation makes itself a slave to its community, it will have all the work it can handle and will never go out of business.

It's other people who are the racists

I will never forget the series in my hometown newspaper, "Race: The Rawest Nerve." The stories chronicled the racial turbulence that once tore up neighborhoods and still troubles the city. A survey of the city and its suburbs revealed that over ninety percent believed that racism is a serious problem here. To the question, "Are you a racist," do you know how many answered yes? Two percent. In other words, it's always other people who are the racists.

Satan seeks to exploit every difference in people to drive them apart. Race is one of his most effective harmony wreckers. "Why do they act like that?" "Our people would never do that."

Realize that racist urges lurk in your heart just as surely as the urges to lie, covet, steal, and commit adultery. The key to healing, as with all sin, is repentance. **"Wash your hands, you sinners, and purify your hearts, you double-minded. Grieve, mourn and wail. . . . Humble yourselves before the Lord, and he will lift you up"** (James 4:8-10).

Forgiven by Christ and indwelt by his Spirit, our hearing improves and we know how our careless race talk sounds to people not like us. Our vision improves and we see how actions and attitudes of our tribe have hurt other people. Fear and suspicion and resentments give way to tolerance, then acceptance, then appreciation and respect.

And then the gospel can move more freely.

I have nothing; I have everything

*I have held many things in my hands, and I have lost them all;
but whatever I have placed in God's hands, that I still possess.*

—Martin Luther

Are you familiar with the terms *P/L statement* and *balance sheet*? These are accounting terms to define a business' profit and loss and a listing of all assets, whether cash or receivables or equipment or real estate, balanced against all liabilities, such as debts or payables.

What does your personal balance sheet look like? What will it look like when you die? I don't mean what your heirs will inherit. I mean what will *you* have when you stand before God? Your money and property on earth will belong to someone else. What will you be able to take with you? **"Whatever was to my profit I now consider loss for the sake of Christ. What is more, I consider everything a loss compared to the surpassing greatness of knowing Christ Jesus my Lord, for whose sake I have lost all things"** (Philippians 3:7,8).

Money, stuff, and real estate are just tools, means by which you can serve God here on earth. They all stay here and soon will be destroyed. What matters, what *lasts,* is your relationship with Jesus Christ. When he speaks the word, your body will leap from the ground and you will be restored. You will then come into your real inheritance.

SEPTEMBER 25
Become children again

Little children are so used to having everything "automatically" provided for them—clothing, food, shelter, transportation—that trust comes naturally to them. This makes it easier for them to believe in Jesus too. They simply know that Jesus loves them. They simply trust that Jesus will help them.

As we grow older, however, and grow more self-sufficient and self-reliant, we lose the "naïve" faith that everything we need will be provided. Adults know that they have to work for everything they get. The problem comes when adults get confused and start to think maybe they have to work for God's love and earn his blessings.

Grown-ups may think if they act better, swear less, drink less, or give more, they might earn a better place in heaven. Perhaps the "achievers" come to think that they are better than other people and deserve everything they plan to get from God. Or worse—perhaps they fear that because they have made so many messes they have forfeited God's favor.

Let Jesus whisper this in your ear. Ready? **"I tell you the truth, unless you change and become like little children, you will never enter the kingdom of heaven"** (Matthew 18:3).

This kind of "second childhood" isn't senility. It's reality; it's a very happy state of mind to live in.

What if I lose my faith?

Love stories will never die out in the movies and on stage. Not only do we all yearn to be loved, but there is also always the undercurrent of fear that the relationship is fleeting, always at risk, and that makes for great drama. We all know what it is like to be let down by someone you long for, and we also know our own fickleness—we ourselves might lose interest in the other person.

What do you tell a young person who is afraid fully to trust God, afraid not so much that God will leave her but that she might leave God? Frankly, by asking that question the young person is telling me that she is safe. Only believers can worry that they might lose their most precious possession. Believers also know that faith comes by hearing the message of Christ, and so they can take preemptive action against Satan's whispers and bribes.

We are indeed often gullible fools, and that's why next to Christ himself our best allies on earth are Christian family members, our Christian congregation, and a circle of Christian friends who will encourage and mentor us. And though our love for God may wobble, his love for us never will. **"God has said, 'Never will I leave you; *never* will I forsake you'"** (Hebrews 13:5).

You're in good hands with your heavenly Father.

I'm a failure

Yesterday a friend told me, "I think my wife and I have lost our teenage daughter. She despises us, is openly defiant day after day, and can't wait to move out of the house." This dear guy feels like a failure. I can only imagine the gloom in his wife's heart.

Know the feeling? Have you blamed yourself for the wreckage of something major in your life? Are you divorced? Been fired? Failed a course? Dropped out of school? Had a child out of wedlock? Ruined a business? Had an abortion? Had to declare bankruptcy?

Among all the great things about Christianity, here is a promise near the top: God does not despise us when we fail. In fact, the heart of the gospel is that God loves losers and the broken. Yes, he loves failures too.

Sometimes we have to be really empty to be ready for God to fill us up. One of life's supreme ironies is that sometimes God gets his best work done through badly broken people whom he is leading out of major crises.

"With your help I can advance against a troop; with my God I can scale a wall" (Psalm 18:29).

_____

_____

_____

_____

_____

Friends help each other

In your efforts to bring someone back to the faith, you are not alone. Sometimes you have to go through some major personal stress to find out that you have more friends than you thought. Ask them for help in your spiritual reclamation project. Ask them to pray for the person on your heart. Ask them to pray for you. **"Devote yourselves to prayer, being watchful and thankful. And pray for us, too, that God may open a door for our message"** (Colossians 4:2,3).

Prayer is not merely something that God *permits* you to do. He invites you to pray. He even commands you to pray, pray often, pray intensely, pray for the same thing repeatedly. He promises on his sacred honor and on the basis of the steady personal intercession of Jesus Christ to process every request you send.

Every time you pray, something moves somewhere. Something changes. The Lord absolutely loves to hear from you, and he loves it even better when friends pray for each other. You are not alone in your mission of being a "soul guard." Bring them back!

St. Michael and all angels

We barely give a thought to the military defenses that protect our nation. Missile silos in cornfields wait quietly, hoping never to be needed. Military satellites watch our borders; silent nuclear submarines prowl the Pacific; worldwide radar tracks everything moving in the air.

Your protectors in the spirit world do their work silently as well, carrying out God's loving orders to keep the believers safe from the evil one and his horde from hell. But even though we can't see or hear their work, the archangel Michael and his heavenly host are engaged in violent spiritual warfare on our behalf: **"There was war in heaven. Michael and his angels fought against the dragon, and the dragon and his angels fought back. But he was not strong enough, and they lost their place in heaven. The great dragon was hurled down—that ancient serpent called the devil, or Satan, who leads the whole world astray"** (Revelation 12:7-9).

It only looks as though evil has triumphed on earth; that good is a fading, spent force. In actuality Satan has been mortally wounded by the mighty blow from Calvary's cross. He and his demons are held in check by the ceaseless patrols of our angel friends.

Someday we will be able to see and communicate with these wondrous creatures. For now, God thinks it enough that we take his word that we are safe.

Thank you, Michael.

_____

_____

_____

Be patient

Americans used to be good savers (10% of personal income went into savings) and now have become terrible savers (0% or even less, which means that people are actually burning up their savings for daily expenses). People who save none of their income probably are suffering from "I Must Have It Now" syndrome.

Waiting for things cheerfully is learned behavior. People who didn't learn it as children can cause some real wreckage as adults.

God tends to ration out his blessings slowly. This keeps us humble, reminds us of our dependence on him, encourages us to thank him for what he has done, and reaffirms our need for his help and blessings.

God can send large amounts of money suddenly into your family. More often he trickles in wealth. But that's okay— with self-discipline and a long-term plan, you can build your family's financial strength. **"He who gathers money little by little makes it grow"** (Proverbs 13:11).

October

I tell you the truth,
he who believes has everlasting life.

John 6:47

I am precious to God

One of Satan's endless deceptions is to get us to think of God in human terms, i.e., that he thinks and acts basically just like us. By those measures God is forgetful, impulsive, evasive, vengeful, and has a temper that can tear the branches off trees.

The Bible describes a different God, one who is patient, steady in love and purpose, and who will never reject or forget the one he has called his child. **"Can a mother forget the baby at her breast and have no compassion on the child she has borne? Though she may forget, I will not forget you! See, I have engraved you on the palms of my hands"** (Isaiah 49:15,16).

This is a God who thinks you're precious and valuable to him, who patiently forgives your sins of the past, and who is far more interested in your future. This is a God who continues to see value in you. This is a God who always takes you back, who will never reject you even if you've given him reason to do so.

If your name can actually be found on the palms of his heavenly hands, you must be precious indeed.

_____

_____

_____

_____

_____

I know it's wrong, but God forgives

I was trying to do some counseling to help a husband and wife whose marriage was teetering on the edge. The husband had had some of his shortcomings pointed out to him, but he was not interested in changing. Neither the threat of a lost relationship with his wife or even the risk of losing his relationship with God seemed to put a dent in his stubbornness. "Okay, so I'm sinning, but you taught me that God always forgives me in the end." Ouch!

The grace of God must never be turned into a license for intentional acts of rebellion. **"If we deliberately keep on sinning after we have received the knowledge of the truth, no sacrifice for sins is left, but only a fearful expectation of judgment and of raging fire that will consume the enemies of God"** (Hebrews 10:26,27). God's mercy should lead us to sorrow, repentance, and a renewed desire to serve and obey him, not be a hall pass for more hell-raising.

When I hear how much he loves me, enough to send his Son to the cross, how can I not love him back? How can I not want to make amends for my past misdeeds? When I think of the horrible fate reserved for unrepentant sinners, how can I not pray, "Speak, Lord. Your servant is listening"?

_____

_____

_____

_____

_____

OCTOBER 3
"At one" with God

The Feast of Yom Kippur (the Great Day of Atonement) does not appear on Christian calendars, but it was one of the three great pilgrim festivals in Old Testament times and is still observed in Judaism today.

The fullest description of God's instructions for this solemn day can be found in the 16th chapter of Leviticus. A young bull, a ram, and a goat were ritually killed and the blood sprinkled. The sins of the nation were ceremonially placed on the head of a second goat (the "scapegoat"), and it was driven out alone into the desert to die, symbolizing the removal of sin from the Israelite camp.

The entire drama was to be reenacted each autumn. **"On this day [yom] atonement [kippur] will be made for you, to cleanse you. Then, before the Lord, you will be clean from all your sins"** (Leviticus 16:30).

You may never have observed Yom Kippur per se. But in a sense, there is a great day of atonement in the Christian church year—we call it Good Friday. On that awe-filled day, God struck his Son with all his force, pouring out his wrath for all human sin on the innocent Lamb hanging on a cross. On that day atonement was made—and all who believe in Christ are once again "at one" with the Father.

There is no more need for the shedding of blood—Christ's great "Kippur" has made the final payment. The atonement is yours to believe; it is yours to share.

_____

_____

_____

_____

Let God handle your baggage

I love people watching at airports. A common sight is a small person dragging a huge load of baggage piled up higher than he or she is tall. Does that sound like your life? Dragging a pile of fear, guilt, failure, and messes that is taller than you?

The Bible's many human stories teach us the dirty secret of life—we're all messes. What about the people who don't look like they have problems? Well, maybe they just hide it better. Can you imagine how long the list would be if we inventoried all our regrets and failures? Maybe you're burdened by maxed-out credit cards. Are you bleeding over the ripping apart of your family? Have your children made such bad choices that you feel like a failure? Or possibly does everything seem overwhelming? You force yourself to put on a happy face, but you are barely holding things together.

Maybe God has allowed your messes to pile up to the point where you are ready to let him be your baggage handler. Behind all of our troubles is sin. Sin makes us fear that God won't help us, or worse, that he will just get angrier and pile on the punishment. Here are some sweet words from the apostle John: **"I write to you, dear children, because your sins have been forgiven on account of** [Jesus'] **name"** (1 John 2:12).

If God forgives you, you can forgive yourself. If God likes you, you can like yourself again. If God will reveal the way out of your problems in his time, you can wait in peace. Baggage? What baggage?

_____

_____

OCTOBER 5

Encourage; don't exasperate

Throughout all cultures and eras, it seems that child rearing is thought of as women's work. There's a reason for that. Childbearing and nursing can only be carried out by the mom, and it is just natural that little ones should be nurtured primarily by her.

But it was never God's design for men to be absent. The apostle Paul has this charter for all Christian dads: **"Fathers, do not exasperate your children; instead, bring them up in the training and instruction of the Lord"** (Ephesians 6:4).

Authority can become controlling, and controlling can become abusive, so Paul reminds fathers to temper their authority with mercy, patience, and kindness so that they won't exasperate their kids. A child damaged by too harsh a home will act out his anger and rebellion for the rest of his life. A father's leadership is supposed to diminish the anger level in a home, not increase it.

Instead, Fathers, *bring them up.* Nourish them. Feed their souls and spirits. Protect them, take care of them, and see to their well-being. Make sure they know the name of their Creator. Make sure they have heard the great stories of their redemption through Jesus Christ. See to it that their faith is fed and the Holy Spirit's wisdom and guiding power are always present.

Everything tangible in your life will be taken from you when you die. The only thing you can take with you to heaven is people.

_____

_____

_____

OCTOBER 6
Don't argue with God

Ask parents to list a few things that make parenting miserable, and near the top of the list will be "lip." My father used to call it "back talk."

In the story of the rich man and poor Lazarus, Jesus tells us that the rich man tried to do some arguing. **"'No, father Abraham,'** [the rich man] **said, 'but if someone from the dead goes to them, they will repent'"** (Luke 16:30).

How often have you argued with God? How often have you chafed at his narrow way? Maybe you think your suffering has gone on long enough. Maybe you have had enough of hardship and are ready for some pleasure. Maybe you've had enough of the wonderful discipline of poverty and are ready for the challenges of wealth for a change. "No, father Abraham!"

Maybe you flinch at having to confess that you are "a poor, miserable sinner." Maybe you don't like Jesus' claim to be the exclusive way to God, which implies that Islam and Hinduism and Zen and Scientology are spiritual dead ends. "No, father Abraham!"

Maybe you're weary of being single and are intrigued by the thrill of taking the shortcut to having someone to sleep with. Maybe you're weary of a marriage that has become hard and unfulfilling and figure you deserve better. "No, father Abraham!"

God's heart is full of love, his mind has laid out great plans, and his Word tells you the truth. Don't argue with him. Practice with me: "Speak, Lord—your servant is listening."

_____

_____

_____

Save and invest

Earning interest on your savings is good. It sure beats stuffing cash under the mattress or slipping twenties into books or slowly filling up a safe deposit box. Because of the steady drip-drip-drip of inflation, though, money that isn't moving is slowly losing its value. Even a bank savings account probably won't keep up with inflation.

Good managers of God's treasures look for investments. Maybe it's investing in equipment that will make your business bigger. **"Where there are no oxen, the manger is empty, but from the strength of an ox comes an abundant harvest"** (Proverbs 14:4). Draft animals are expensive to acquire and maintain, but they multiply your farm output many times over.

Business activity that is well run and meets people's needs will grow faster than savings passbook interest. Jesus not only described this timeless process but speaks approvingly of a man's industry and drive: **"There was a landowner who planted a vineyard. He put a wall around it, dug a winepress in it and built a watchtower. Then he rented the vineyard to some farmers"** (Matthew 21:33).

Do you have an investment strategy? You will almost certainly benefit from having an adviser coach you to make the most of your assets. God indeed loves and helps the poor, but that doesn't mean that you should make poverty a life goal.

_____

_____

_____

_____

I feel so guilty

The story of Judas is a miserable one, and I don't mean for the reasons you think. True enough, Judas was a greedy, selfish, money-hungry, lying, betraying weasel. But that is not the worst part. The worst is that his massive guilt made him think that he was a bigger sinner than Christ was a Savior.

You can't approve of what Judas did, but you can understand his miserable conclusion. So could David: **"My guilt has overwhelmed me like a burden too heavy to bear"** (Psalm 38:4). Do those words sound familiar to thoughts of your own? "Done it too often, too long. The badness inside me proves I'm no good. I'm too far gone."

David had good reasons to despair: lies, theft, adultery, murder. He also believed this: **"My soul finds rest in God alone; my salvation comes from him"** (Psalm 62:1). The crucifixion of Christ, pre-enacted for centuries by the shedding of animal blood in place of people's, bought total forgiveness for David and all other sinners retroactively, backward in time, and also proactively, forward in time, setting up a tidal wave of mercy that covers us as well. There is no condemnation for those who are in Christ Jesus.

_____

_____

_____

_____

_____

OCTOBER 9
It's not the size

Gideon was a man who knew no fear when he knew that he had the Word of the Lord behind him. A gigantic coalition of nomadic peoples headed up by the Midianites had rolled into Israel like an invading army of locusts, stealing their animals and destroying their crops. Their camels "could no more be counted than the sand on the seashore." Their army numbered 135,000.

Gideon mustered 30,000 Israelites, but the Lord didn't like those numbers. He thought Gideon had way too many. He led Gideon to reduce Israel's force to a small battalion of 300. He gave Gideon a positive sign, allowing him to overhear a Midianite man's dream of Israelite victory.

"When Gideon heard the dream and its interpretation, he worshiped God. He returned to the camp of Israel and called out, 'Get up! The LORD has given the Midianite camp into your hands.' [He divided] the three hundred men into three companies" (Judges 7:15,16).

Not only did Gideon welcome the sign and believe the Lord's promises; he actually *divided* his tiny force into three companies. The Lord didn't even need the three hundred—he simply drove the Midianites and their allies to attack and kill one another. Through Gideon's strong leadership, Israel had peace for 40 years.

It pleases the Lord to do great things through small people, to make extraordinary happen from the ordinary. Never say, "We are too small." Never say, "God can't."

_____

_____

_____

The core of my self-esteem

Do you like pain? I sure don't. In fact, one of my life philosophies is "no pain, no pain." But one of the things I've learned in life is that not all suffering is bad. When God is not involved, or when you don't learn anything, it is just miserable and pointless. But when the scalpel is held by a skillful and loving surgeon, it leads to blessings.

When we realize the frailty and vanity of sinful people, we will come to appreciate God's steady love for us all over again. Here is healthy thinking—to let God's unconditional love for us be the core of our self-esteem. Here are his wonderful words: **"I have loved you with an everlasting love; I have drawn you with loving-kindness. I will build you up again"** (Jeremiah 31:3,4).

The stories of the ups and downs of Old Testament believers and the insights given through prophets like Jeremiah help us see that God's overriding purpose for our lives is to have a love/faith relationship with us. Anything that helps deepen and strengthen that relationship is a good thing in God's eyes.

When God's Word has built confidence in your heart that you are loved by and valuable to your Father and Savior, everything else will flow out of that. He will build you up again.

_____

_____

_____

_____

_____

Get your oil now!

One of the most painful snubs people have to undergo these days is being "unfriended" on Facebook. Suddenly you are no longer welcome in someone's virtual "house," and that person's personal news, comments, and pictures no longer flow through your "feed." Oh, well. There are other people to be friends with.

Can you imagine what a disaster it will be for people on judgment day who hear *Jesus'* voice disavowing and unfriending them? Jesus once told a striking story about members of a wedding party who needed to have their oil lamps filled so they could join the nighttime bridal procession. Some of the bridesmaids were too self-centered or distracted to prepare in advance.

The procession left without them. **"Later the others also came. 'Sir! Sir!' they said. 'Open the door for us.' But he replied, 'I tell you the truth, I don't know you!' Therefore keep watch, because you do not know the day or the hour"** (Matthew 25:11-13).

Jesus' earnest warning: get your oil *now.* The oil you need is an attitude of repentance for your many sins, open-hearted listening to God's Word, and faith in the gospel message of your forgiveness through his blood. Do it now. You don't know when the Bridegroom will choose to come.

I'm angry all the time

You know, of course, that there are support groups for abusers, just as there are for alcoholics. Batterers Anonymous has done some great things to help violence-prone people to grow in the grace of self-control.

But you don't have to be physically violent to have an anger problem. Persistently angry people also beat up other people *verbally,* and they probably beat themselves up internally every day as well.

Anger is planted by Satan, whose anger at God seethes more with the passage of every day. Anger is pure emotion, and as such often does not even need a reason. During the Milwaukee riots in 1967, John Oraa Tucker loaded up his .12-gauge shotgun and unloaded blast after blast into the street. Weeks later, when asked why he did it, he answered, "I don't know."

"Refrain from anger and turn from wrath; do not fret—it leads only to evil. For evil men will be cut off, but those who hope in the LORD will inherit the land" (Psalm 37:8,9).

Did you know that through the Spirit of the Lord you have the power to let go of your anger?

_____

_____

_____

_____

Wait for God's reward

Why do husbands and wives not serve each other more willingly? Why do people hesitate to volunteer for ministry and social projects at church? One guess: they expect an insufficient reward. It just doesn't seem worth their time and energy.

Here is where church leaders can show some leadership: in clearly outlining what needs to be done, in ceaseless recruiting to bring in new talent, in training and encouraging, and in constant thanking.

But God's people can find joy in serving even when their leaders seem disorganized, when the same people seem to get stuck with the same jobs, and when nobody says thank you. We can always remember that we're really working for God and that labor is never in vain. **"Humble yourselves, therefore, under God's mighty hand, that he may lift you up in due time. Cast all your anxiety on him because he cares for you"** (1 Peter 5:6,7).

God always pays off. Always.

_____

_____

_____

_____

_____

God is patient

"Revenge is a dish best served cold." Those words first appeared in the novel *Mathilde* by French author Marie Joseph Eugène Sue and were quoted approvingly in movies like *The Godfather*, *Star Trek II*, and *Kill Bill*. The point is that your vengeance will be more effective if you go slow, brooding and planning.

God calls himself "slow" as well. But the slowness is not in his brain processes or his revenge fantasies, but in his temper. He is patient with foolish sinners like you and me, giving us time to hear his diagnosis of what's really wrong with us and to hear what he has done about it. **"The Lord is compassionate and gracious, *slow* to anger, abounding in love"** (Psalm 103:8).

People with hair-trigger tempers usually aren't very thoughtful. Impulsive people usually aren't known as planners. Your God goes slowly because he is patient and wants as many people in his heaven as he can draw in. Aren't you grateful for all the extra time he has given you to learn and grow?

Judgment day will come without warning. Who in your life is benefitting from God's slowness to anger? How can you share the great message of God's abundant love with the urgency it deserves?

_____

_____

_____

_____

_____

Spirit gifts: Prophesying

When Jesus ascended into heaven, he was not abandoning the believers. In fact, he assured them repeatedly before he "left" that his eyes would be on them, his heart with them, and his ears open to their prayers. Furthermore, he promised to send a mighty deluge of the Holy Spirit, who would strengthen and enlighten them for their lives of ministry.

The Spirit also brings gifts, and each believer has a unique combination. Nobody can say, "I've got nothing" or "God doesn't need me." **"We have different gifts, according to the grace given us. If someone's gift is prophesying, let him use it in proportion to his faith"** (Romans 12:6). The word *prophesy* in Scripture has various meanings. In its narrowest sense, it means to have the ability to foretell the future, a rare, special gift that God chose to give occasionally in Bible times. In a wider sense it simply denotes the ability to proclaim and explain God's Word publicly and clearly and compellingly.

That's where the church today is so blessed—when it recognizes people gifted for communicating the Word and puts them to work. Do people recognize that gift in you? Have you ever led a Bible study? Who in your life is the best Word-proclaimer? Thank you, Holy Spirit, for all who prophesy well.

Spirit gifts: Serving

When I hear it said of someone, "She is so gifted" or "What a gifted young man!" people are always speaking about overachievers, out-front leaders, or outstanding performers. I never hear it said of people for their humility. And yet a humble servant-attitude is a priceless gift of the Holy Spirit. **"We have different gifts, according to the grace given us. . . . If it is serving, let him serve"** (Romans 12:6,7).

In a world that admires ego, chest-thumping, and personal autonomy at all costs, how refreshing is it to be around someone who is interested in helping you? Who makes you feel important? Who will lend you a hand without complaining or calling a lot of attention to it? Who finds satisfaction in bringing joy to other people?

Our Savior Jesus is also our personal hero and role model. He told his disciples once that he came not to be served but to serve. He asked nothing less of his followers. He told them also that the nonnegotiable trademark of an authentic follower of his is love—your willingness to spend yourself on someone else's behalf. He told them that the attitude he and his Father most admire is best exemplified by that of a humble child.

Does your congregation have a reputation for cheerful voluntarism?

_____

_____

_____

_____

_____

Spirit gifts: Teaching

One of my all-time favorite bumper stickers reads, "If you can read this, thank a teacher." Can you even imagine the thousands of hours that a small army of caring adults spent with you so that you could learn to decode the symbols on a page? make sense of an array of numbers? learn the intricacies of musical notation?

I know that in theory people could read the Bible all by themselves, be brought to faith, and grow to Christian maturity self-taught. In theory, yes, but I have never met any real person like that. I personally have benefitted from hundreds of Christian teachers who shared their insights, experience, passion, talents, scholarly work, and stories and helped me develop my faith and understanding. **"We have different gifts, according to the grace given us. . . . If it is teaching, let him teach"** (Romans 12:6,7).

Some teachers have the extra patience needed to work with preschoolers in Sunday school. Some bring great depth and scholarship to college-level studies. Some saints actually love mentoring teenagers. Some are linguistic whizzes who lead seminary students into the Hebrew Old Testament and Greek New Testament. And some have the special gift of opening up the Word to senior citizens.

Holy Spirit, thank you for our teachers. They are your gifts to us!

Spirit gifts: Encouraging

The little girl came home from school beaming. Her mother asked, "Did you get a part in the school play?" "Yes!" she said. "I've been chosen to clap and cheer!" Some genius teacher was obviously anointed with the gift of encouragement, and she helped a child to discover the joy of encouraging others early in her young life.

You know what it's like to feel unappreciated. Boy, do you know! Sometimes it seems like you give and give and nobody notices. Your work seems not to matter to anybody. And then God sends someone with a kind word, and it's like water to a parched throat in the desert. **"We have different gifts, according to the grace given us. . . . If it is encouraging, let him encourage"** (Romans 12:6,8).

Have you ever noticed how people's faces light up when you praise them? Have you ever pondered what a few words of encouragement cost you? Nada. Encouragers have an inner self-confidence. They aren't emotionally needy and insecure, waiting for others to notice them. They have been given the gift of humility, happy to make somebody else look good. They can genuinely enjoy someone else's good fortune without cursing their own lot in life.

When you spot an encourager, you will probably find a crowd. Encouragers have a lot of friends.

Spirit gifts: Generosity

Maybe you know this already from personal experience, but people's generosity has little to do with their degree of wealth. Social scientists confirm that there is no correlation between wealth and generosity.

There is, however, a strong correlation between generosity and the Spirit of the Lord, one of whose most valuable gifts is a willingness to share resources. **"We have different gifts, according to the grace given us. . . . If it is contributing to the needs of others, let him give generously"** (Romans 12:6,8).

Why is that so hard?

Because we think it's *our* money. Because we are afraid we won't have enough for ourselves. Because we think other people's problems are their problems. Because we are driven by our own agenda, not God's. Because we think that sharing means we will have less.

In fact every one of those beliefs is untrue. In fact all we have really belongs to God and we are just his managers. In fact generosity in the lives of God's people moves him to release even more resources to us. In fact we were created for the sole purpose of giving glory to God and serving his agenda. In fact the Bible promises that those who refresh others will themselves be refreshed.

_____

_____

_____

_____

_____

Spirit gifts: Leadership

In real estate, as you probably know, the top three criteria for price are—ta-da!—location, location, location. In the world of the church, the top three criteria for a healthy and growing congregation are leadership, leadership, leadership.

Good leadership and governance are unfortunately not automatic in a Christian organization. Is your church well led and well governed? If it is, give thanks where thanks are due—to the Holy Spirit, who built those gifts into your leaders. **"We have different gifts, according to the grace given us. . . . If it is leadership, let him govern diligently"** (Romans 12:6,8).

Serving on a board of directors is often invisible and thankless work, but a strong board is critical for providing necessary checks and balances to staff, to represent the members' interests, and to clarify and articulate mission. Managing people and money well is way harder than it looks and usually involves late nights, aggravation, and hard decisions. Good leaders inspire people, know what needs to come next, have a nose for talent, and know how to say thank you.

May I invite you today to identify the three best people in leadership and governance in your church and find a way to give them your thanks personally? Also—send up a prayer flare to heaven to thank the Spirit who gave them to you.

_____

_____

_____

_____

_____

Spirit gifts: Showing mercy

"All people will know that you are my disciples if you love one another," said Jesus, right after he had washed his disciples' feet, right before he offered his life for their sins. Loving somebody else means that you choose to see his or her worth, that you value your relationship, that you wish to imitate Christ himself.

"We have different gifts, according to the grace given us. . . . If it is showing mercy, let him do it cheerfully" (Romans 12:6,8). Think for a minute how patient and kind our Lord has been with sinful jerks like us. Only one word will suffice: *mercy.* He saw our weakness and sorry condition *and didn't despise us.* The gospel's message of unconditional love is what made us believers; that message also inspires us to show that same kindness and mercy to people around us.

But do it in the right spirit. Grudging kindness does not please God. Freely have we received; freely should we give. A truly generous spirit doesn't calculate what he or she might get back from the act of mercy but simply enjoys passing on God's resources to someone whose need is urgent. A truly generous spirit knows that we are blessed to be a blessing.

This week you will probably come into contact with someone who is ill, broken, exhausted, or struggling. May God bless the time, money, and love that you invest in them.

What if I can't forget the past?

Communicating, listening, showing compassion, and emotional bonding are all things men in general need to work on. Holding grudges is one for the ladies. It can be wonderful to have a memory like an elephant when it comes to remembering anniversaries and distant relatives' names. It can be an anger prison when your thoughts are dominated by old hurts.

Some person long ago invented the cliché forgive and forget. That's impossible. You can't expunge pain memories from your mind as though tapping the Delete key. The key to moving on is to learn how to forgive *while remembering.*

St. Paul has some splendid advice for grudge holders: "[Love] **is not easily angered, it keeps no record of wrongs**" (1 Corinthians 13:5). In other words, you may indeed remember your partner's old sins, but you can choose not to continue blaming him. It's sort of like being a judge and ruling that the statute of limitations applies.

Choosing to keep no record of wrongs is learned behavior. You can do it.

_____

_____

_____

_____

_____

OCTOBER 23
I want to be happy

Some people hate shopping and venture out only to purchase what is absolutely necessary. Other people are almost addicted to the rush they get when they spend money. You know the drill: "When the going gets tough, the tough go shopping." What is it about spending money on ourselves that is so compulsive?

Well, we're all materialistic to some degree. If getting stuff makes me happy, then getting a lot more stuff will make me a lot happier, right? If we view happiness as something outside of us that we can acquire by getting stuff, we will end up chasing status symbols and designer toys and never have enough.

Here is God's wisdom: **"He who loves pleasure will become poor; whoever loves wine and oil will never be rich"** (Proverbs 21:17). There is nothing wrong with pleasure. God invented it. There is nothing wrong with wine and oil either; nor is there anything wrong with liking and appreciating the fruits of God's marvelous creation.

Here's the danger: when your likes become loves and your loves become cravings. Be careful.

_____

_____

_____

_____

_____

Tell me more

Does the Bible's brevity sometimes drive you batty? Are you as curious as I am for the "rest of the story"? Do you wish that God had been more generous with the content of his Word so that you would know the complete biography of Jesus, for instance, with a stenographic record of all of his teachings?

St. John, biographer #4, knows you do. Here's how his account ends: **"Jesus did many other things as well. If every one of them were written down, I suppose that even the whole world would not have room for the books that would be written"** (John 21:25). Our Lord, speaking through John, realizes that you and I would never have enough. The full history of every individual's encounter with God and his agenda would overwhelm even a library.

And so God gives us clippings and snippets (which— admit it—you could stand to read more often). He thinks we have enough Word for everything we need. The Bible is sufficient; it is able to make us wise for salvation and prepare us for every good work. It reveals the incredible identity of our Savior and tells us what we need to know about his wonderful saving work. Instead of pining for more, let's read more earnestly what we've got.

We can get the rest of the story in heaven.

_____

_____

_____

_____

_____

It's hard to be a minority

May I confess that I dislike the term *minority*? It's from the Latin word *minor*, which means "lesser" or "smaller." Just because you live or work or study in a place where you are outnumbered doesn't make you of lesser value.

Some brave people, like students studying abroad or entrepreneurial business agents, are completely surrounded by people not like them. That must be how Abraham felt. **"I am an alien and a stranger among you"** (Genesis 23:4), he said to the Hittites from whom he bought a burial plot.

It is a tremendous personal growth opportunity. When you are immersed in another culture or language, you have to adapt and learn to survive. People in the minority become bicultural—fluent and knowledgeable in an environment beyond their own. What a gift! It is also intensely lonely. It can be a perfect time to look for people connections to make up for the absence of family and old friends.

Christians who are open to God's opportunities for accepting one another can pay special attention to the "minorities" in their midst. That's how God connected Philip with an Ethiopian. Believers who are "aliens and strangers" can also use their differentness to get attention for their message. That's how Jonah connected with the Assyrians and what started Daniel on his rise to influence in Babylon.

_____

_____

_____

_____

_____

Victory for the whole world

If you live outside the U.S. and Canada, it probably sounds prideful for us to call the grand finale of the Major League Baseball season the World Series. After all, only North American teams are allowed to play. It's not like soccer's World Cup, which truly draws teams from all over the globe.

Jesus was an Asian male living in Israel in the first century A.D. But his victory over sin, death, hell, and Satan was not just for first-century Israelite Asian males. It was a truly universal redemption. **"If anybody does sin, we have one who speaks to the Father in our defense—Jesus Christ, the Righteous One. He is the atoning sacrifice for our sins, and not only for ours but also for the sins of the whole world"** (1 John 2:1,2).

Here are talking points when you have a chance to share your faith with someone on his or her way to a miserable eternity. First, the Savior has already made payment in full for all the person's sins of thought, word, and deed. Second, that payment is a gift. It does not have to be earned or deserved by the sinner.

Best of all, it is a sign of God's endless and universal love for all people. It is his greatest passion that every sinner on earth will embrace the gift, be forgiven, and be reunited forever with the Father.

_____

_____

_____

_____

_____

Your faith makes you beautiful

From what the women in my life tell me, flipping through a magazine makes them feel beaten down and ugly. The models are always skinny, and their hair and makeup are always perfect. Reading these magazines is as likely to be torture as pleasure.

I'll tell you what—when you flip through God's Book, you will find reminders that he is not interested in your outsides but in your insides: **"Charm is deceptive, and beauty is fleeting; but a woman who fears the LORD is to be praised"** (Proverbs 31:30).

Do you know why the external stuff doesn't matter to God? Because people can so easily turn charm on and off. Charmers are often users. Unscrupulous women ever since Delilah have been using looks and sexuality to get what they want. Do you need any convincing that beauty is fleeting? Have you looked closely in the mirror lately? How fast the wrinkles come!

But a woman who fears the Lord is a different story. How happy the home where the woman seeks first to please her Lord with words and actions. How happy the home where the Word of God guides the way she treats her husband and children. How happy the home where the woman lives, prays, and sings her faith.

You know, the list of virtues of the woman in Proverbs chapter 31 is not intended to intimidate women. Its intent is to get her husband and children to notice her worth and cherish especially her heart of faith. Let's hear it: "Mom, we all think you're awesome!"

God and my ignorance

Back when Jay Leno was on the *Tonight Show*, one of his most reliable gags was called "Jaywalking." He hiked around the streets of Los Angeles with a microphone, asking passersby basic questions about America, things middle-school students ought to know. The horrible ignorance of American history and government that he found was hysterically funny at first, but sad and depressing later.

You don't want to know how bad the average American Christian's basic Bible knowledge is. Surveys show that we struggle to name half of the Ten Commandments; get only some of the books of the Bible; and struggle to identify and distinguish the main characters of the most important Bible stories like Noah, Abraham, and Moses.

What's even worse than deficient Bible knowledge is deficient spiritual commitment. Learning about God's mighty acts in human history and about what he did through people is important not just for head knowledge of facts but to grow in faith and zeal to use your life to be useful to God's global rescue plan.

Here is a prayer for all who know that they need to grow both in Bible knowledge and in spiritual commitment: **"Teach me, O Lord, to follow your decrees; then I will keep them to the end. Give me understanding, and I will keep your law and obey it with all my heart"** (Psalm 119:33,34).

To the ends of the earth

Some people are offended and embarrassed when Christians send missionaries to other countries. In their view it shows disrespect to local religious beliefs when "Westerners" arrive and expect indigenous people to abandon their ancestral beliefs and accept theirs.

If the missionaries' vision was merely to change people's political system or diet preferences, that would indeed be cultural imperialism. But the dilemma of human sin and condemnation is global, and so is the rescue that Jesus Christ brought about.

The Bible says, **"He [Christ] is the atoning sacrifice for our sins, and not only for ours but also for the sins of the whole world"** (1 John 2:2). Do you see the beauty of it? Christ made the payment. Christ gives the benefits. Christ's work is universal.

The message that we entrust to our missionaries is the same message you need: the Creator of all saw the sins of all, sent his Son for all, and through him atoned for all. What remains is for us to announce the plan and for people to believe the plan and find the joy of living the plan.

_____

_____

_____

_____

_____

Till death us do part

It seems like a romantic thing to craft your own wedding vows and then say them while looking into your fiancée's eyes. I attended a wedding once where the young man got off to a great start with his customized vows, but then under the severe pressure, sweating profusely, it became obvious to all of us that he was freelancing halfway through. "And I pledge, uh, you my faithfulness, for, uh . . . as long as we shall be together."

Well, he didn't promise much of anything, did he? Just to stay together as long as they were together? Alas, the movie stars who set the standards for moral behavior in America today seem to be willing to promise no more than that. Any marriage that makes any claim to respect God's institution is a vow "until death us do part."

Easy divorce was a feature of Israelite life in the fifth century B.C. just as it is in ours. God's voice thundered, **"Has not the LORD made them one? In flesh and spirit they are his. . . . Do not break faith with the wife of your youth. 'I hate divorce,' says the LORD God"** (Malachi 2:15,16).

God hates divorce. His children do too. When you make your vows, say 'em right and mean what you say.

_____

_____

_____

_____

_____

OCTOBER 31
Zombies

American participation in and interest in religion is in steady decline (especially "organized" religion), but "spirituality" is big. The annual observance of Halloween has never been bigger. A friend of mine who operates an online costume rental/purchase service does 80% of his business in the month of October.

The dark side of spirituality also has never been bigger. TV shows and books about vampires and other creatures are always popular. Voodoo never went away, and ever since 1968's movie *Night of the Living Dead*, people have been fascinated with zombies.

Zombie is an African word that came to America through Haiti and refers to legends of corpses brought back to life through occult means. Michael Jackson's "Thriller" video notwithstanding, the bodies of the dead will stay dead and return to the dust of which they are made.

But the dead *will* live again, and whether or not they come back to life to an eternity of misery or ecstasy will depend on their relationship with Jesus Christ. **"Multitudes who sleep in the dust of the earth will awake: some to everlasting life, others to shame and everlasting contempt"** (Daniel 12:2).

What will you experience when you awake?

_____

_____

_____

_____

_____

November

Our citizenship is in heaven.
And we eagerly await a Savior from there,
the Lord Jesus Christ.
Philippians 3:20

The Lord's Prayer: The Address

Jesus' public ministry lasted for three years. He spoke to many different people on many different occasions. The four gospels preserve only relatively small amounts of his precious words. He clearly spoke about the same topics in similar language at different times. Both Matthew and Luke record slightly different versions of the magnificent prayer he taught his friends to use.

"One day Jesus was praying in a certain place. When he finished, one of his disciples said to him, 'Lord, teach us to pray, just as John taught his disciples.' He said to them, 'When you pray, say "[Our] Father [in heaven]"'" (Luke 11:1,2; Matthew 6:9).

The platform upon which all true prayer rests is to remember who you are and remember to whom you are speaking. You are addressing not an admiral or general, not a president or superhero, but your Father, your heavenly Father. You are related to him. He gave you birth and rebirth. He loves you more than you love your own children. You may claim his attention with childlike confidence because he has publicly claimed you through your baptism.

When you pray, you are not filling out a grant request to a heavenly charitable foundation. You are talking to your Father. And he loves taking care of his children.

_____

_____

_____

_____

_____

The First Petition

To get more out of the praying experience, Jesus leads you away from you. Have you noticed how most of the petitions in his model prayer lead you to think about *God's* program instead of yours? It's not that material things are unimportant. It's that God's Word and ways are far more important.

Jesus' first sentence has only four words. Don't rush when you say them. They are a mouthful. **"When you pray, say: 'Hallowed be your name'"** (Luke 11:2). God's "name" refers not only to the various proper names that the Scripture reveals to us, like Lord or Christ. God's name in its fuller sense is his self-revelation. It's the sum of what we know about God's person and work.

The word *hallow* has mostly faded from contemporary English. It means "to consider holy." You can't make God any holier than he is already, can you? But you *can* ask for God's help to lift up his holiness in your heart and make him look good to the people around you in your life.

That means no idols. That means taking out the trash in your mind and recommitting yourself to the *one* Creator, *one* Savior, *one* Counselor. That means radiating the conviction to all around you, "I'm proud of my God."

_____

_____

_____

_____

_____

The Second Petition

It is a mistake to think of God's kingdom as just a place. The whole earth is the Lord's and the heavens too. The Bible uses the term to refer to Christ's ruling activity, his "reigning" in people's hearts through their faith in him. **"When you pray, say: ' . . . Your kingdom come'"** (Luke 11:2).

When you utter that powerful prayer, you are urging on the Holy Spirit to do his wonderful work of creating and strengthening faith in more and more people's hearts. You are also committing yourself to that mission as his field representative.

I guess you could say that this petition is a mission prayer. You are praying that hell will be emptier and heaven fuller. You are praying that the Spirit will claim minds and hearts where the darkness of Satan used to lie like a poisonous night fog. You are praying that people who are born, live, and die slaves of sin and Satan will become citizens of the kingdom of the light of Christ.

Every material thing that you can touch with your hands will soon be taken from you as you die. The only thing you can take with you to heaven is people. Pray for them. Help them find out how wonderful it is to belong to King Jesus.

_____

_____

_____

_____

_____

The Third Petition

"Your will be done on earth as it is in heaven" (Matthew 6:10). Doesn't this sound backward? You come to God in prayer to tell him what you want, and then Jesus says that a better way is to come to God in prayer and first ask him what *he* wants.

Wise counsel. The point is that you won't know what is good for you until you are tuned into his goodness. You won't know what is the smart thing to pray for until you are first tuned into his wisdom.

Jesus modeled this humble, healthy attitude all the way to the cross. As he himself fought the terrible spiritual struggle to stay committed to the plan that he offer up his life, he went to his Father in prayer in the Garden of Gethsemane. He prayed, "Not my will but yours be done." The result was a strengthened resolve that led to Satan's crushing defeat and forgiveness won for the whole world.

The greatest and most satisfying moments in your life will occur when you are carrying out God's will as his joyful agent on earth.

_____

_____

_____

_____

_____

The Fourth Petition

Finally—Jesus invites us to ask for material things. After reorienting our priorities to put God on the throne of our lives, recommitting ourselves to his saving agenda, and vowing obedience to his will, we are ready to talk about physical things. **"When you pray, say: 'Give us each day our daily bread'"** (Luke 11:2,3).

It is a delightful practice to pray when sitting down to eat. It is totally appropriate that we give God credit for so richly and consistently supplying us with not only bread but all our food. Soil, rainfall, seeds, and sunshine all come from him. It is humbling but accurate to see God as the originator of every meal you eat.

"Daily bread" is also a metaphor for everything that you need to have a healthy and productive life. Jesus' choice of the lowly word *bread* is a reminder that God obligates himself to give you everything he thinks you need, though perhaps not everything you want.

Daily is also an allusion to the Israelites' *manna,* the miracle bread that appeared every day while they lived in the wilderness after the exodus from Egypt. "Daily bread" reminds us that God generally doesn't front us our supplies in advance. He prefers to dribble it out on an as-needed basis.

_____

_____

_____

_____

_____

The Fifth Petition

Only Christianity gives it away.

Every human being who has ever lived has a conscience and knows two things for sure: there is evil within me, and I am in some kind of trouble with the holy Power out there. When people make up their own religious systems, they always put the pressure on the individual to make amends. There are rules to keep, rituals to observe, propitiations and sacrifices, pilgrimages, and various acts of devotion and obedience. But only Christianity *gives* forgiveness away. Jesus invites you to ask for it.

"When you pray, say: 'Forgive us our sins, for we also forgive everyone who sins against us'" (Luke 11:2,4). Jesus Christ, on Calvary's cross, did all the obeying, sacrificing, and paying that was necessary. He bought forgiveness of sins for the whole world, and everyone who believes it has it. He gives it away.

He also charges his believers to show that same mercy to the fools and sinners who surround them each day. How can the first half of that prayer be so easy and the second half so hard? When you pray the Fifth Petition, pray it with all your might. Don't let Satan steal your absolute confidence of forgiveness, and don't let a shabby spirit withhold that same forgiveness to people who ask it of you.

_____

_____

_____

_____

_____

The Sixth Petition

Your heavenly Father watches your progress on the road to everlasting life and eagerly desires your success. He takes no delight in watching some fall away. Jesus urges you to ask the Father's help in staying strong: **"When you pray, say: '. . . Lead us not into temptation'"** (Luke 11:2,4).

James 1:13 shows us that God never tempts anyone to sin; he hates the very notion. The five little words in this petition are shorthand for a plea that God would have mercy on us because of our many sinful weaknesses and keep us from committing spiritual suicide. We are all prone to becoming careless, stubborn, hard of hearing, and reckless in the way we live, and we must keep imploring God to send his angels of protection.

You can help God answer that prayer. The Bible is a mighty resource to keep us out of temptation. It is armor for our hearts and a helmet for our brains. I hope you read some of it each day. He also sends other Christian people into your life—listen to them when they speak words of warning to you.

One of God's greatest gifts to you is your congregation. Cherish it and thank God for the strength you draw from it. Your pastor cares about your spiritual well-being, prays for your safe journey, and will help you watch out for the ditches.

_____

_____

_____

_____

_____

The Seventh Petition

Call me naïve, but I'd like to think that I don't have any enemies. I mean real enemies—people who would like to assault or kill me.

That's what Satan would like me to think. The Bible calls him a dragon, a lion, a serpent, always prowling about looking for people to devour. He is indeed a deadly enemy. He would like to attack us physically; invade our minds; re-enslave our wills; and trap us forever in the burning, sulfurous dungeon that is his destiny.

"When you pray, say: '. . . Deliver us from the evil one'" (Luke 11:2; Matthew 6:13). Mean this when you pray it. The words *devil* and *hell* have lost much of their meaning in the way people talk today. They are joke words, rude emphasis words. But they contain a deadly reality—that the prince of darkness is seeking whom he may devour, and he's coming for you.

Jesus crushed the serpent's head when he died and rose again. All people who trust in him as their Savior are forgiven and immortal, safe and secure. Claim your forgiveness from Christ, grow in knowledge and power from the Word, and pray for the final deliverance. When you are in heaven, you will never need to pray this petition again.

_____

_____

_____

_____

_____

The Doxology

The conclusion to the Lord's Prayer as we speak it in church is not found in the Bible. Protestants almost universally end it by saying, "The kingdom and the power and the glory are yours, now and forever."

Even though that *doxology* (a statement of praise to the Trinity) is not in the Bible's prayer, it still makes a great finishing statement to Jesus' teaching. It explains why we have confidence that all we ask for will be granted. It reaffirms our promise to make the Lord's name hallowed, work to extend his gracious rule in people's hearts, and make obedience to his will a life priority.

St. John heard a magnificent song from angels who surround the throne of God: **"Worthy is the Lamb who was slain, to receive power and wealth and wisdom and strength and honor and glory and praise!"** (Revelation 5:12).

A doxology like that one is a great way to end any prayer:

- We affirm that God is our supreme Ruler, our King.
- We affirm that God is able to do all we ask and more.
- We pledge to give him the honor and glory when he takes care of us as we ask.

And when you say "Amen" at the end, you put your personal exclamation point on what you just said. "That's the truth!"

_____

_____

_____

_____

_____

Bring healing

"You are so stupid." "You're worthless." "You will never amount to anything." "I hate you." "You are such a loser." I hope you've never heard those words, and I hope that you've never said them. But a great many people you know have been beaten down with words like those.

Words like those can damage people permanently. They crush the human spirit, maybe permanently. Our world is full of wounded adults who were badly hurt as children long ago, and sadly they perpetuate the abuse on others. But that's where you come in: **"Reckless words pierce like a sword, but the tongue of the wise brings healing"** (Proverbs 12:18).

Our wounded spirits have been healed, and are still in the process of being healed, by the gospel's love messages from God. Don't believe the abusers in your past! Believe the God of your present and future. And what a thrill it is to be useful to God by passing on his kindness to people who are starving for it. Let's practice: "Great job!" "I really like what you've done with your home." "I appreciate you so much." "Thanks for being my friend." "I value your advice." "I love you."

_____

_____

_____

_____

_____

Parent heartbreak

Years ago I was complaining to an older friend about the burden of raising small children. He grinned patronizingly, "Little children, little problems. Big children, big problems." How our children can hurt us! God told that to Eve already in Genesis chapter 3, and little did she know what was in store. She became the first in what would become a long stream of weeping mothers with sons who were murdered.

How our children can hurt us! We are so emotionally open to them—we can't protect our hearts when they are in trouble or have caused trouble for others. King David undoubtedly knew that his weak parenting was partly to blame for his rebellious son Absalom's treason, and that made his death hurt all the more: **"The king was shaken. He went up to the room over the gateway and wept. As he went, he said: 'O my son Absalom! My son, my son Absalom! If only I had died instead of you—O Absalom, my son, my son!'"** (2 Samuel 18:33).

When our children stray, what can we do but pray that the seeds of the Word that we planted in their youth will not be forgotten, that after a time they will be recalled and believed. We can pray that after a time God will use whatever size two-by-four he needs to get their attention and lead them to repentance before it's too late.

_____

_____

_____

_____

_____

The future matters more

The first two mentions of Mark in the New Testament are not particularly flattering, and sometimes I wish I were not named after him. He is probably the young man who happened to be without an undergarment in the Garden of Gethsemane. As guards tried to seize him, they caught his outer garment. He fled naked, leaving the garment in their hands (Mark 14:51,52).

It gets worse. He accompanied Paul on his first missionary journey, but he did not prove worthy. **"Barnabas wanted to take John, also called Mark, with them, but Paul did not think it wise to take him, because he had deserted them in Pamphylia and had not continued with them in the work"** (Acts 15:37,38).

So he's a runaway and a deserter. But he matured and changed. As he grew up in his faith, he grew also in perseverance and spiritual stamina. Peter so valued his work that in 1 Peter 5:13 he called him **"my son Mark."** Most scholars think that Peter provided eyewitness source material for the biography of Jesus Christ that Mark wrote and which became the second book of the New Testament.

Here's what I love about "John" Mark—he did not let the failures and breakdowns in his earlier life characterize him permanently. When God let him know that he still had use for him, Mark answered the bell. God's grace helped him back on his feet. Mark helps me remember that my God is more interested in my future than in my past. Yours too.

_____

_____

_____

_____

Is your money for rent?

The concept of interest on saved money has a strange history as it relates to religion. Many Muslim scholars believe that the Quran forbids usury, by which they understand the charging of any interest from one Muslim to another. This tends to make banking almost impossible, and enterprising Muslim businesspeople who need capital have to find all kinds of creative and contorted ways to borrow and save.

Historically many influential Christian teachers in times past also have thundered against the evils of "usury," by which they meant any charging of interest on loaned money. Since Jews weren't bound by that peculiar teaching, they would be willing to rent capital, which unfortunately tended to associate medieval Jews with money lending (like Shakespeare's character Shylock).

No less an authority than Jesus himself told a parable in which he put words in his own royal mouth, advising a savings account as a basic form of investment: **"You should have put my money on deposit with the bankers, so that when I returned I would have received it back with interest"** (Matthew 25:27).

On your Federal Form 1040, our government calls this unearned income. I think it's mighty hard work to keep your mitts off your savings so that these hard-earned funds can generate a return. You've earned your interest income.

_____

_____

_____

_____

Appreciating the artists

Some Christians long for simplicity, even stark and severe plainness, in their churches. I can appreciate their desire to reserve all their focus and attention for the Word of God, that they want their worship space to look like everyday life, not like a theater or hotel ballroom.

But that's not me. I long for a separate space, a sanctified, other worldly space, where designers and artists have been commissioned to use the materials of God's world—the copper, oak, glass, fabrics, stone, gold leaf, and paint—to express God's wonderful works and our great joy in worship. I thrive on visuals, on color and form, to lift up my spirit from the dust to the skies.

I celebrate and appreciate people like the man whom King Hiram of Tyre sent to King Solomon of Israel to assist in the construction of the grand temple in Jerusalem, a place of worship where the God of gods and Lord of lords would make his earthly home: **"I am sending you Huram-Abi, a man of great skill. . . . He is trained to work in gold and silver, bronze and iron, stone and wood, and with purple and blue and crimson yarn and fine linen. He is experienced in all kinds of engraving and can execute any design given to him. He will work with your craftsmen"** (2 Chronicles 2:13,14).

To all designers, artists, and crafters in service to the Lord, thank you! Love your work.

_____

_____

_____

_____

Devoted to fellowship

Golfing by yourself is not a lot of fun. It's okay for practicing, but it pales next to playing in a foursome. What's the fun of making a hole in one—or even just hitting a good shot—when you're golfing by yourself? First of all, nobody will believe you and second, you want to be with people to celebrate the PGA-level shots and to groan and laugh together about the lame ones.

Expressing and sharing your faith isn't for loners either. One of the best parts of a Christian family is that you get to be with people. People who love Jesus. People who are motivated by Jesus' love for them and as a result find it possible to love you. People who help carry your burdens when you're sad and celebrate the very best times in your life when you're happy.

The Bible says, **"As we have opportunity, let us do good to all people, especially to those who belong to the family of believers"** (Galatians 6:10).

This week, look at the believers around you. God sent them to make your life better. Or perhaps he sent you to them to make their lives better. Or both. See if you can figure out how.

_____

_____

_____

_____

_____

I feel useless

I used to visit a sweet little old man named Alex. He was a dear guy, but pretty self-centered, with a perpetually gloomy outlook. At some point in every conversation he would say, "Ah, I'm no good no more." He saw no purpose in his continuing existence. He had defined the minimum for a satisfied life, and in his mind he was sure he would never again reach even that minimum.

Do you ever suffer from Alexitis? Have you doubted that your life had a purpose any greater than just survival? Are you just consuming air, water, and food and taking up space?

You exist for the same reason God created Adam and Eve and the rest of his children: to be loved by God and to love him back . . . to have his value system and attitudes become yours . . . to adopt his agenda for spending your resources and energy. The more we turn inward and care only about ourselves, the more we will get sick of life. "Meaningless," Solomon says over and over in the book of Ecclesiastes.

There is a better way. The more you serve other people, the more you spend yourself to make other people's lives better, the more fulfilled you will feel. At the top of the pyramid is sharing the message of Christ. **"I will not die but live, and will proclaim what the LORD has done"** (Psalm 118:17).

Ministry failure

As a child I enjoyed hearing about the amazing missionary journeys of St. Paul and the astounding successes he had in one city after another, planting congregations in spite of ferocious hardships, recruiting and training new leaders, and performing amazing miracles.

But it wasn't all seashells and balloons. Just as Jesus' own ministry initially yielded more unbelievers than believers, Paul also suffered some severe setbacks. **"Their teaching will spread like gangrene. Among them are Hymenaeus and Philetus, who have wandered away from the truth. They say that the resurrection has already taken place, and they destroy the faith of some"** (2 Timothy 2:17,18).

Your congregation probably has some great stories of triumph and progress. But you may also have experienced days of bitter disappointments. People you thought were solid in the faith wandered off or—worse—stayed and caused divisions in the group.

These setbacks do not mean that there's something wrong with the gospel message or something wrong with you. Jesus predicted that these things would happen. Expect them. Stay dialed into the Word as your personal source of truth and your personal source of strength and let God sort out the macro picture.

He will take care of people like Hymenaeus and Philetus in his own way and his own time. Don't panic. He will protect you and get you safely home.

_____

_____

_____

I'm lost

You've heard the proverb, "You can't go home again." Can prodigal daughters and sons go back to God after they have run away for a long time?

Am I talking about you? Or maybe someone you know? How do you get back with God? What if it's been years, or even decades, since you've been in church? Is it too late? What if you don't even know what to think or how to believe anymore? What if you've forgotten the path once learned in Sunday school eons ago?

Here's the beauty of it: you may have forgotten God's voice, but he still knows yours. Your love for him may have cooled, but his for you is greater than ever. You may have lost track of him, but he knows exactly where you are. Here is a prayer you can pray when you feel lost: **"O LORD, you have searched me and you know me. You know when I sit and when I rise; you perceive my thoughts from afar"** (Psalm 139:1,2).

It's back to the gospel. Remember: God's love for you is based not on your performance but on Christ's. His mercy is bigger than your folly. His arms are still stretched out wide. No, it's not too late. Come home before it is.

_____

_____

_____

_____

_____

What are you morphing into?

Do your kids or grandkids like to watch Transformers cartoons or play with Transformers action toys? These mechanical marvels look like robots but can transform themselves into vehicles or aircraft. There is ceaseless war between the good Autobots and the Decepticons, led by the evil Megatron.

You and I may enjoy the fantasy that we are sovereign and independent agents in life, clearheaded and in control, but in actuality we are all changing into something or another and the only question is what we are changing into. The war between good and evil is real, and Satan, the true Megatron, is trying to morph us into copies of himself—people who throw off God's authority and despise his Word; people who love money, worship power, and use other people as stepping-stones or props.

Heads up! **"Do not conform any longer to the pattern of this world, but be transformed by the renewing of your mind. Then you will be able to test and approve what God's will is—his good, pleasing and perfect will"** (Romans 12:2).

Would your family members say that the ways in which you've changed in the last five years are good? What are you allowing into your mind today? How might you let the Spirit of the Lord influence your thinking?

Looking for joy

You know the old phrase that says you get what you pay for. Long ago some Christian amended that proverb to this: you get what you pray for. I'd like to add a third: you find what you're looking for.

If you have a basically pessimistic outlook on life, if you expect to be disappointed by people, encounter moral and ethical failures, run into financial hardships, and suffer rejection, you will find all those things. If on the other hand you choose an optimistic worldview, if you believe that Christ has risen, that all things are possible in him, that every day you will meet awesome people, that God's help and support will keep coming from a variety of angles, that there is a solution for every problem, then that's what you will experience.

Are you looking for joy? Do you believe that there still is goodness in the people God is sending into your life? "[Love] **always protects, always trusts, always hopes, always perseveres**" (1 Corinthians 13:7). That isn't blind faith. It's eyes-wide-open faith, because it's not based on naïve and wishful thinking. It's not a foolish projection of one's own fantasy life. It's based on God's clear promise. Jesus' resurrection made him a winner. Your faith in Jesus makes you a winner too.

Look for joy today and you will find it.

Grateful for grace

One of life's bitterest ironies from God's point of view is that the lowlifes of Jewish society, the tax collectors and prostitutes and "sinners," were more likely to listen to Jesus and welcome his message of grace and forgiveness. The church people, the Pharisees and teachers, didn't need him and didn't want him.

It's because they weren't aware of their many sins and because they rated themselves proficient and advanced in personal holiness by comparison with the lowlifes that they were uninterested in the message of a Savior. "Saved from *what*?" they thought. "I'm fine!" Then there were people like the woman who had lived a sinful life, who wet Jesus' *feet* with her tears, wiped them with her *hair*, and then anointed him with some of her perfume. Criticism broke out like water from a ruptured dam, but Jesus shushed them: **"Therefore, I tell you, her many sins have been forgiven— for she loved much. But he who has been forgiven little loves little"** (Luke 7:47).

People on the margins of society know their failures. They are *painfully* aware of their failures. Their thirst for hope and a rescue makes the gospel sound sweet in their ears. They are grateful for grace. People whose pride keeps them unaware of their own need, not so much. Jesus' observation back then is still true today—people who know they've been forgiven much will love much.

_____

_____

_____

_____

You are able to resist temptation

TV dramas and movies generally portray sexual excitement only between people who are not married to each other. "Falling in love" is exciting because you can't control those desires—you can only obey them. "Out of control" sexuality seems to make better video.

Genesis chapter 39 brings us the unbelievably wonderful story of a manservant with enough self-control to resist the allure of a quickie with a wealthy and beautiful married woman who was throwing herself at him. **"Now Joseph was well-built and handsome, and after a while his master's wife took notice of Joseph and said, 'Come to bed with me.' But he refused. . . . 'My master has withheld nothing from me except you, because you are his wife. How then could I do such a wicked thing and sin against God?'"** (Genesis 39:6-9).

Our sexed-up culture bombards us all with the message, "Resistance is futile. Go for it, and who cares about consequences." Joseph is a hero who shows that we can indeed resist. *¡Si se puede!* ("Yes, we can!") Imagine how different our world would be without all the adultery. Imagine all the damage that adultery has done—fatherless children, broken marriages, and STDs.

Sexual love is fulfilling and guilt free only when it is expressed by a man and woman who are married to each other. Do you believe that?

_____

_____

_____

_____

I'm afraid of being found out

Everybody has secrets, things we are glad other people don't know. But some people are sitting on past secrets that would drop a bomb on their lives if the information ever got out. What's in your closet? Maybe it's a felony for which you were never caught. Maybe you are an illegal alien. Maybe you cheated on your spouse.

Maybe you got your job under false pretenses. Maybe your kids have been in major trouble with the police, but your family doesn't know it. Yet. Maybe the college degree(s) you claim are phony. Maybe your life looks normal on the outside, but you are so deeply in debt that you could lose your home.

How many people know your darkest secret? Do you live in fear that someone could rat you out? This is a timeless problem. **"A gossip betrays a confidence"** (Proverbs 11:13).

Where can you go with these fears? Lord, have mercy! Lord, help me! Pray that the Lord of compassion and mercy will keep the lid on that destructive information. If it was your carelessness or evil deed that put you at risk, learn from your error, fix what you can, and give the rest to God. But if it is you who holds power over someone else, remember what God thinks of those who betray confidences. Show to others the same mercy God has shown you.

_____

_____

_____

_____

_____

NOVEMBER 24
I don't know

For us pastors, three words that come very hard from our lips are *I don't know*. We try so hard to have answers from the Word for all your questions, but God's activity in human history is so vast and his Word is often so very terse, that we need to exercise some humility about the limits of our understanding. And that's okay.

An example: Genesis chapter 5 hints at the life of an amazing man named Enoch, an ancestor of Christ, a powerful witness to the Word, one of the seventh generation of humans on earth. **"By faith Enoch was taken from this life, so that he did not experience death; he could not be found, because God had taken him away"** (Hebrews 11:5). Enoch went straight to heaven and bypassed the grave. Why is he an exception to the iron law of human death? Ahem . . . I don't know.

God has demonstrated such integrity that even if I don't know the reason, I know there is a good reason. I look forward to meeting Enoch and hearing more of his story. There's much, much more that I do not know. But I do know this—God made me, God loves me, Christ died and rose for me, the Spirit lives in me, and my name is written on the palm of his hand so that he's never, ever going to forget me.

_____

_____

_____

_____

_____

Pray for its prosperity

In Daniel's visions of the four great empires that were to rule the Middle East for the next millennium (chapter 7), the Babylonian Empire, in whose government he was serving, was depicted as a beast. Daniel himself had been deported from Judea as an unwilling captive following the crushing defeat of the Judean armies. Babylonian soldiers had looted the temple and carted the sacred worship vessels back east.

And yet the prophet Jeremiah had this to say to those exiled in Babylon: **"Seek the peace and prosperity of the city to which I have carried you into exile. Pray to the Lord for it, because if it prospers, you too will prosper"** (Jeremiah 29:7).

If the Israelites were expected to pray for Babylon, how much more should our hearts overflow on behalf of America? What a wonderful place to live! How precious are our personal and religious freedoms! How blessed we are! Thank you, Lord!

_____

_____

_____

_____

_____

Will I be recognizable in heaven?

Of course you will. Your personality, skills, abilities, and relationships were all designed by God to last beyond the grave. You may look a little different from the way you appeared in your casket—Scripture promises that you will undergo complete physical restoration—and so you might have to wear a name tag at first.

The Bible calls Jesus the first installment of the resurrection from the dead, and so a peek at the resurrection stories is instructive. The risen Christ looked like himself, had his memory, and rose with a fully functioning human body. He ate fish with his disciples and touched them. He used his lips and tongue to communicate with them in human speech.

Or consider Elijah, given the extraordinary gift of avoiding death altogether. **"Jesus took with him Peter, James and John the brother of James, and led them up a high mountain by themselves. There he was transfigured before them. His face shone like the sun, and his clothes became as white as the light. Just then there appeared before them Moses and Elijah, talking with Jesus"** (Matthew 17:1-3).

Like Moses and Elijah, we will be recognizable as ourselves and enjoy an eternity of being with our families, our friends, and with the Lord. And have plenty of time to make a lot of new friends.

_____

_____

_____

_____

Discipline them

Scripture has some miserable examples of men who were not engaged in the lives of their boys. The priest Eli was one. His sons ran the worship life of the tabernacle like their personal racket and committed adultery with women from the Service Guild. King David was a great warrior but had some miserable failures among his boys. Even the prophet Samuel had two wild children, enriching themselves through bribery and illicit gain.

The Bible tells us, **"Discipline your son, and he will give you peace; he will bring delight to your soul"** (Proverbs 29:17). So what exactly does that entail?

Discipline begins with a parent's willingness to spend time and energy to shape attitudes and behaviors. Love sets boundaries so that a child knows what is good and bad, what he or she is free to do and not free to do. Discipline involves punishment, because sometimes people learn best through pain. It isn't simply punishment though; it is a process in which you help to shape a person's attitudes and values and behavior to reflect God's ways.

Lord, grant peace in our homes and delight in our souls!

_____

_____

_____

_____

_____

Shop till you drop

Do you know people who get into the sales and shopping hype at this time of year? You know, the ones who get up really early to get the deals? How about you—do you love or hate the big sale days?

People just can't resist getting lured into the frenzy. The media enjoy whipping us into a lather—"must shop . . . must get to sale . . . must buy more . . . must go now . . ." People push and shove and fight over the last sale item. Somehow the occasion of the birth of our Savior, the annual festival of the incarnation of the Son of God in human likeness, has become the critical factor in whether or not business in America finishes in the black or red.

Christians must manage their time, their value system, and their priorities, or they too will be sucked into the craziness. Do you feel pressured by relatives to perform? Do you feel that you have to "give a great Christmas" to someone? What really matters this month and next, and what can you let go of? Who's on your list? What's in your wallet? Who's in your heart? Is it the One who said, **"Watch out! Be on your guard against all kinds of greed; a man's life does not consist in the abundance of his possessions"** (Luke 12:15)?

_____

_____

_____

_____

_____

Stretch

Nobody mends clothes anymore. Machine-made fabrics and mechanical sewing and assembly on a huge scale have made clothes so cheap that when something tears you just pitch it out and buy another. Even the poor can go to a thrift store and outfit their kids for a few dollars.

But in the days when all clothes were painstakingly made by hand from cloth woven by hand from yarn spun by hand from fleeces sheared by hand, the cost of a garment was so high that most people owned only one or two changes of clothes. If something tore, you patched it.

Jesus used that sewing metaphor to help Christians, and perhaps especially the organized church, to prepare to flex and change. **"No one sews a patch of unshrunk cloth on an old garment, for the patch will pull away from the garment, making the tear worse"** (Matthew 9:16). The message that the church has been entrusted to share is nonnegotiable. It must never change. But the style by which it is communicated, and the way in which ministries are organized, are infinitely negotiable. Changing demographics and changing culture and changing technology mean that the church must always be reexamining and reinventing its ways of connecting with people.

Too much old cloth and the times will rip a hole in it.

_____

_____

_____

_____

_____

NOVEMBER 30

Desertion

Military commanders hate desertion. It drains the fighting strength of their unit and is terrible for morale. It is also contagious if not dealt with, and so historically deserters who were arrested were often in for severe punishment— imprisonment, flogging, or even execution.

Ministry leaders hate desertion too. Not only does it deprive the church's ministries of someone's talents, relationships, and energy, but people are concerned about the spiritual state of the soul and heart of the deserter. St. Paul recruited and trained a phenomenal core group of workers for the Lord, but he wasn't able to keep them all. He wrote to one of his top assistants named Timothy: **"Do your best to come to me quickly, for Demas, because he loved this world, has deserted me"** (2 Timothy 4:9,10).

How it must have pained Jesus to lose Judas. How it pains me to see once spiritually active people drop out of regular worship. But I must say that one of my greatest joys as a pastor is to see someone respond to loving invitations and come back to the Lord.

Does your congregation have a board of elders or spiritual care team that seeks after at-risk members? Today would be a good day to pray for them and their work.

_____

_____

_____

_____

_____

December

Give thanks to the God of heaven.
His love endures forever.
Psalm 136:26

DECEMBER 1

Expect hostility

In theory we know that there won't be heaven on earth, that we won't experience heaven until we're in heaven, but we just can't stop fantasizing and wishfully expecting that since we're Christians all conflict and trouble will die down in our lives.

David was such a faithful follower of the Lord that God called him a man after his own heart. But even a wise king and phenomenal warrior like David experienced life blowups, like the time he had to flee from his rebel son Absalom. To make matters worse, he had to experience the howling abuse of a man named Shimei as he fled: **"As King David approached Bahurim, a man from the same clan as Saul's family came out from there. His name was Shimei, son of Gera, and he cursed as he came out. He pelted David and all the king's officials with stones, though all the troops and the special guard were on David's right and left."** The king said, **"Leave him alone; let him curse"** (2 Samuel 16:5,6,11).

Though with one royal command his enraged soldiers would have put Shimei down like a rabid animal, David bowed his head and endured the abuse. He was absolutely confident that the Lord would turn his troubles inside out, and he walked ahead into the future without fear.

Expect hostility. Trust the Lord. Don't be afraid.

_____

_____

_____

_____

_____

Build up your leaders

Much of the Christian life involves stringing your hammock between two seemingly contradictory ideas. Are we sinners or saints? Well, er, the truth is we're both. Should we plant and build for the next one thousand years or assume that the world could end tomorrow. The answer is yes.

Are we kings and priests of God, free to serve him as we will, or part of an authority structure? You know the answer—both are true. A congregation is a family of ministers who gives leadership roles and a promise of loyalty and cooperation to certain qualified people in their organization.

How you treat them shows what you think of God. **"Obey your leaders and submit to their authority. They keep watch over you as men who must give an account. Obey them so that their work will be a joy, not a burden, for that would be of no advantage to you"** (Hebrews 13:17).

Leaders can't lead if people will not choose to follow.

_____

_____

_____

_____

_____

DECEMBER 3
Silence is not an option

During their three-year training period, Jesus' disciples were not particularly good ambassadors for him. The remarks they blurted out revealed men who were often confused, personally vain and ambitious, and vengeful. They talked when they should have been listening, and they fell silent and even ran away when their testimony was needed.

But the Lord stuck with them. He sent his Spirit upon them and transformed them from cowards into champions of the faith. Even when threatened with imprisonment, physical abuse, and death, they knew that silence was not an option: **"We cannot help speaking about what we have seen and heard"** (Acts 4:20).

We are all raw material like them at first. But the more we let God speak to us in his Word, the more we let him use us in his agenda, the more our confidence will grow, and the more we will agree that silence is not an option. We have been blessed with the knowledge and understanding of the outcome of the great war between good and evil, Christ and Satan, life and death.

How can we not speak about what we've seen and heard?

_____

_____

_____

_____

_____

Hidden treasure

Stories abound in the settlement of the American West of people who rushed to establish clear legal title to land they were sure was valuable—land with grazing rights, water rights, and especially mining rights. Prospectors in particular tried their best to keep anyone else from finding out about a lucky strike until they had solidified their ownership. They didn't want anyone "jumping" their claim.

Jesus told a story once about a man's lucky find and what he did to secure it: **"The kingdom of heaven is like treasure hidden in a field. When a man found it, he hid it again, and then in his joy went and sold all he had and bought that field"** (Matthew 13:44). This doesn't mean that when you discover God's amazing grace through Jesus Christ you keep it a secret. The gospel is meant to be shared.

Jesus meant that so valuable is a living relationship with God, the forgiveness of your sins, a clean conscience, clear guidance to a happy life, and the promise of immortality in heaven that it is worth whatever you may have to sacrifice in order to live that life.

Is there anything keeping you from following God? Are the friends you hang with boat anchors for your soul? Does the pursuit of money leave you with no time or energy for the pursuit of understanding God and his Word?

_____

_____

_____

_____

_____

DECEMBER 5
You owed God a tithe then

Psalm 24 says that the entire earth is the Lord's and
everything in it. Psalm 50 says that the cattle on a thousand
hills all belong to him. God brought that concept home to his
minor children in Old Testament times by "taxing" them
10% of their income.

That 10% was called the tithe. **"A tithe of everything from
the land, whether grain from the soil or fruit from the
trees, belongs to the Lord; it is holy to the Lord. . . . The
entire tithe of the herd and flock—every tenth animal that
passes under the shepherd's rod—will be holy to the
Lord"** (Leviticus 27:30-32).

There were various opportunities for the Israelites to give
freewill offerings of livestock, produce, or money to the
Lord, but those would have to be given on top of the base
tithe, which they were not free to ignore.

Christians today, and especially Christian ministry
leaders, need to be very careful in their use of the term *tithe*.
A return of 10% to the Lord, if freely chosen, is a wonderful
thing. But the law of the tithe belongs to the Old Covenant,
and God's people today must feel free to choose their gifts to
the Lord, even if church leaders are nervous about making
their budgets.

_____

_____

_____

_____

_____

Give gifts from your heart now

It's sad to hear stories of people who have dropped out of church life because of money issues. The church should not treat its members like children, making rules for their faith lives. It shouldn't act like a country club either, charging membership fees. God's people are royal priests and need to be treated as such.

God is still the Creator and Owner of everything on earth. He is still the Giver of everything you own and every dime of your income. But he invites you to honor him with gifts of your choosing, and he waits to see what you will do with your freedom.

St. Paul gave some wonderful guidance (note: not rules) on how to make your giving decisions in the advice he gave the Christians in Corinth who were gathering an offering for famine relief in Judea: **"Now about the collection for God's people: Do what I told the Galatian churches to do. On the first day of every week, each one of you should set aside a sum of money in keeping with his income"** (1 Corinthians 16:1,2).

Here's how to think about your giving decisions: (a) *Each one.* Giving is for all. (b) *First.* Make your giving decisions first before your check is gone. (c) *Regularly.* Give as often as God gives to you. (d) *Proportionately.* You choose the percentage as a spiritual adult. Give it to God's glory, and give it with a heart full of rejoicing to the one who has given you everything.

Crooked or straight

A meaningful Christmas experience will not come to you. You must go to it.

If you do nothing, all you will notice is that most stores are closed on December 25 and there isn't much traffic. If you are interested in an encounter with the Savior of all mankind, listen to the public relations agent that God himself commissioned during the first Advent time of preparation: **"Prepare the way for the Lord, make straight paths for him,"** John the Baptist said (Luke 3:4). What on earth does that mean?

It means using the precious days before the celebration of the birth to straighten out crooked thinking in our minds, to fill in the ditches of despair and fear, and to level the obstructing hills of pride. It means recognizing that what drove God's Son to come to earth as a human being was the wretched and damnable evil that lurks in every human heart. It means humbling yourself before a love so great that it agreed to be born in a barn.

Has your house preparation begun? Have some fun with all you do. Spend within your means; take on what you can handle joyfully. Shop, decorate, wrap, bake, give with a smile.

Has your heart preparation begun? Will Jesus Christ feel like the most important treasure there?

_____

_____

_____

_____

_____

Show compassion

Some of the wisest words ever uttered about building great family relationships came from a career bachelor—St. Paul. Inspired by the Holy Spirit, though, he identified Christlike qualities to cultivate in yourself that will make you a joy to live with. Even though he wasn't speaking specifically about marriage, there are few passages in Scripture that better contribute to a "happily ever after" marriage.

He uses the analogy of putting on clothes. Not wedding clothes. Marriage clothes. Here's one of those qualities: **"As God's chosen people, holy and dearly loved, clothe yourselves with compassion"** (Colossians 3:12).

Compassion comes from two Latin words meaning "suffering along with someone." It is the wonderful characteristic in a loving spouse that makes one willing to hear a partner's bad news, share a partner's pain, go through a partner's stress.

This one is primarily for the men. Guys, when you ask her how her day went, look at her the whole time, listen to it all, don't look at a clock, and let her know that your heart resonates with everything she's been through. Don't try to fix it or fix her. Don't interrupt. Just listen and let her bond emotionally with you. That's compassion.

_____

_____

_____

_____

_____

They will come streaming in

It's hard for the old guard when they realize that the ethnic group that founded their community/congregation/school/whatever is drifting away and being replaced by "people not like us." It's easy to criticize the insularity of the first generation of Jewish Christians, who were dismayed about letting Gentiles into their congregations. Realize, however, that for centuries the Jews had thought they were the only believers (and would always be the only ones). They were the chosen.

Two dysfunctions arise from such insularity. One is that as your tribe fades, you think all is lost. The other is that as new peoples pour into your community, you fear that the heritage and traditions will be lost and soon the message itself will be lost. Isaiah assures fearful Jewish believers and nervous old guardians today: **"Lift up your eyes and look about you: All assemble and come to you. . . . Then you will look and be radiant, your heart will throb and swell with joy"** (Isaiah 60:4,5).

Outreach works. If you really care about reaching out to people not like you, it will happen, and new believers sooner or later will outnumber the original ethnic group. *Pssst*—wanna know a secret? It's okay. In fact, it's God's ongoing plan.

_____

_____

_____

_____

_____

Joseph, husband of Mary

Joseph is my hero. The Holy Spirit brought about a virgin pregnancy in his fiancée, but God allowed Joseph a miserable stretch of time in ignorance during which he must have assumed that his dear Mary had been unfaithful to him. How bitter it is for a man to think that another man's baby is growing within the woman he loves.

At just the right time, God sent an angel messenger to bring Joseph into the plan. Even though the details were unbelievable, Joseph believed. **"When Joseph woke up, he did what the angel of the Lord had commanded him and took Mary home as his wife"** (Matthew 1:24).

I love this man. He stuck with Mary and endured the looks and comments of the Nazareth peanut gallery. He put his career on hold to take the family to Bethlehem for the Roman tax registration. When Herod's death threats made Bethlehem unsafe, he took the little family to Egypt to lie low until Herod's death. He cheerfully accepted his role as stepfather.

He himself, not Mary, was of the royal bloodline of the kings of Judah, and he gave to his stepson the right to be called the Son of David, the last and greatest King of the house of Judah.

_____

_____

_____

_____

_____

God works great things

What a change takes place in your mind and imagination when it dawns on you that you are not the star of your own play, when it dawns on you that you are actually working for God and not vice versa. You are an employee in his company! That means that he sets up your job description, assigns you a salary, and determines your benefit package.

What a relief it is when it dawns on you that your earthly life is not the be-all and end-all. This is training time. God is using us as he needs us, and we often can't see our influence or roles clearly. Sometimes we serve his agenda by being strong, sometimes by being broken. Sometimes we serve his agenda by being famous as achievers and sometimes by "failing." What matters is to accept his guidance eagerly and accept his place and opportunities in life cheerfully.

Here is the bright hope that draws us on: **"Instead of their shame my people will receive a double portion, and instead of disgrace they will rejoice in their inheritance; and so they will inherit a double portion in their land, and everlasting joy will be theirs"** (Isaiah 61:7).

God always gets the last word. Even when you feel like a failure now, his last word is *Winner!*

_____

_____

_____

_____

_____

DECEMBER 12
Leave a legacy

The potential client was listening to the life insurance guy and interrupted: "So let me get this straight. If I die . . ." He couldn't finish the sentence because the salesman was laughing. "What do you mean, *if* you die?"

Call me naïve, but I'm a family guy, and I've always kind of assumed that most people have given some serious thought to getting their financial records in order for the time when they die, so that their estate can be passed on to their heirs in an orderly way and so that they can give a gift to the Lord's work one last time.

How wrong I was. State probate officials report that almost 70% of Americans die intestate (without a will). How is it possible for otherwise reasonably bright people to push that important planning into perpetual mañana?

Wouldn't you like to leave your children and your church something besides debts? **"A good man leaves an inheritance for his children's children"** (Proverbs 13:22).

DECEMBER 13
Share your toys

Have you noticed by now how many teachings of Christ are paradoxes (that is, they seem to contradict established principles of human life)? When Jesus said that in God's world "the last shall be first and the first shall be last," he really meant it. God's economics sometimes require a leap of faith, but here's the amazing thing—his principles work just as he promises!

Here's an example: **"A generous man will prosper; he who refreshes others will himself be refreshed"** (Proverbs 11:25). You'd think that this is absurd. After all, if I give my stuff to other people, I will automatically have less. But in Godonomics, people who trust his words and dare to live them will find his magic and "refreshing" all over the place.

God loves it when you show hospitality . . . share food with the hungry . . . contribute to a homeless shelter . . . volunteer at a thrift store . . . mentor a fatherless kid . . . hire a disabled adult . . . guard a school crossing . . . drive an elderly person to the doctor . . .

_____

_____

_____

_____

_____

How do I love thee?

Elizabeth Barrett Browning had simply titled her poetry "Sonnet 43," but her 14 lines made it one of the most famous poems in the English language.

How do I love thee? Jewelry stores are buying immense amounts of TV airtime right now, helping the concept to dawn on romantically minded men young and old to purchase gifts at their stores that will thrill the hearts of the females whose attention these men desire. Black Friday kicked off the mad annual rush of "Santamas," stoking the crazed materialism of our culture to an even greater degree. Is your life still sane, or do you fear that it is out of control? Do you feel the pressure mounting, or are you enjoying this month?

How much does your God love thee? This much: **"This is how God showed his love among us: He sent his one and only Son into the world that we might live through him. This is love: not that we loved God, but that he loved us and sent his Son as an atoning sacrifice for our sins"** (1 John 4:9,10).

If your Christmas is built around that kind of love, everything else will fall into place.

_____

_____

_____

_____

_____

Church yeast

Only bakers really appreciate the usefulness and function of yeast. Bread made without it stays flat and compact, and it is not particularly enjoyable to eat unless baked in thin sheets. Yeast in dough reacts with the starches and produces carbon dioxide, which causes the whole ball of dough to expand and rise. When baked, the yeast dies, but the air pockets remain, creating fluffier and tastier bread.

That's how the Spirit works among people. Jesus **"told them still another parable: 'The kingdom of heaven is like yeast that a woman took and mixed into a large amount of flour until it worked all through the dough'"** (Matthew 13:33). When yeast is kneaded into dough, it is invisible; nothing happens right away. But in its own time the dough expands and rises, driven by the yeast.

In the same way we are not able to see the Spirit as he moves through groups of people. Sometimes it may seem as if nothing is happening, but when you look at the steady growth of the church from the handful at Jesus' time to the millions of believers today, all you can do is marvel.

God doesn't want us thinking that we can do his job, and he absolutely refuses to do ours. We can't convert people but can certainly share the yeasty Word that does.

_____

_____

_____

_____

_____

Sing a new song

We try so hard to get our lives under control—our finances, our family, our jobs—but things keep breaking down. You know what it's like to sing the blues, when the lyrics are groans, sighs, and bitter complaints. Maybe some of those blues lyrics have been part of your prayers that you were sending to heaven, imploring God to intervene and change your world.

But then—shock! He does answer your prayers in the way you'd hoped, or even better than you'd thought possible. Suddenly your song lyrics change: **"I waited patiently for the Lord; he turned to me and heard my cry. He lifted me out of the slimy pit, out of the mud and mire; he set my feet on a rock and gave me a firm place to stand. He put a new song in my mouth, a hymn of praise to our God"** (Psalm 40:1-3).

The Bible uses that phrase "new song" at least eight times to describe the worship response from a believer who is grateful for grace, grateful to be pulled out of a pit he couldn't escape on his own. When your financial stresses ease, when a friendship is restored, when you hear "I love you" instead of "I hate you," when your hear words of pardon for your miserable sins, there can be no better response than to give God the credit and sing him a new song.

The Lord is our light

Some communities have been sued into getting rid of their public Christmas trees and crèches, but other places allow them as long as Jewish menorahs can be displayed as well. Perhaps a few cynics simply assume that Hanukkah provides Jewish kids a chance to get presents like their non-Jewish friends, but the annual December festival has its origin in an important historical event.

From 586–167 B.C. the Jews were not a truly independent nation. They were a vassal state for centuries to the Babylonians, Persians, Egyptians, and then to the Syrians. As a gesture of imperial contempt, the Syrian king dedicated the temple in Jerusalem to the worship of Zeus and sacrificed a pig on the great altar. The Jews revolted successfully, gained their independence for a century, and rededicated the temple to the God of Israel. The multibranched oil lamp (menorah) is used as a Hanukkah symbol to commemorate a legendary story that the temple lamp burned miraculously without oil those first eight days.

Jesus himself observed the feast. **"Then came the Feast of Dedication at Jerusalem. It was winter, and Jesus was in the temple area walking in Solomon's Colonnade. The Jews gathered around him, saying, 'How long will you keep us in suspense? If you are the Christ, tell us plainly'"** (John 10:22-24).

In the Advent season, Christians light four candles to mark the weeks of waiting for the One we believe is the Christ, the Messiah long promised, the Savior of the world.

_____

_____

_____

Wise builders

Home builders who do not spend serious time studying the construction site and taking proper steps in the excavation and foundation phases are asking for trouble (and lawsuits) later. Special steps need to be taken if you're in a flood plain or in tornado or hurricane or earthquake country. Even more important—what kind of spiritual foundation is underneath your *life*? How can you prepare yourself so that the storms that *will come* won't ruin your life and destroy your eternity?

Jesus himself has something to tell you: **"The one who hears my words and does not put them into practice is like a man who built a house on the ground without a foundation. The moment the torrent struck that house, it collapsed and its destruction was complete"** (Luke 6:49).

Will you let God's Word tell you the difference between right and wrong? Do you take seriously God's warnings about your violent adversary, the devil? Do you fear the horrible consequences of rebelling against God? Do you believe his message of grace and forgiveness through Jesus? Do you believe that God intervenes to bless and prosper those who trust in him? What do you want most in life? How will you measure if your life is successful?

Whose approval do you want most?

_____

_____

_____

_____

_____

Tell the truth

I've been lied to plenty in my life, but there is one person from whom I absolutely must have the truth and nothing but the truth—my doctor. If I have a problem, I want straight talk.

It is indeed important to be gentle and respectful when we talk to people who seem to be slipping away from the Lord. But we still need to communicate clearly and passionately that the wages of sin is death but eternal life is God's gift.

The congregations in the region of Galatia had been taught that the forgiveness of their sins was a gift of God, received by faith alone. But they had begun to backslide into ritualism and ceremonialism, and Dr. Paul needed to deliver some straight talk and strong medicine: **"You foolish Galatians! Who has bewitched you? . . . I am astonished that you are so quickly deserting the one who called you by the grace of Christ and are turning to a different gospel—which is really no gospel at all"** (Galatians 3:1; 1:6,7).

I am certain that there will be people in hell complaining bitterly, "Why didn't someone tell me?"

_____

_____

_____

_____

_____

DECEMBER 20

Are believers destroyers?

I can never read the third chapter of Ecclesiastes without hearing the Byrds' version of Pete Seeger's folk song "Turn! Turn! Turn!" in my head. King Solomon's original words are a poetic and honest summary of the often paradoxical opposites of life. We can readily understand some of these pairs—such as "there is a time to be silent and a time to speak"—but is God really giving his blessing on "a time to kill" and "a time to hate"?

Are believers sometimes supposed to be destroyers? **"There is a time for everything . . . a time to tear down and a time to build"** (Ecclesiastes 3:1,3). Well, yes. Israel's golden calf needed to be torn down. The better kings of Judah periodically had to launch spiritual reformations that included tearing down altars built to idols.

Sometimes the tearing down is just something old and small and worn-out to make room for something bigger and better. Sometimes it is the times in our lives when we need to downsize, to travel lighter. Or perhaps it's a part of our lives that is destructive, like heavy drinking and a party lifestyle, that has to go if you are going to follow Christ.

Is this a time for tearing down or building in your life?

The magic of Christmas

Is the glass of your life half full or half empty right now? Is your heart full of optimism or regrets? Do the coming days of Christmas fill you with joyful anticipation or sad memories? The more you put pressure on yourself to make things happen, the more frustrated you will be. **"I consider everything a loss compared to the surpassing greatness of knowing Christ Jesus my Lord, for whose sake I have lost all things. I consider them rubbish, that I may gain Christ and be found in him"** (Philippians 3:8,9).

Here is the true magic of Christmas—not what you are doing for your family or friends or yourself or even for Christ, but rather what *he* has already done for *you*. Through Christ you are forgiven of all your sins. If you are forgiven, then you are loved by God. If loved, then you will be protected, fed, sheltered, and blessed. If you are blessed, then you will always have enough. If you are forgiven, then you are immortal.

The Christmas story guarantees that Christ really came as he said he would. If your family has the sweet custom of lighting candles for each week of the four weeks of advent, then light that fourth candle and celebrate Christmas hope.

_____

_____

_____

_____

_____

Clothed in humility

Looking backward is a dangerous indulgence. It turned Lot's wife into a pillar of salt. It can turn your marriage salty and sour if you keep looking backward, wondering if you should perhaps have chosen a different spouse from former boyfriends or girlfriends.

Pride is deadly in all relationships, including marriage. When you start feeling that you've been cheated in life, that your spouse owes you, or that you could have done better, it's time for a new "marriage garment": **"As God's chosen people, holy and dearly loved, clothe yourselves with . . . humility"** (Colossians 3:12).

Humility means realizing that you can be a chore to live with sometimes. Humility means that you thank and praise God for giving you a spouse with as many great qualities as yours. Humility means thanking your spouse for putting up with you, realizing that your spouse's irritations with you are probably three or four times greater than you think they are.

Need some humility therapy? Consider Jesus Christ, King of the angels, who was born in a barn and executed on a vertical instrument of torture, all to make your life and your eternity better, all so that you could live happily ever after with him.

_____

_____

_____

_____

_____

DECEMBER 23
God's POV

Normally a ministry of a year and a half would be thought of as terribly short. But for St. Paul it was a huge investment of time and demonstrated a mission field that was unusually productive. Paul was a rapid traveler and planter; he left it to others to do the longer-term teaching and harvesting.

He had encountered severe hostility early on in Corinth, and he might have left early but for this amazing revelation given to him in a vision at night: **"'Do not be afraid; keep on speaking, do not be silent. For I am with you, and no one is going to attack and harm you, because I have many people in this city.' So Paul stayed for a year and a half, teaching them the word of God"** (Acts 18:9-11).

Imagine that—God can see great potential in a certain place and correctly anticipate openness to the gospel. We never know in advance where to do effective evangelism and mission work because our point of view (POV) is so clouded. Unlike God, we can't read minds and hearts. But God's POV senses people movements and openings, and he steers human resources where they are needed.

Lord, show us today where the opportunities are. When you see a place where you have many future believers, move us to be there.

_____

_____

_____

_____

_____

Christmas matters for you

It's amazing, isn't it, how much extra baggage has been piled onto the stories of Christmas? Singers can put out a "Christmas" album and never once mention the baby in the manger. Somehow you can make a whole season out of mistletoe, Yule logs, Frosty, Rudolph, and chestnuts roasting on an open fire.

Santa Claus can't do a thing for you because he's just part of the myth. The only way that the "holiday" will be a holy day for you is if you center your thoughts on the incredible truth that the second person of the Trinity, God from God and Light from Light, thought enough of you to become fully human, just like you.

Here is why Christmas matters: **"Since the children have flesh and blood, he too shared in their humanity so that by his death he might destroy him who holds the power of death—that is, the devil—and free those who all their lives were held in slavery by their fear of death"** (Hebrews 2:14,15). Imagine that. He needed a human body so it could be nailed to a cross. He needed human blood so it could be poured out as a sin offering for the world. For you.

And it all started in Bethlehem. What can you say to that but "glory to God in the highest!"

_____

_____

_____

_____

_____

Your first Christmas

Christ's first coming surprised everybody.

Zechariah was surprised. Mary and Joseph were surprised, first by the angelic announcements and surprised again at the terribly inconvenient time that Mary's labor pains began. Third-shift shepherds were surprised by the sound and light show that they alone experienced. As they knelt at the manger and peered in at the little bundle on the straw, their worship of God would never be the same.

I guess you aren't surprised at the birthday celebrations this December 25—you've had all year to prepare. But what you may not have expected is the satisfaction that comes from worshiping Jesus as though this were your first Christmas. There before you, wrapped in his little strips of cloth, is the ultimate paradox: God and man, Co-Creator and yet begotten, helper and helpless, frail and mighty, brand-new and ancient. There before you lies your salvation—the One who would put himself, his body, between you and death. How can you not love him?

"At the name of Jesus every knee should bow, in heaven and on earth and under the earth" (Philippians 2:10).

_____

_____

_____

_____

_____

Love to serve

When we enter into some kind of personal interaction with other people, it's generally because we expect to get something out of it—isn't it so? If shopping and dating weren't pleasurable, if we didn't get a lot out of it, we wouldn't do it.

Here's the heart of a happy home (and it comes as a rude shock to many): *neither marriage nor parenting works if you are not willing to become somebody else's servant.*

That's hard. Oh, man, that's hard. I'm still working on it. But a servant attitude not only works; it is the only proper attitude for people who have been saved from death and hell by a servant named Jesus Christ. The Bible says that he emptied himself of all his divine glory and perks and made himself our slave. He dares to call us not only to faith in him but also to a life like his.

Here are hard words but healing words: **"Do nothing out of selfish ambition or vain conceit, but in humility consider others better than yourselves. Each of you should look not only to your own interests, but also to the interests of others. Your attitude should be the same as that of Christ Jesus"** (Philippians 2:3-5).

Tell me the truth—do you think of yourself as a servant in your home?

_____

_____

_____

_____

_____

You have gifts

Over the years I have met some Christians with a very broken spirit. "I'm of no use to God. I deserve to be fired from the team. I've got nothing. Basically I'm just killing time until I die." I fear that unless something major happens to change their thinking, they will live out their lives as disappointed, frustrated, crabby individuals, depressed and hating themselves.

If only they had read 1 Peter. God's Word assures us that each of us has great worth in God's eyes and also important gifts to be used in his service. ***"Each one* should use whatever gift he has received to serve others, faithfully administering God's grace in its various forms"** (1 Peter 4:10).

The Lord not only saved you to live with him someday, but he saved you also to be useful to him right now. If you are having trouble identifying your unique God-given gifts, do two things: First, ask the people around you what they appreciate about you. You might be surprised. Second, listen to your heart and identify where you have a passion for helping people.

Now bring to the Lord whatever you've been given and give it back to him.

_____

_____

_____

_____

_____

The Father's plan

The gospel message is based on mysteries and paradoxes that seem illogical and unbelievable to outsiders to the faith. Take the Trinity, for example. How can God be three and one at the same time? Is there one mind or three? one will or three? one power or three?

God tells you about himself not to explain enough so that you understand but rather so that you appreciate and worship him. He tells you of his essential unity, but he reveals that three distinct persons are at work in the universe.

It is the Father whom Scripture describes as the grand Planner. In servant mode during his earthly ministry, Jesus gave 100% of his attention and respect to the Father's saving design: **"When you have lifted up** (i.e., crucified) **the Son of Man, then you will know that I am the one I claim to be and that I do nothing on my own but speak just what the Father has taught me. The one who sent me is with me; he has not left me alone, for I always do what pleases him"** (John 8:28,29).

From all eternity, even before mankind's fall into sin, the Father lovingly predesigned the rescue he foreknew his Son would need to carry out. The greater our lives are aligned with his plan, the greater our satisfaction and joy in life.

The Son's mission

Did St. Patrick really use a shamrock (three-leafed clover) to teach the Irish Celts about the mystery of the Trinity? Who knows? The earliest historical evidence linking Patrick and the shamrock dates only from the 1600s, 12 centuries after the legendary missionary walked the Auld Sod bringing Christianity to the people.

But it's a sweet way to visualize the Three-in-One. Jesus Christ, the Son, is one with Father and Spirit, and yet has his own distinct personhood and holy work. Jesus himself explained to his disciples once why he was on earth: **"The Son of Man came to seek and to save what was lost"** (Luke 19:10). Only the Son was conceived of the virgin Mary by the Holy Spirit; only the Son was born fully human; only the Son placed himself under the Law in order to demonstrate perfect obedience on our behalf; only the Son was convicted of the crimes of the human race; only the Son bled out on that horrible cross; only the Son was buried, rose again, and triumphantly returned to heaven.

The glorious result? The Father's forgiveness and mercy were pronounced on the whole world. Whoever believes in him shall not perish but have eternal life. Mission accomplished: he sought us and he saved us.

_____

_____

_____

_____

_____

The Spirit's renewal

Scripture says that we are saved by grace (Christ's work) through faith, and here's where the Spirit comes in. It is the Spirit's great work to connect spiritually dead people with their living Savior by creating faith in their hearts. He also sustains our faith through his Word and the Holy Supper.

Let St. Paul explain: **"When the kindness and love of God our Savior appeared, he saved us, not because of righteous things we had done, but because of his mercy. He saved us through the washing of rebirth and renewal by the Holy Spirit"** (Titus 3:4,5). Through the washing of your baptism you actually experience spiritual *rebirth* and come alive.

You are spiritually *renewed* as well, and that process continues throughout your life on earth. Your Christian progress may look like the jagged ups and downs of the Dow Jones averages, but through Word and Supper you will grow stronger and steadier over time. The Spirit helps you think straight, renews your determination to resist Satan, strengthens your willpower, awakens the gifts he placed within you, makes you useful to his agenda for healing and reconciliation, and restores your joy and optimism.

His annual festival is the Feast of Pentecost. Remember to wear red in his honor!

_____

_____

_____

_____

_____

Persians need a Savior too

Everyone in the ancient world assumed that religion was regional. Each nation and tribe had its own deities. And while you were loyal to yours, you would probably accept the existence and power of the gods of others.

The one who was born in Bethlehem is the One. The only One. There is only one Creator; in his great love for mankind, he ordained only one rescue plan. His Son was incarnate and born as we all were, born to live as our substitute and born to have a body to offer as the ultimate sin offering.

Some true believers in the ruling class of the Parthian Empire, which included much of the old Persian (Iranian) Empire, were honored with a miraculous divine birth announcement. A specially created bright light in the heavens, visible like a star apparently only to them, led them to Jerusalem to seek the One. **"After Jesus was born in Bethlehem in Judea, during the time of King Herod, Magi from the east came to Jerusalem and asked, 'Where is the one who has been born king of the Jews? We saw his star in the east and have come to worship him'"** (Matthew 2:1,2).

Parthia was far bigger and much more powerful than little Israel. The Magi were far wealthier and socially loftier than low-income Mary and Joseph. But they believed God's message that their rescuer, the only One, was in the cradle before them. They bowed low and gave gifts, gifts fit for a king. Their King.

_____

_____

_____

Devotions for Special Days

Heavenly royalty

No country does the pageantry of royalty better than Britain. The new monarch arrives in regal procession, following the Lord's High Steward with St. Edward's solid gold crown, later to be invested with the golden spurs, royal glove, golden orb, and golden scepter.

How different was Jesus' royal ride around the Mount of Olives into Jerusalem. His mount was a donkey colt, a small animal that would barely have lifted his head above the crowd. And yet so many people in that crowd recognized him as royalty that they got a chant started: **"Blessed is the king who comes in the name of the Lord!"** (Luke 19:38).

The royal robe awaiting him was only an old Roman army cloak; the scepter he was given was a puny reed; the crown put on his head was made of thorns. The blood that came down his face was both the blood of a man and the blood of God, powerful to purchase and redeem.

The Mount of Olives served as another important royal coronation procession. It was from that very place that the resurrected Christ ascended into heaven. His humility is now replaced with glory; his attendants are now ten thousand times ten thousand angels; his presence and Spirit fill the universe; he rules all things for the benefit of his brothers and sisters. Through faith, you are royalty too. Heavenly royalty.

_____

_____

_____

_____

_____

You will live too!

We all love stability in our lives. We all like to assume that everything will stay the same, stay *manageable*. We fear disruptive change—getting laid off or fired, suffering injuries in a car accident, being hospitalized with some disease. Worse—we fear having to live in a nursing home, being moved to a hospice.

Martha's nightmare came true—Jesus the Healer arrived in Bethany too late to save her sick brother, Lazarus. **"'Lord,' Martha said to Jesus, 'if you had been here, my brother would not have died.' . . . Jesus said to her, 'Your brother will rise again'"** (John 11:21-23).

That's just empty talk coming from one dying mortal to another. But those words come from Jesus, Lord and Master of sin, sickness, death, and hell. His resurrection gives him the power and authority to undo death. He demonstrated that power at Lazarus' mausoleum by commanding the dead man to come forth and live. That dead man restored is a demo version of what Jesus will do on a grand scale at the end of time.

The resurrection of Jesus Christ calms our deepest fears. The resurrection of Jesus Christ guarantees the forgiveness of your sins. There is no condemnation for those who believe in Jesus. The resurrection of Jesus Christ guarantees yours. He lives. You will too.

_____

_____

_____

_____

_____

Hearts with no walls

When God needed to impress on Adam and Eve how their sinful rebellion was going to hurt their lives, he had a different message for each. To Adam (and all men) God described how work itself would become frustrating and difficult. To Eve (and all wives and mothers) God announced that their children would cause them pain.

The "Song of Simeon" has become a powerful hymn in the Christian liturgy, and its text has furnished comfort to thousands of Christian funeral mourners. But Simeon also had something somber to say to mother Mary: **"This child is destined to cause the falling and rising of many in Israel, and to be a sign that will be spoken against, so that the thoughts of many hearts will be revealed. And a sword will pierce your own soul too"** (Luke 2:34,35). Through his prophetic foresight Simeon predicted Mary's anguish of spirit at having to witness her Son's crucifixion.

A dear friend of mine, also named Mary, told me once, "Women's hearts have no walls." That is, they are open and vulnerable to the people they love, especially their children.

This Mother's Day, think of all the things for which you are grateful for your mom. Don't forget to pause and appreciate the fact that she loves you in spite of all the pain you have caused her.

_____

_____

_____

_____

_____

A father's prayer

"Blessed is the man you discipline, O Lord, the man you teach from your law; you grant him relief from days of trouble, till a pit is dug for the wicked. For the Lord will not reject his people; he will never forsake his inheritance" (Psalm 94:12-14).

Lord, I am honored that you made me a father. It was not I who joined a male cell to a female cell and made a new living creature. It was not I who engineered the spectacular event of childbirth. I can't make my child grow even one inch—it is all you. I am humbled and grateful to be a steward of your wondrous creation.

I am also painfully aware of my own shortcomings. Forgive me for my many acts of selfishness, for being slow at seeing and meeting the needs of my children. Thank you for your discipline; thank you even more for your promise never to forsake me.

I need more wisdom than I have now. Please grow my capacity to see, understand, remember, care, and lead like a servant. I need more strength than I have now. Please grow my stamina, patience, resilience, trust, and courage.

Father, help me to be a father like you.

_____

_____

_____

_____

_____

THANKSGIVING DAY
Cause and effect

There is a reason why our culture has so enthusiastically embraced annual birthday and wedding remembrances. Time slides by, and we tend to take one another for granted. Birthdays and anniversaries are helpful reminders about the importance of the dear people whom God has sent into our lives.

An annual call to national thanksgiving is just as urgent and helpful. President Lincoln knew that America badly needed God's help, and even in a time of terrible war, he wanted Americans to pause and express their gratitude for all the divine interventions and blessings that made their lives better.

Sinners like us need periodic wake-up calls to notice God's working in our lives. Our instincts are either to take his gifts without noticing or thinking or to suppose that everything good in our lives comes from our own achievement.

St. Paul knew how engaged our Lord is in the lives of each believer, and he urged a Greek congregation and he urges us to pause, notice, understand cause and effect, and make a joyful noise of thanksgiving: **"Be joyful always; pray continually; give thanks in all circumstances, for this is God's will for you in Christ Jesus"** (1 Thessalonians 5:16-18).

What three treasures in your life can you trace back to God's kindly giving?

_____

_____

_____

_____

About Time of Grace

Time of Grace is an international Christian outreach media ministry that connects people to God's grace through Jesus Christ so that they know they are loved and forgiven. The ministry uses television, print, social media, and the web to share the gospel with people across the U.S. and around the world. On the weekly *Time of Grace* television program, Pastor Mark Jeske presents Bible studies that are understandable, interesting, and can be applied to people's lives. The program is broadcast on more than 150 local stations; 4 satellite networks, including American Forces Network; and airs on ABC Family, which is carried by virtually all cable providers in the U.S. For a complete broadcast schedule, visit timeofgrace.org. Watch *Time of Grace* or visit timeofgrace.org, where you will find the program via streaming video and audio podcasts, as well as study guides, daily devotions, blogs, a prayer wall, and additional resources. You can also call 800.661.3311 for more information.

TIME OF GRACE®
WITH PASTOR MARK JESKE

P.O. BOX 301
MILWAUKEE, WI 53201
800.661.3311 | 414.562.8463
info@timeofgrace.org
timeofgrace.org